TELEVISION FRAUD

Recent Titles in
Contributions in American Studies
Series Editor: **Robert H. Walker**

TELEVISION FRAUD

THE HISTORY AND IMPLICATIONS OF THE QUIZ SHOW SCANDALS

Kent Anderson

Contributions in American Studies, Number 39
GREENWOOD PRESS
WESTPORT, CONNECTICUT • LONDON, ENGLAND

Library of Congress Cataloging in Publication Data

Anderson, Kent.
   Television Fraud.

   (Contributions in American studies ; no. 39 ISSN: 0084-9227)
   Based on the author's thesis, University of Washington.
   Bibliography: p
   Includes index.
   1. Quiz shows—United States. 2. Fraud—United States. I. Title.
PN1992.8.Q5A5   791.45'7   77-94755
ISBN 0-313-20321-0

Library of Congress Catalog Card Number: 77-94755
ISBN: 0-313-20321-0
ISSN: 0084-9227

First published in 1978

Greenwood Press, Inc.
51 Riverside Avenue, Westport, Connecticut 06880

Printed in the United States of America
10 9 8 7 6 5 4 3 2 1

CONTENTS

ACKNOWLEDGMENTS

I am grateful for the opportunity to thank the people who helped me with the initial stages of this book. First I must thank my friend, Bill Mullins, who suggested the idea. I also want to thank Eric F. Goldman for his early encouragement in the project. More than any other, though, Otis Pease deserves the most gratitude for his intellectual guidance, patience, and many fine editing suggestions. I also wish to thank Robert Burke and Donald Pember for their aid.

I am grateful to Erik Barnouw for suggesting Greenwood Press as a publisher and James Sabin and Nancy Clements for their continuous editorial assistance in bringing this work to print.

PREFACE

This is a tale about television, the most pervasive of all mass media, the one whose instantaneous entry into our homes has been met with the greatest acceptance. Without discussing McLuhanesque theories about the nature of television viewing and its effect on us, it is noteworthy that the first of the big-money quiz shows, *The $64,000 Question*, produced a mass media event rivaled only by the radio show *Amos 'n' Andy* of the early 1930s in terms of audience addiction, and also by the recent series *Roots* in terms of enormity of audience and subsequent attention showered upon its participants from all media. As with *Amos n' Andy*, *The $64,000 Question* produced a cessation of other adult activity during the time it was being aired. Movie theaters stopped their shows, and bar patrons riveted their attention en masse to the quiz show as most adult Americans within proximity of a television set were captured by *The $64,000 Question*. As with *Roots*, this first big-money quiz had such an astoundingly large viewing audience that the show became an event in itself and in the eyes of all other media. Throughout the summer of 1955 and beyond, the quiz's participants, both on screen and off, were liberally publicized and displayed in newspapers, magazines, and radio before a highly interested public.

Because this is a story about television, it is also a comment on the uses of leisure time in America. The big-money quiz show occurred at that period in our recent social past when the rate of televisions coming into American homes was at its most rapid. By 1955, approximately 70 percent of all households had television sets; at the start of the decade, the figure was less than 15 percent. As a leisure activity created by and dependent upon technology, watching television has drastically altered our recent social history by becoming, by a large percentage, the primary free-time activity for Americans.[1]

Television is a technological pastime, and the quizzes used and manipulated technology as part of their appeal, all the while containing the baser elements of show business. Props and paraphernalia such as an IBM sorting machine, soundproof booths, the apparent random-sample contestant and question, and a modern bank vault complete with guard combined on the shows with pretty women, neon signs, and all the tinsel and glitter that would make Las Vegas proud.

Several older concepts that have permeated American social life and thought present themselves in the form of subtle strains in the fabric of the big-money quizzes. Although it is difficult to imagine a less likely location than *The $64,000 Question,* the ideas of Protestant (or capitalist) work ethic, upward mobility, and self-help surfaced on that show. These notions have been ever-present in American popular art and literature, as well as in more seriously regarded sources, such as sermons, primers, and Franklin's aphorisms. Therefore their extension onto a very electronic palette is not surprising. A byproduct of the work ethic and upward mobility in America is the dream of limitless riches, a legitimate goal of the American individualist who was willing to strive for them as surely as windfall profits were the honored goal of Gilded Age corporate life. The analytical leap from the novels of Horatio Alger, Frank Norris, and Ayn Rand to the personages of Charles Van Doren, Gino Prato, and Herbert Stempel of quiz-show fame is neither lengthy nor illogical.

More obvious than the previous ideas is the profound influence the big-money quizzes held for the value of knowledge. The debate prompted by *The $64,000 Question* and its successors as to what constitutes useful knowledge has been a longstanding argument in American society. Educators displayed ambivalent feelings toward the quizzes. Was not the knowledge used to answer a question, and thereby earn capital, a crass example of Dewey's instrumentalist knowledge carried to an outrageous extreme? The obvious rejoinder was that the very construct of the quizzes determined what constituted useful knowledge in purely monetary terms, which, in our capitalist society, produced a public empathy and fascination that swept the nation. Closely related to this was the question of what constituted an educated person in America. Did most television viewers of the quizzes perceive the successful contestants as well educated, wise, or merely well trained? The nature of the knowledge that spewed forth from the quizzes was a source of consternation to many educators, serious television critics, and societal commentators who resented the application of dollar signs as reward for snippets and bits of knowledge devoid of having demonstrated any evidence of reasoning from those who supplied it and who thought the entire process represented a debasement of accumulating knowledge for its own sake. Another body of opinion held the big-money shows more in wonder than in scorn. Some teachers hoped that the shows increased the motivation for learning in youngsters, while other critics viewed the programs in truly positive fashion laden with worthwhile and heroic personages.[2]

Since this is a story about commercial television, the institution of American advertising figures prominently. The responsibility of advertising for what occurred is debatable only by degree. The late David M. Potter once said that the primary influence exerted by the institution of advertising was not upon our economical system but rather upon the values of our society.[3] This study looks at that supposition. Advertising is but one large component in the business process, however; others explored in some detail here are the television industry and its regulatory bodies, the Federal Trade Commission and the Federal Communications Commission. (In fact it could be argued that this study is more a business history than a social history, but the reader will make that determination.)

The ideas and areas of American study thus far discussed were reflected in varying degrees in the short-lived institution of the big-money quiz show. Had there been no subsequent scandal connected with these shows, their study still would have been an interesting project; but what makes this story doubly fascinating was the extraordinary amount of fraud unearthed in their structure. This was, indeed, a scandal without precedence, and the questions and comments it raised about the television industry in particular present an intriguing scope of speculation about American society in general. There were moral questions involved with the quiz scandal. The contestants and producers who participated in the fraud pelted the American media and its public with a series of case studies in individual morality. Admittedly to take the chicanery of a few score people and transform it into a comment on national mores is a risky venture, but that is precisely what occurred in the late 1950s from practically every variety of commentator and philosopher, and that hue and cry deserves to be reexamined.

The final chapter of this book will provide a wide variety of comment on the scandal. Much of the discussion does not focus on the deceptions themselves but rather on the meaning of the public reaction to the frauds and what this portended for American society. There are few concepts more tenuous to which a historian can address than national character. Fortunately, though, one cannot begin a discussion of national character with a better intellectual foundation than the ideas of David Potter. Leaving his economic considerations aside, is it not possible to argue that the big-money quizzes were a product of the twentieth-century American characteristic of abundance? Or that the alleged public apathy in the wake of the scandals was the result of society's belief that money was plentiful and the means for attaining it of secondary importance?

NOTES

1. Thomas M. Kando, *Leisure and Popular Culture in Transition* (St. Louis: C. V. Mosby Co., 1975), pp. 95–96, 191.

2. Arthur M. Schlesinger, Jr., "Sources of the New Deal," in *Paths of American Thought*, ed. Arthur M. Schlesinger, Jr., and Morton White (Boston: Houghton Mifflin, 1963), pp. 377–379.

3. David M. Potter, *People of Plenty* (Chicago: University of Chicago Press, 1954), p. 188.

TELEVISION FRAUD

1 | "EVERYBODY'S SMART AT SOMETHING"

I've always been interested in people and I've never sub-scribed to the belief that the average American radio and TV listener has a 12-year old intelligence. The average American has a brain and an integrity that's really wonderful. You just have to look for it. Everybody's smart at something. [1]

—Louis G. Cowan

During its brief history, the television broadcasting industry has devised a wide variety of programs to attract both audiences and sponsors. Much of what has appeared on the airwaves has been derived from other media. From film and the theater, television has offered documentaries and drama, both live and filmed, of varying duration and quality. The content of television programming, however, probably owes more to radio than any other medium or form of entertainment. At the beginning, the television networks were mere extensions of the earlier radio networks, frequently having the same personnel. Radio performers behind the microphone had only to step in front of the camera. It seemed natural to network executives that entertainment that had been successful on radio should be attempted on television. Such attempts were made in abundance, from weekly situation comedies to on-the-spot sports broadcasts. One of the staples of radio, particularly during the 1940s, was the question-and-answer format, better known as the quiz show. It was also brought to television, and, as it did with everything it borrowed, the new medium transformed the quiz show. The first change was visualization, but in the mid-1950s something else occurred: enormous sums of money were injected into the format, and the big-money television quiz show was born. Its new popularity was phenomenal.

More than any other person, the man responsible for this television phenomenon was Louis George Cowan. Born in Chicago in 1909, Cowan was the only child of a successful building contractor. He attended the University of Chicago, and, after an academic career that included classes taught by John Dewey, he graduated in 1931 with a bachelor's degree in philosophy. He remained in Chicago after college and launched a career as a publicity agent. Many of his accounts were charities, such as Hull House and the Salvation Army. Then he got a job as a press agent on the Big Band circuit. First he managed publicity accounts for the orchestra of Wayne King; then he went to work for bandleader Kay Kyser, with whom he developed the musical quiz program, *The College of Musical Knowledge*, which put the band on radio for several years. Cowan had discovered his forte. His career as publicist gradually gave way to that of a radio programmer. After a few regional successes with Chicago radio stations, in 1940 he created and produced his first network quiz show, *Quiz Kids*. This program was comprised of a panel of highly precocious preadolescents who amazed listeners with their ability to answer questions. *Quiz Kids* ran fourteen years on radio and was only the first of many programs Cowan conceived.[2]

World War II interrupted Cowan's show business career when he headed the Office of War Information in New York City. After the war he went back to packaging formats for possible sale to the networks. Calling himself an "idea man," Cowan was not particularly interested in staying with any one show or retaining control of production once a program had secured a position on the air.[3]

Radio was satiated with game and quiz shows immediately after the war. Programs with such resounding titles as *Mr., Mrs. and Miss Hush, Stop the Music* (a Cowan creation), and *Sing It Again* more often gave successful contestants appliances, vacations, and other material gifts than relatively small money prizes. The quiz craze was even strong enough to force such competition as comedian Fred Allen off the air, leading him to remark: "If I were king for one day, I would make every program . . . a giveaway show; when the studio was filled with the people who encourage those atrocities, I would lock the door. With all of the morons in America trapped, the rest of the population could go about its business."[4]

As the 1940s wore on, the appeal of quiz programs dwindled. Part of the decline can be explained by the fact that airtime quizzes had reached the satiation point, and their attraction quickly faded. The competition from the new medium of television also brought an overall decline in interest in radio programming. Quizzes faced legal pressure in addition to the other factors, as the Federal Communications Commission attempted, unsuccessfully, to rule them as lotteries, thereby making them illegal. Louis Cowan was not deterred. Not limiting his airtime creations to the quiz format, he continued to produce. He moved into television easily enough, and by the mid-1950s he had packaged and produced nearly fifty programs for radio and television. Quizzes, though, were still his inventive specialty.[5]

At the beginning of 1955, Cowan was an unqualified success and an acknowledged master of his craft. He had a spacious Park Avenue apartment in New York City, a large estate in Connecticut, and four programs on radio and television, including the George F. Peabody Award-winning radio show, *Conversation*, hosted by Clifton Fadiman. One January morning Cowan arose at his usually early hour. (He preferred to do most of his work at home and normally found that time of day to be his most productive.) This particular morning he had Mount Everest on his mind. He was also thinking about quiz shows. Mount Everest and quizzes . . . why not combine the two and create the ultimate quiz program?[6]

As he pondered over the structure of such a definitive show, Cowan thought back to his days in radio. He remembered *Take It or Leave It*, with which he had no connection and which left the air in 1952. *Take It or Leave It* and its accordian-playing emcee, Phil Baker, added to American colloquialisms "the $64 question." This amount was top prize on the show after a contestant had successfully answered a series of relatively simple questions and doubled his winnings, beginning with one dollar. Cowan liked the double-or-nothing format of *Take It or Leave It* but thought the stakes no longer impressive. As he recalled: "The $64 wasn't enough to make news. Although it once was. $640? That's nothing either. Nor is $6,400. But $64,000 gets into the realm of the almost impossible." With "the audacity of those three zeroes" attached to the frame of an extinct radio program, Louis Cowan created his masterpiece, *The $64,000 Question*, the first big-money television quiz.[7]

Devising the format was only the first step. The basic business of television is conducted between a network and an advertising agency, the latter representing the sponsor or advertiser. The advertiser pays the price of production for a program, as well as a fee to the network for airtime. The price a network can charge for airtime varies with every half-hour time slot and is determined by the popularity of the show as determined by television ratings. A fee (usually 15 percent of the network fee) is also paid to the advertising agency for negotiating with the network and for the production of commercials. *The $64,000 Question* had to find a sponsor.

The Columbia Broadcasting System show *Danger* was leaving the air at the end of the television season in June, and its sponsors, Revlon Products Corporation and Nash-Kelvinator Corporation, were interested in finding a new program to maintain their national television advertising. Cowan contacted both firms and told them about *The $64,000 Question*. Each was offered half of the sponsorship, or alternating the cost of production every other week as had been the case with *Danger*. Revlon quickly accepted through its advertising agency, William H. Weintraub and Company (which soon after became the firm of Norman, Craig, and Kummell), while Nash-Kelvinator eventually declined, thereby making the cosmetics company sole sponsor.[8]

Unlike most other program packagers, Cowan was an independent producer; he had no network affiliation. Working closely with Walter Craig of the Weintraub agency, Cowan had the additional burden of having to sell his creation to the network. CBS did not immediately agree to televise *The $64,000*

Question upon hearing that Revlon had bought the package, but rather deliberated a few days. The publicity announcements of the show that Cowan released to the press no doubt hastened CBS's reasonably rapid acceptance of the show. To prevent any copyright problem that might have arisen, Cowan had already purchased rights to *Take It or Leave It* from the advertising executive Milton Biow. *The $64,000 Question* was scheduled to take over the thirty-minute time slot beginning at 10:00 P.M., June 7. Not even Cowan was aware of how much his latest production would overwhelm not only the slack summer television season but the entire direction of television programming as well.[9]

When *The $64,000 Question* made its debut that Tuesday evening, much of the specific structure of the show was unveiled to the viewing public. Little about it was very original. There were twelve categories of questions, from which a contestant picked one. A new category was then placed into the selection to replace the old one, affording the opportunity of a variety of question topics. *Newsweek* described the appearance of the set as, "vaguely sleazy . . . compounded of beaverboard and sequins, liberally decorated with the name of the sponsor." There was the usual pretty girl (coincidentally named Lynn Dollar) to escort contestants onto the stage and the usual host, actor Hal March, who combined the right amount of enthusiasm with the correct dosage of sincerity.

The $64 that was the grand prize on *Take It or Leave It* was merely the starting point for *The $64,000 Question*. As long as a contestant correctly answered the question, he could risk his winnings on a more difficult question and double his amount, or leave. The initial winnings or "plateaus" were $64, $128, $256, and $512. Then the amount leveled off at $1,000. The next series of winning amounts were $2,000, $4,000, and $8,000, the maximum a contestant could win on one appearance. The contestant could come back in one week and decide whether to try for a $16,000 question. If he answered it correctly, he waited another week to attempt the $32,000 question, then another week until the ultimate plateau of $64,000. Thus the Mount Everest of quizzes could be reached in four weeks. After answering the $32,000, the contestant was given several reference books in his category and was allowed to bring any expert to assist him if he chose to tackle the $64,000 question. [10] Amid the familiarity of an old format, there were some new devices. A large IBM sorter shuffled all the question envelopes, though it was used only for the early questions. At the $1,000 plateau, the questions were kept by Ben Feit, a bank officer of the Manufacturers Trust Company, which had the Revlon banking account. Feit sat conspicuously behind a desk flanked by two uniformed security guards and gave the higher-valued questions to March. If a contestant wished to attempt the $8,000 question and others beyond that amount, he had to enter what was called the isolation booth, a soundproof compartment built in a style one critic called "juke-box baroque." The consolation prize for failure to answer an isolation booth question correctly was a Cadillac convertible. [11]

The first night of The $64,000 Question featured a Trenton, New Jersey, housewife, who missed at $8,000, and a New York City policeman, Redmond O'Hanlon, who succeeded in reaching the plateau of the first week by answering questions on Shakespeare. One critic called the debut "outlandish." But if the initial show was not particularly impressive to some, others saw its future. The CBS program that followed The $64,000 Question was the weekly news show, See It Now, produced by the paragon of CBS News, Edward R. Murrow. His longtime friend and partner, Fred W. Friendly, described the newsman's reaction: "Murrow, who seldom watched any show preceding ours, was riveted and horrified by what he saw. His instincts, accurate as usual, made him realize before the half-hour was over that the carny, mid-way atmosphere heralded by the big-money quizzes would soon be dominating the airwaves." [12]

Murrow's premonition was correct. Within a few weeks, The $64,000 Question became the talk of television and then of the country. John P. Shanley, the critic who dubbed the premier show "outlandish," said after the third viewing, "The formula may not be original, but the results are absorbing." The audience for the latest Cowan creation swelled at an incredible rate. Newsweek called it "the greatest question and answer routine... since Socrates packed them in on the Agora." By mid-July The $64,000 Question was the top-rated program on television. In early August the approximately 32 million American television sets had what the American Research Bureau estimated to be 47,560,000 viewers for the show, or nearly one-third of the nation, all during the traditionally lagging summer months for television. The quiz, astoundingly, had yet to achieve its peak of popularity. Few entertainment enterprises ever experienced such a phenomenal surge in appeal as *The $64,000 Question*. [13]

Possibly a public familiarity with the basic structure of the quiz coupled with the strikingly high stakes precipitated the extraordinary interest in the show, but also, an enormous factor was the amazing popularity of the series of successful contestants that *The $64,000 Question* produced. Overnight folk heroes were created, accompanied by all the attention such heroes deserve and which the eager mass media can deliver to a fascinated public. Each contestant had endured the same highly pressured quiz process in front of millions of people. Each winner, however, also retained his own distinctiveness, and his personality was publicized as fully as the amount of prize money.

The first folk hero was Redmond O'Hanlon, who stayed on the show two weeks and was the first to win $16,000. As "the cop who knew Shakespeare," he said the reason he declined to try for more riches was because he put "the conservatism of a father of five children" above "the egotism of the scholar" (he had a master's degree from Fordham). Next came Catherine Kreitzer, a fifty-four-year-old grandmother from Camp Hill, Pennsylvania, who worked as a clerk-typist at a naval depot. Her category was the Bible. Saying that she was guided by the Bible throughout her progression on the program, Kreitzer advanced to the $32,000 plateau after answering an increasingly difficult series of biblical identifications. Her massive audience tuned in July 24, 1955, hoping that she would be the first to try for $64,000. Her opening statement to Hal March, "I am confident I can answer the $64,000," brought wild applause. "But," she continued, "I am balancing that confidence with a quotation from Ephesians, 'Let your moderation be known unto all men,' so I am going to let my moderation be known... and accept the $32,000." The audience was naturally disappointed.

The producers of the show and March had no way of knowing whether a contestant would choose to go on unless they were told so. There was always another contestant in the wings ready to come forward in decisions such as Kreitzer's. Ironically Catherine Kreitzer had made what may have been her first mistake about the Bible; the quotation she had used was not from the Ephesians, but Philippians. [14]

As the summertime audience swelled, each successive winner received greater attention than the one before. Undoubtedly the most prominent contestant *The $64,000 Question* produced that first summer was Gino Prato, a bespectacled Bronx cobbler with an amazing expertise in opera. Prato also stopped his run after winning $32,000. According to one report, his halt somewhat angered the producers, who had hoped that he would be the first to attempt the top amount. [15] Prato's ninety-two-year-old father sent him a cablegram from Italy telling him to stop. Prato, like the other contestants, exemplified what happened to successful contestants on *The $64,000 Question:* a brief, publicity-laden life of tours, awards, endorsements, and commercial requests, all in a familiar pattern of American merchandising. [16]

The instant celebrity status of the contestants was attained usually after successfully completing the first plateau of $8,000. While appearing on the show, Prato was forced to close his small shoe repair shop as the store-blocking throng of well-wishers and confidence men made business impossible. This adversity was short-lived for Prato, though, as the process of contestant commercialization began quickly. Even before he left *The $64,000 Question,* the American Biltrite Rubber Company, a rubber heel manufacturing concern, offered Prato a $10,000-a-year job as a traveling "good will ambassador" for their product, an offer the humble cobbler accepted. After leaving the program, Prato's fame and fortune continued. He was given a season pass to the New York Metropolitan Opera and was visited by such fans as Wanda Horowitz, the daughter of Arturo Toscanini. A travel agency paid his way on a tour of Italy, including a trip to the little village of Statale where he visited his father for the first time in thirty-three years. His Italian tour also included dining in Rome with the United States ambassador to Italy, Clare Booth Luce, and baseball star Joe DiMaggio. When Prato returned to America, he included the mayor of Genoa in his entourage. Later he capped his popularity by appearing on a variety of radio and television programs such as the *Perry Como Show*.[17]

Prato was only one of many ordinary and previously unknown people who were changed materially by *The $64,000 Question*. The first hero of the quiz, Redmond O'Hanlon, was the guest of honor at four Shakespearean festivals, and Lehigh University offered him a job as lecturer on his literary avocation. Elderly baseball expert Myrtle Power, winner of $32,000, was hired by the Hearst International News Service to cover the World Series and by the CBS *Morning Show* to be its sports commentator for one week. Catherine Kreitzer was named Bible Lady of the Year by the New York Bible Society and was hired on a semiregular basis by the Ed Sullivan program, *Toast of the Town*, to do Bible readings for upward of $2,000 an appearance. All winning contestants were besieged with pleas for money, but none more than Kreitzer. Possibly because of her category or her kindly manner, she received requests for aid totaling $150,000. The heroes and heroines created by *The $64,000 Question* were subjected to near-endless commercial uses. Endorsements, new careers, opportunities to publish, pictorial life stories in popular magazines, and the meeting of dignitaries were all part of the success story of quiz champions as well as the accompanying loss of privacy. Unexpectedly the new celebrities received a recognition rich in fame and wealth sometimes well beyond their televised dollars, with a degree of commercialization and public relations processing obtainable only in America.[18]

The task of supervising the questions to be devised for use on *The $64,000 Question* belonged to Bergen Evans, a professor of English at Northwestern University. Evans was no stranger to television; he had been the moderator of a game show, *Down You Go*, a panel verson of the parlor game "hangman." *Down You Go* was a Louis Cowan creation, and Evans had presided over the program for five years. On *The $64,000 Question* Evans was assisted by associate producer Merton Koplin and three anonymous experts in sports, music, and science. Occasionally Evans flew to New York City to discuss the questions with the executive producer, Steve Carlin, probably the person most responsible for the decisions of detail on the program. Sometimes Evans supplied Koplin with a large body of material on a particular subject and let him make up the questions. Devising a particular question for the quiz might take anywhere from two days to two weeks. In discussing the reasoning behind his choice of queries, Evans said: "The earlier questions should be simple, but not too simple, the later ones progressively harder and in several parts to build up the tension. The ideal question is one that gets a gasp from the audience and yet stands a fair chance of being answered by someone who knows his field." Evans then outlined a sequence in American history to indicate what a $64,000 question might be like. After the emcee gave some details about the ride of Paul Revere, a comparatively simple question would begin the series: "How many lanterns were hung in the steeple of Old North Church?" Harder questions would follow: "Who rode with Paul Revere?" "Who lent him his horse?" "Was it a mare or a stallion?" Finally, for $64,000, "What was the horse's name?" The important fact about Evans's position was that, even though the public may have believed him to be the man behind the questions, he did not select which questions were to be asked on the quiz. That crucial job was usually left to Mert Koplin.[19]

If the selection of questions for The $64,000 Question seemed complicated, the picking of contestants was in some ways more complex and more carefully done. There were three routes by which a person could become a contestant. Most were chosen by the letter writing process. Within weeks of the premiere of the program, The $64,000 Question was receiving from ten thousand to twenty thousand letters per week. Catherine Kreitzer's initial letter had read, "Add the Bible to those categories and I'll give you a chase for your money." The show employed from four to eight full-time sorters who whittled down the weekly batch of aspirants to about 10 percent of the total, or they hoped, no more than five hundred, and sent them a form letter requesting information about their work, educational background, hobbies, reading habits, the all-important special knowledge of interest, and how they would spend the potential prize money; the applicants were also requested to write a short paragraph on why they thought they would make a good contestant. In addition, three references were requested, preferably including a spiritual adviser, landlord, employer, or banker.

About half of those who received form letters returned them. From the several hundred replies, the total was narrowed down to a more manageable twenty or so, at which stage Steve Carlin and his associates entered the selection process. These remaining few were interviewed by telephone or in person by either Carlin, Koplin, or Ben Kagan. The executive producer made the final choice for all contestants. At the interview when the specialties of knowledge were discussed, Carlin decided which categories were to be added to the selection. In this sense, part of the behavior of the contestant on the quiz was predetermined, as it was assumed the category most preferred in the interview would be chosen on the first airtime appearance. By the letter-writing process, approximately two contestants per week were selected.

The other main entrance onto *The $64,000 Question* was by the studio audience, who were given the form letters and asked to fill them out. Returnees received no more consideration than the hundreds of letter-writing finalists. Getting a seat in the studio, however, was not simple; on more than one occasion, police reinforcements had to be sent to break up the mobs of people trying to enter.

The third method in becoming a contestant was the most devious since it bypassed any sort of formal application. One merely had to be recommended by someone at the studio and then pass the interview. This side door technique was used very rarely, yet it did produce some notable quiz champions. Redmond O'Hanlon got onto the quiz by writing directly to the president of Revlon, Charles Revson. Gino Prato came to *The $64,000 Question* by way of a letter from his daughter. Unbeknown to him, she wrote a letter to the show describing the Italian upbringing of her father and how he saw his first opera when he was only eight years old. The letter was so intriguing that a program official cased Prato's Fifty-seventh Street shop, and after watching him, he became convinced that Prato would make a great contestant. Another person to forego the usual process was a twelve-year-old black girl from Baltimore, Gloria Lockerman, whose expertise was spelling. As a National Spelling Bee runner-up, she was slated originally to appear on a television version of *Quiz Kids*, which Louis G. Cowan, Incorporated, was in the process of preparing. She was noticed by an official from *The $64,000 Question* who immediately transferred her to the potential for bigger money. Gloria eventually won $16,000 for spelling "The belligerent astigmatic anthropologist annihilated innumerable chrysanthemums."[20]

Of the general type of contestant sought by *The $64,000 Question*, executive producer Carlin said: "We don't want hard cases, whiners, or smart alecks. We'd rather have someone who would spend the $64,000 on a trip around the world or a new house. We want good, honest, three-dimensional people.... We want personable, although not necessarily good looking, people. Nice people, intelligent people—people who look like your neighbors." Creator Louis Cowan reiterated much the same in describing the ideal contestant:

In the first place, these people cannot be mistaken for charity cases. They have what we insist upon in a contestant for this show—a feeling of well-being. It is clear that they can use the money to good advantage if or when they win, of course, but it is also clear that should they lose at any juncture, they can and will continue to engage in a good, useful life.

We don't want anyone to mistake *The $64,000 Question* as one of those awful microscope-on-misery programs. This show makes its point much more simply and cleanly. No one is picked just for the purpose of passing out money to bare medical or neurotic tragedies.

Everyone concerned with *The $64,000 Question* agreed that the worst possible letter to write for the purpose of getting onto the show was a hardship letter. No hint of personal adversity was to be broadcast or promoted as the contestant climbed the various plateaus. Catherine Kreitzer had many personal problems in her background; she had lost her home and job during the Depression, and five of her six sons were serving in the armed forces. But none of this distress was mentioned on the quiz nor was she chosen because of it.[21] Cowan's "microscope-on-misery" remark was directed at several earlier game shows that had appeared on television, particularly the programs created by Walt Framer.

Framer had created and produced *Strike It Rich* and *The Big Payoff* which, along with *Queen for a Day* (a non-Framer creation), exploited and used the hardships of its contestants as a basis for a show. All three had players who had to state the recent adversity in their lives prior to answering some relatively simple questions. *Queen for a Day* could not even be considered a quiz: the matron whose tale of woe received the loudest and most sustained audience applause won the day's prizes. Cowan thought such a heart-on-sleeve approach degrading and embarrassing to both contestant and viewer. Instead *The $64,000 Question* sought the common man, minus the misery that befits charity and devoid of the artificial glamor that already glutted the television airwaves. In letting the common man win large amounts of money through his individual expertise and with all his natural charm, however, the show created a host of most uncommon celebrities.[22]

August and September 1955 were particularly important months for *The $64,000 Question*. In one way they were the crest of the wave of popularity for the show; in another they were the crucial months of reaction by scores of other television producers, leading to decisions that would eventually shake the foundation and threaten the future of commercial television.

For Louis Cowan that first summer of the program was a milestone in his life, as he went from his freelance independent packaging of television formats to a vice-presidency at CBS. For a while it looked as if the incredible success of Cowan and *The $64,000 Question* would spark a new interest in non-network programming, thus relieving the networks of much of the burden of having to invent television shows to fill up airtime. Indeed as the 1950s wore on, this hope was fulfilled. For Louis Cowan, however, as is the case with much of the history of the television industry, creativity is more easily purchased than cultivated and thus Cowan joined the fold of CBS. Hired by the head of programming, Hubbell Robinson, Jr., Cowan was allowed to retain a small profitable interest in *The $64,000 Question* and all his other endeavors, but was, in the future, to devote himself entirely to the interests of CBS. Advertising agencies that had asked Cowan for program packages now would have to go through CBS. The network hoped that Cowan would continue to create formats that would capture a larger share of the ever-expanding television audience.[23]

With Cowan gone, Harry Fleischmann became president of Louis G. Cowan, Incorporated, which soon changed its name to Entertainment Productions, Incorporated. Fleischmann was an old colleague of Cowan's and the first person to whom Cowan broached the idea of *The $64,000 Question*. Steve Carlin was made executive vice-president of the organization.

The sponsor of the quiz also enjoyed success. Charles Revson announced that the third-quarter grosses for 1955 were the highest in the company's twenty-four-year history. By the end of the year, gross earnings had risen nearly 200 percent over the previous year, and Revlon stock had gone from twelve dollars a share to thirty dollars in three months. Cosmetic products such as "Love That Pink," "Living Lipstick," and "Touch and Glow" were up 50 percent in sales since the show started in June. In fact Revlon's lipstick sold so rapidly that production and distribution could not keep up with consumer demand; for one week in September, the company ran out of lipstick and decided not to advertise it on the program that week.

Success also touched those who were only marginally associated with *The $64,000 Question*. Even Ben Feit, the banker who held the higher-valued questions for Hal March, was promoted from assistant vice-president to full vice-president, quite probably because of his continued exposure on the enormously popular show.[24]

The most important aspect about the months of August and September 1955 in the life of *The $64,000 Question* was the beginning of a gradual policy of controlling contestants. Coincidental with the departure of Louis Cowan was the beginning of a subtle and gradual form of question selection that would enable the new electronic folk hero and heroine to emerge. The quiz was conceived and had begun as a totally honest contest of knowledge. The show's original producer, Joe Cates, however, left even before Cowan. Even Mert Koplin, a key figure hired after the fifth program to evaluate potential contestants and assist in the process of devising questions, was at first unaware of the implementation of contestant control. Koplin later testified:

> We had no idea of controls or when I entered the scene, the controls had not been formulated. We had a desire for people to do well. We fumbled. It evolved. We tried to create techniques that would insure people doing well and continuing without having recourse to such things as giving questions and answers . . . we tried to determine what they knew but not coach them into knowing something they had not known. . . . It was really in these early days an attempt to have a contestant do well. The public had taken contestants on the show itself to their hearts. They liked to see people win. We liked to see people win. Determining their background was an attempt to further this mutual desire.[25]

The technique used on *The $64,000 Question* for control was to determine the specific expertise of the potential contestant at the interview stage. In a casual conversational manner, Koplin would elicit bits of knowledge from his interviewees to discover the strengths and weaknesses of their avocations, or as he described:

> They [the potential contestants] would come in and either want to demonstrate their knowledge or be elated at having an opportunity at displaying their knowledge and they would talk at some length about what they liked, what they had studied, why they were interested in it, the books they had read, the trips they had taken to further this study.
>
> In short, they gave us a complete outline of their particular area of knowledge.

These prescreening interviews were not question-and-answer sessions, but occasionally Koplin would ask a question to stimulate further discussion, as well as to give the interviewer a more general idea of the area of knowledge. Questions were then constructed from the information gathered and inferred from the prescreening interviews, as well as from the body of questions Bergen Evans provided. Invariably during the course of a contestant's run on *The $64,000 Question*, particularly if it was a long run to one of the higher plateaus, a question would be asked that had been asked at least indirectly during the prescreening, or the information required for the answer had been volunteered by the contestant during that initial interview. Koplin estimated that two-thirds of all the contestants who appeared on the show after controls had been instituted received a minimal amount of aid in that manner. A major part of the process was inference, as Koplin described:

While 60 to 70 percent of the people at one time might receive a question they previously had answered before, our questions were multi-part; three, four, five, or six part questions. The question asked on the air might concern itself with only one part or two or three of which we knew he had knowledge. The rest of them were inferential or tangential questions, or questions that I had the feel they would do well with.[26]

Koplin called his primary method of interviewing a "playback," or the drawing out from a potential contestant, through conversation, the strengths and weaknesses of his or her area of knowledge. For example, during the course of the interview with Gino Prato, it was discovered that he was relatively ill informed on German and French opera. Therefore virtually all the questions he received on *The $64,000 Question,* particularly the highest-valued ones, were on Italian opera, even though the category he chose simply read "opera" to the viewing audience.

There was no collusion on *The $64,000 Question.* At no time was a contestant ever made aware of the controls being exercised upon him. He was never told that what was discussed during the prescreening might appear on the show in the form of a question. This was deliberate effort on the part of the producers to keep the contestant as spontaneous as possible. Unlike later imitators of the first big-money quiz, there was never any coaching of contestants for dramatic effect, and no agreements were made between contestant and producer. The number of persons aware of controls was small. Louis Cowan was never involved in the process, nor was the master of ceremonies, Hal March, aware that contestants had been aided to such an extent. None of these controls, though, could have continued without the reinforced belief of Steve Carlin and Mert Koplin that the sponsor of the quiz show, Revlon, approved the questionable methods, a crucial perception on the part of the producers. *The $64,000 Question* might not be called "rigged" or "fixed," but there was an unethical—though well-intentioned—effort on the part of a few showmen to have their contestants do well. The seeds of later deceit were sown. [27]

The quiz program flourished. On September 13, Marine Captain Richard McCutchen became the first person to answer the $64,000 question. Throughout the summer it had appeared less and less likely that someone would attempt the top amount, for the contestants and the viewing public became more aware of the tax disadvantage in making such a move. Winning the $64,000 question meant the Internal Revenue Service would take out approximately $31,150 in taxes, leaving the contestant with only slightly more than the second-best winning amount. A contestant who stopped at $32,000 in winnings paid only $11,910 for taxes, giving him a little more than $20,000 remaining. Thus a contestant who tried for the $64,000 question was risking nearly $20,000 to gain an extra $12,000. Even *Fortune* editorialized on the situation as it praised the shrewdness of Gino Prato to stop at $32,000:

It is entirely possible that a Bronx cobbler by the name of Gino Prato has done more to dramatize the workings of the high-bracket income-tax laws than all the learned treatises ... on the subject. ... The U.S. Chamber of Commerce and the N.A.M., which have so often argued that over-progressive taxation discourages risk-taking, owe a vote of thanks to the Pratos. [28]

Despite the risk, Captain McCutchen went ahead. His category was food and cooking, and he brought his father along, from whom he learned his initial gourmet skill, as his expert. The television audience was estimated at 55 million viewers, 84.8 percent of all American television sets. For the $64,000 McCutchen was asked to name and describe five dishes and two wines from the world-famous menu of a royal banquet given in 1939 by King George VI of England for French President Albert Lebrun. The dishes he named and described were consommé quenelles, filet de truite saumoneé, petits pois à la francaises, sauce maltaise, and corbeille. Then he told something about the characteristics of the two wines, Château d'Yquem and Madeira Sercial. When McCutchen first heard the question, he cracked his knuckles in delight. He knew the courses immediately and answered fully. The news that Richard McCutchen had done it flashed around the world as the grinning naval ROTC instructor from Ohio State University emerged from the isolation booth. Hal March added tritely, "If you're symbolic of the Marine Corps, Dick, I don't see how we'll ever lose any battles."[29]

In the best tradition of successful contestants on *The $64,000 Question*, Captain McCutchen received his share of commercial and publicity offers. State fairs besieged him with pleas to appear, and many publishers asked him to write cookbooks for them. McCutchen did write a series of cooking articles for the *New York Journal-American* and most of the other Hearst newspapers. The by-line invited readers to be "Captain Cook's" guest. The commandant of the Marine Corps ordered the young captain to come to Washington, D.C., to dine with him and to review a parade with him. *Life* magazine even went so far as to bring famed French chef Louis Diat out of retirement to recreate the entire meal that McCutchen described and then invited the captain and his wife, along with members of *The $64,000 Question* staff, to eat it. The original menu of the royal banquet included nine courses, comprised of fourteen dishes, and nine kinds of wine.[30]

In all instances, the office of Louis G. Cowan, Incorporated, voluntarily acted as the agent in handling all the offers that followed in the wake of winning on *The $64,000 Question*. The program staff advised contestants which public relations endeavors to take and which profit-making schemes might prove most beneficial. All of this unanticipated work above and beyond the actual quiz itself was done without any fee to the contestants and with little enthusiasm on the part of the staff. Steve Carlin called this aspect of his job a "headache." No one had expected the popularity of the show to deluge the contestants with such unprecedented commercial and publicity uses.[31]

The reaction of the press to *The $64,000 Question* was both a measure and a cause of the phenomenal interest in the quiz show. No television program in history ever had received as much newspaper coverage. The press reporting was worldwide. Gino Prato became a cultural hero to most televiewers in Italy. When Richard McCutchen won the top amount, the headline for the *Paris Presse* read "Pres. Lebrun's Green Peas Won $64,000 for Captain Richard."[32]

The attempts of the press to criticize and analyze the show beyond mere reportorial journalism varied greatly. Some criticism was rather harsh. The magazine *Christian Century* doubted that the appearance of Catherine Kreitzer on *The $64,000 Question* would promote any worthwhile interest in the Bible. Then, when it later appeared that the quiz program would spawn other quizzes of the big-money variety, *Christian Century* said:

> The American people are about to be subjected to the most blatant and sustained attempt to aggravate their covetous instincts that has ever been turned on an entire people . . . they will inundate the nation with an orgy of gambling and turn most of the national TV audience into a money-bedazzled mob, pantingly hopeful that at last the magic has been found that will lead them to the pot of gold at the rainbow's end.[33]

Others were less harsh but saw ominous signs in the hugely popular quiz. *Time* magazine called the final appearance of Gino Prato "one of the vastest audiences ever assembled for the purposes of unabashed materialism." Wendell Brogan of the *New Republic* queried, "What may one fairly take from this phenomenon? That in a tax-shadowed era people are peculiarly fascinated by the dream of a lump sum?"[34] Criticism of *The $64,000 Question* also took the form of abundant satire. Commenting on the contribution to television to be gained from the appearance of Paddy Keough, one of the several baseball experts who appeared on the quiz, John Lardner said, "I have known barflies who would answer those questions for the price of a beer."[35]

Two of the most respected critics of television, Jack Gould and Robert Lewis Shayon, had relatively kind words to say about *The $64,000 Question* at the outset of the quiz phenomenon. Gould of the *New York Times*, the dean of television critics (and also the least apologetic in the infant profession), was perhaps the first to identify the big-money quiz show as making a hero of the common man. Gould's populistic viewpoint distinguished the *The $64,000 Question* as a program unique in its "voice of the people" presentation and chastised television for not capitalizing upon the masses sooner. "Television complains continually that it doesn't know where its material will come from next. . . . Yet, meanwhile it overlooks the bottomless reservoir of intelligent people."[36]

Shayon analyzed the program in terms of a much older medium, drama, specifically Sophoclean tragedy. Shayon, probably the most colorful writer among television critics, called the quiz the "Revlon rites" and thought the comparison with the plays of the ancient Greeks to be quite valid. Like Sophocles, *The $64,000 Question* used nonprofessional actors for its participants; people pulled from the modern amphitheater to act out an "unconscious community ritual." Said Shayon: "There on the Revlon stage . . . a modern scapegoat is to be offered who will purify us of our baser lusts for certified checks, harmonize our obscurities and frustrations, and render our unpublicized, individual lots palatable till 'the next plateau'." Tongue halfway in cheek, he compared Gino Prato to *Oedipus at Colonos,* particularly in the wake of his postprogram publicity. The cobbler, he said, "became a sort of sacred relic, like the bones of a saint; perilous, but 'good medicine' for the community that possessed him." To Shayon, a contestant in the isolation booth grappling with difficult questions had all the basic elements of Sophoclean drama: struggle, dismemberment, death, and renewal. In the best Shayon style the critic described the ordeal:

He is face to face with the very meaning of his life, with the most desperate crisis of his aspiration. And the community, the audience, the 50,000,000 who pity and fear, who echo the unutterable prayer of a Mammon—culture—observe (courtesy of the clever, naked, searching camera's eye) how they are dismembered by the trial, the suspense, the unendurable torment of the hero who is expiating publicly their private unacknowledged sin of greed.[37]

Unlike Gould, Shayon put emphasis upon the huge prize money potential of *The $64,000 Question* as a factor for its popularity. The materialistic part of this analysis, however accurate it might have been, also contained a cynicism, which soon turned even more bitter. One year after the big-money quiz phenomenon began, upon hearing rumors of a possible million dollar quiz show called *Twenty Steps to a Million* (which never appeared), Shayon said, "Like all entertainment programs, quizshows deal in illusion, the illusion, in this case, of making the common man look smart." Little did he realize how accurate his judgment was. He also stated that any real experts would shy away from such shows because of the possible loss of face upon not knowing an answer. The addition of such a gigantic amount of money, however, might change the pattern. Shayon posed the question: "What price a lifetime devoted to scholarship when with a common man's cloak of memorized data and a little artfully feigned color in the personality a philosopher may become a plutocrat?"[38] Although the million-dollar quiz never developed as Shayon feared, the inevitable imitation of *The $64,000 Question* produced sufficient thousands of dollars to make the quiz business a richly rewarding vocation for contestants and television producers alike. While the money increased, however, the means of attaining it in television sank to new depths of venality.

NOTES

1. "The $64,000 Question," *Newsweek*, September 5, 1955, p. 42.

2. *New York Times*, August 7, 1955, sec. 2, p. 11; Eliza Merrill Hickok, *Quiz Kids* (Boston: Houghton Mifflin, 1947), pp. 193–199; *New York Times*, August 21, 1955, sec. 6, p. 30; "Moderation," *Time*, July 25, 1955, p. 68; "$64,000 Question," p. 42.

3. *New York Times*, August 21, 1955, p. 30; "$64,000 Question," p. 42.

4. "$64,000 Question," pp. 41–42.

5. U.S., Congress, House, Committee on Interstate and Foreign Commerce, *Investigation of Television Quiz Shows*, before a subcommittee of the Committee on Interstate and Foreign Commerce, House of Representatives, 86th Cong., 1st sess., 1959, Doerfer testimony, pp. 510–511 (hereafter cited as *Investigation*); "High Court Takes Giveaway Issue," *Broadcasting*, October 19, 1953, p. 44; *New York Times*, August 21, 1955, p. 30; "Moderation," p. 68; "$64,000 Question," p. 41.

6. *New York Times*, August 21, 1955, p. 30; "Moderation," p. 68; *New York Times*, March 19, 1955, p. 21; "$64,000 Question," p. 43.

7. Goodman Ace, "The $64,000 Answer," *Saturday Review*, August

13, 1955, p. 23; *New York Times,* March 9, 1955, p. 35; *New York Times,* August 7, 1955, p. 11; Anne W. Langman, *Nation,* April 28, 1956, p. 370; *New York Times,* August 21, 1955, p. 30; "Moderation," p. 68; "$64,000 Question," p. 42.

8. *New York Times,* March 16, 1955, p. 48, March 9, 1955, p. 35; Clark Agnew and Neil O'Brien, *Television Advertising* (New York: McGraw-Hill, 1958), pp. 47–51, 62–63, 68–74; Les Brown, *Television: The Business Behind the Box* (New York: Harcourt Brace Jovanovich, 1971), pp. 15–16, 33–35, 58–62; Jacob Evans, *Selling and Promoting Radio and Television* (New York: Printers' Ink Publishing Company, 1954), pp. 112–116, 122; "Now the Sponsors Call the Tune," *Business Week,* April 19, 1958, pp. 53, 56; *Variety,* June 29, 1955, p. 31.

9. *New York Times,* March 16, 1955, p. 48, March 9, 1955, p. 35; Wendall Brogen, *New Republic,* August 8, 1955, p. 23; *New York Times,* August 22, 1955, p. 30, June 8, 1955, p. 59.

10. *New York Times,* March 16, 1955, p. 48, June 8, 1955, p. 59; "64,000-Dollar Carpenter," *American Magazine* (July 1956): 43; "$64,000 Question," p. 42; "Think Hard," *Newsweek,* June 13, 1955, p. 102.

11. "Banker," *New Yorker,* September 24, 1955, pp. 35–36; "Poor Loser," *Newsweek,* April 23, 1956, p. 58; "$64,000 Question," p. 42.

12. Fred W. Friendly, *Due To Circumstances Beyond Our Control* (New York: Vintage Books, 1967), p. 77; *New York Times,* June 8, 1955, p. 59.

13. *New York Times,* August 7, 1955, p. 11, June 8, 1955, p. 59, June 22, 1955, p. 59; $64,000 Question," pp. 41–42; *Variety,* June 29, 1955, p. 31.

14. Richard Gehman, "How to Think Big," *Cosmopolitan* (December 1955): 79; *New York Times,* July 13, 1955, p. 53; "The Philippian Way," *Newsweek,* July 25, 1955, p. 59; *New York Times,* June 22, 1955, p. 59.

15. Gehman, "How to Think Big," p. 79.

16. "Fort Knox or Bust," *Time,* August 22, 1955, p. 47; Gehman, "How to Think Big," p. 79; *New York Times,* August 10, 1955, p. 51; "Papa Said Stop," *Newsweek,* August 22, 1955, p. 85.

17. *New York Times,* August 7, 1955, p. 11, August 10, 1955, p. 51; Hal March, "Could You Answer the $64,000 Question?" *American Magazine* (December 1955): 82; *New York Times,* September 2, 1955, p. 3, September 6, 1955, p. 53; "Papa Said Stop," p. 85; "$64,000 Question," p. 44; *New York Journal-American,* August 9, 1955, p. 3.

18. Gehman, "How to Think Big," p. 81; March, "Could You Answer," p. 82; *New York Times,* July 13, 1955, p. 53, July 17, 1955, sec. 2, p. 12; "The Philippian Way," p. 59; "$64,000 Question," p. 44.

19. *New York Times,* August 7, 1955, p. 11; *Investigation,* Koplin testimony, pp. 772–773; *New York Times,* October 16, 1959, p. 20; "$64,000 Question," p. 43.

20. *New York Times*, August 7, 1955, p. 11; Gehman, "How to Think Big," pp. 77–78, 80–81; *New York Times*, August 31, 1955, p. 47; *New York Journal-American*, July 20, 1955, p. 4.

21. Gehman, "How to Think Big," p. 80; March, "Could You Answer," p. 81; *New York Journal-American*, July 19, 1955, p. 9; July 20, 1955, p. 4; "$64,000 Question," p. 43.

22. John Sharnik, "Giveaways: Little Men, Big Money," *House and Garden* (November 1956): 46-47; Dan Wakefield, "The Fabulous Sweat Box," *Nation*, March 30, 1957, pp. 270-271.

23. George Rosen, *Variety*, August 3, 1955, p. 25; "The Ultimate Responsibility," *Time*, November 16, 1959, pp. 78–79; *Variety*, July 24, 1955, p. 25.

24. "Banker," pp. 35–36; "Fort Knox or Bust," p. 47; Gehman, "How to Think Big," pp. 77, 81; "No Question That It Sells," *Broadcasting*, September 19, 1955, p. 46; Daniel Seligman, "Revlon's Jackpot," *Fortune* (April 1956): 236; "Semper Chow," *Time*, September 26, 1955, p. 17; "$64,000 Question," p. 44.

25. *Investigation*, Koplin testimony, pp. 743, 748, 761, 770.

26. Ibid., pp. 744, 746, 776–777, 779.

27. Ibid., Abrams testimony, p. 985, Carlin testimony, pp. 791, 798, and Koplin testimony, pp. 770, 776–777, 779, 787.

28. *New York Times*, September 11, 1955, sec. 6, p. 18, September 14, 1955, pp. 1, 71; "$64,000 Question," p. 44; "Stop Wherever You Are," *Fortune* (September 1955): 85.

29. "Semper Chow," pp. 17–18.

30. "A Rich Marine Eats His Words," *Life*, September 26, 1955, pp. 181–183; "Semper Chow," p. 18.

31. Gehman, "How to Think Big," pp. 77, 81.

32. "Semper Chow," p. 18; *Variety*, July 13, 1955, p. 28, July 20, 1955, p. 25.

33. "All Aboard for Rainbow Land!" *Christian Century*, September 14, 1955, pp. 1044–1045; "Another $64,000 Question," *Christian Century*, August 3, 1955, p. 885.

34. Brogen, p. 23; "Fort Knox or Bust," p. 47.

35. John Lardner, "The Summit of Culture," *Newsweek*, September 26, 1955, p. 72, and "Take It, Myrt, Take It," *Newsweek*, October 10, 1955, p. 104; see also *New York Herald Tribune*, July 17, 1955, sec. 9, pp. P1–P2; Nat Hiken's thoughts in "The Big Money," *Time*, September 3, 1956, p. 38; Marya Mannes, "The Million Dollar Surprise," *Reporter*, December 1, 1955, pp. 38–40; parts of Robert Lewis Shayon, "Come and Get a Million," *Saturday Review*, June 16, 1956, p. 34.

36. *New York Times*, August 10, 1955, p. 51.

37. Shayon, "The Tragedy of $64,000," *Saturday Review*, September 24, 1955, p. 26.

2 THE FIRST FULL SEASON OF QUIZ MANIA: 1955-56

...one of the all-time American insanities, ranking well up there with dance marathons and flagpole sitting.'' [1]
—John Crosby

Beginning in the fall of 1955, within weeks after Louis Cowan departed, a series of weekly meetings was instituted in Revlon's offices, which continued virtually for the life of *The $64,000 Question* well into 1958 and which solidified the control exercised over the quiz's contestants, a process already begun by the producers. The meetings were held in the office of Martin Revson, executive vice-president and director of Revlon. The president of the company, Charles Revson, attended the sessions only infrequently and rarely stayed long. Always present from EPI were Steve Carlin, Harry Fleischmann, and Mert Koplin. Also attending were George Abrams, Revlon's vice-president in charge of advertising, and his assistant, William Mandel, as well as a representative from Revlon's advertising agency (it had several; the turnover was rather rapid). [2]

Martin Revson chaired these meetings, called for the purpose of discussing the progress of the program in extensive detail. Rarely has a sponsor shown the interest and influence with a television program as did Revlon with *The $64,000 Question* and its later quizzes. According to Steve Carlin, every minute detail was discussed at the sessions. The first part of the meetings would usually have a discussion of the previous show and covered such questions as whether the show had been interesting that week. Then there would be some talk about the specific contestants and their appeal or why they failed to generate any attractiveness. The walls of Revson's office had weekly ratings charts coupled with the names of the contestants, the inference being that if a rating declined a particular week, the type of contestants who had appeared on the quiz was largely at fault. Other topics for discussion included the introduction of new categories of questions and the ongoing search for future contestants. No subject was too trivial or minute for Revson to introduce (he had lengthy criticisms about the staging of the commercials), but the bulk of the time was spent discussing contestants, specifically how more picturesque contestants could be found to increase ratings.

These meetings gave substantial reinforcement to the producers of *The $64,000 Question* to continue, if not strengthen, their deceptive methods of control. Although Martin Revson later vehemently denied that the purpose of the meetings was contestant control, it is not difficult to envision how the volatile sponsor's expressed hopes and fears regarding the quiz at these sessions might be interpreted as implicit demands to producers only too eager to justify their actions. For example, if Revson speculated aloud, "I sure hope so and so stays on," the producers would infer that further manipulation was in order. Unintentionally and unknown to himself, Martin Revson fostered the initial deceit in the first and later big-money television quizzes by his "emphatic suggestions" and force of personality. Although Steve Carlin and Mert Koplin later testified that they believed Revson was aware of the controls used on the show, the actual circumstances surrounding the meetings seem to be that the producers presumed the sponsor had implicitly suggested that his wishes as to the progress of the show be transformed into an exact program blueprint. The word *control* was never used at any of the meetings. Nor was there any candid discussion on the part of the producers as to the specific methods of question writing and contestant selection being conducted. George Abrams said it was his understanding that the producers were to carry out the sponsor's wishes as to writing relatively difficult or simple questions. Said Abrams: "We understood that the technique used for controlling the destiny of a contestant was to employ questions ranging from tough to easy, based on the producer's knowledge of the expertness of the contestant in certain areas within his chosen category as determined in their screening operation." The details of control, according to Abrams, were never discussed but were left to the discretion of the producers. He testified that he never knew that screening answers might reappear in the actual contest. Revson later denied that he knew his suggestions were carried out by Carlin regarding the destiny of contestants on the show. James Webb, president of the advertising agency of C. J. LaRoche and Company, which was Revlon's agency of record for a short while, attended most of the weekly conferences in 1955 and 1956. His version of events confirms Revson's testimony: "From time to time, Martin Revson or George Abrams of Revlon expressed the hope that uninteresting contestants would leave the show. But to me this meant that EPI should reevaluate the contestants and not encourage them to try for the higher level." Webb said he knew nothing of controls or that the sponsor's wishes should have ever been interpreted as anything beyond mere hopes, certainly not as instructions. The complicity of the sponsor, then, in the questionable behind-the-scenes conduct on *The $64,000 Question* was there only by implication. During the early life of the quiz in particular, Martin Revson's suggestions and criticisms were few compared to later years when the ratings were lower. The only thing not in question in 1955-56 was that *The $64,000 Question* was the most meteoric event in television's brief history.[3]

Nothing breeds imitation in television like success. It was inevitable that *The $64,000 Question*, the most rapidly successful program of its time, would bring about a slew of other big-money quizzes. Unfortunately for the possible competition, most of the fall programming for 1955 had been established and scheduled when the show made its debut in June of that year. There were a number of efforts to get another big-money quiz on the air after Louis Cowan announced his latest creation, particularly after it became apparent that the show would be the hit of the season. Often these rumored productions and reported efforts were more intriguing and more outlandish than what actually ever appeared on the television screen in the wake of *The $64,000 Question*.

One of the earliest attempts to match Cowan was made by promoter Sumner Rosenthal of General Artists Corporation who devised the quiz show *The Big Moment*. The ultimate prize a contestant could win was $100 per week for life. Panel-and-game-show producers Mark Goodson and Bill Todman, creators of the very successful *What's My Line?* investigated the possibility of airing a $50,000 quiz program, *Beat the Jackpot*, but their work on this project never went beyond the planning stage. The Mutual Radio Network tried to promote an unnamed radio quiz on which a person would receive a telephone call at random, be given a question, and upon correctly answering be given $250,000. This quiz would have required at least three and possibly as many as eight sponsors but none came forth to place it on the air.[4]

Other big-money quiz programs that never were aired on television as a rapid response to *The $64,000 Question* included *Texas Tycoon*, a complicated mixture of auction and quiz, which provided for a top prize of $100,000 in oil royalties and consolation prizes of hundreds of silver dollars; *The Big Board*, which had prizes of from ten to a hundred shares of the favorite stock of the contestant, and *Get Out of Debt*, which was "a quiz show for the improvident" and which the prizes, such as a new house, would depend upon how deeply in debt the hard-luck contestant was. Some of these proposals failed to attract sponsors; some were probably too preposterous to succeed; but all of them came too late. The saturation of big-money quiz programs would have to wait until the fall of 1956.[5]

A few imitative quizzes did surface during the 1955–56 season; not too surprisingly, the majority of them came from EPI. First was *The Big Surprise* in October 1955, created by Steve Carlin shortly after Cowan left to join CBS. It was an unusually complicated program with a seemingly indefinite format. Originally it was speculated that a contestant might win from $1 to $100,000 in the course of only one evening. When the show finally premiered on the National Broadcasting Company, though, the first week maximum amount was $10,000; it jumped to $25,000 the next week, then $50,000, and finally

$100,000 with special rules for a second chance at the top money. If a contestant missed the high-valued question, a second chance was available if a stand-in came forth. In other words, if someone who strongly resembled the contestant in appearance came to the studio the next week and correctly answered a question from another category, then the original contestant would be afforded another opportunity. This complex procedure was hoped to foster brotherhood as complete strangers might come forth to help fallen contestants on the road to riches.[6]

Mert Koplin also produced *The Big Surprise* and remained with the show for approximately six months. Early in 1956 Koplin hired a new assistant, Shirley Bernstein, to work on the new program. Bernstein had originally been working for Louis Cowan, who had hired her as a researcher in September 1955 and later she did some interviewing for *The $64,000 Question*. Her new job at *The Big Surprise* was similar to Koplin's at the parent quiz. She interviewed potential prize winners and devised many of the questions for the lesser levels of the quiz. Koplin and Bernstein continued the same form of contestant control on *The Big Surprise* that had been initiated on the older show. With Bernstein and the successors to Koplin, the interviewer grew gradually less subtle. They more than likely turned away from his conversational approach and changed the contestant screenings into blunt question-and-answer sessions. Also assisting Koplin and Carlin in the new quiz was a continuity writer, Albert Freedman, who occasionally interviewed in Bernstein's place. As new practitioners in the ethics of big-money quizzes, Shirley Bernstein and Albert Freedman learned their craft quickly and soon expanded their positions, hers within the confines of EPI, his in a future quiz show, *Twenty-one*. Since *The Big Surprise* was not under Revlon's control (it was sponsored by Spiedel and Purex corporations), it is most noteworthy that Carlin and Koplin continued the controls minus the supposedly crucial weekly reinforcement of Martin Revson.[7]

Steve Carlin preferred that *The Big Surprise* be labeled not a quiz show but a "novelty show with human interest as a major factor." The method of contestant selection seemed almost as complicated as the process of winning money on the program. People were chosen on the basis of some unusual act they had performed, such as "either a small act of kindness or a heroic deed." Police sergeant Barney Arluck, the first contestant on the show, had freed a man wrongly accused of murder. Categories on *The Big Surprise* depended upon the hobby or chief interest of each contestant. The procedure for answering questions initially involved solving riddles rather than answering direct questions, but this format evolved into questions submitted by celebrities or other public figures. The first contestant to win the $100,000 amount, Ethel Park Richardson, answered six questions on American folklore devised by the governor of California, Goodwin Knight. The queries Richardson successfully answered included naming the 1825 canal that opened the West, identifying the river in the song "El-a-noy," naming the girl in the song "Colorado Trail," and also identifying Shenandoah. She had to sing a verse and chorus from the folk song "Sacramento" and sing one stanza from "The Streets of Laredo."[8]

The program was a success, although it was never as popular as *The $64,000 Question.* Jack Gould called its debut a "crashing bore" and severly criticized the complexity of the quiz, as well as its emcee, Jack Barry, whom he said, "displayed all the warmth and charm of a headwaiter who had not been tipped." Barry was soon replaced by newsman Mike Wallace early in 1956. Undoubtedly the most popular contestant on *The Big Surprise* the first year was a ten-year-old asthmatic child from Tujunga, California—Lenny Ross, wizard on questions on the stock market. Even though he was the fourth contestant to win $100,000 on the show, his popularity was greatest. Keith Funston, president of the New York Stock Exchange, gave $2,500 worth of any listed stock of his choice as well as let the young expert open the Exchange, the first outsider ever to do so. Lenny Ross was one of the exceptional contestants who occasionally confronted EPI as being so well informed in his subject that virtually no assistance was necessary to help him on his way to winnings. In his initial interview Ross poured forth with so much knowledge on the stock market that Carlin and Koplin felt confident that they had a winner. Not long after leaving *The Big Surprise* Ross received a job from a Brazilian cartel to study and report on coffee prices in the United States. [9]

The capitalization upon the success of *The $64,000 Question* and its contestants was most obvious in *The $64,000 Challenge,* which pitted former winners against new contestants in a dual isolation booth quiz. In the first show, Redmond O'Hanlon faced fireman Richard Van Outryve in the familiar category of Shakespeare. The idea appeared early with Cowan and his organization. After he went to CBS, he and Carlin packaged the quiz for the network. There were numerous sponsor problems as Revlon haggled with its co-sponsor, the tobacco firm of P. Lorillard Company, represented by the advertising firm of Young and Rubicam. P. Lorillard withdrew from the venture; it was already sponsoring an hour of prime time on CBS and decided not to enter into contract with a different network. For a while it was resolved that there would be no cosponsor, but when the new quiz eventually premiered (April 1956), the makers of Kent cigarettes were present alongside Revlon. A name for the show was slow in coming. The adman Norman Norman of Norman, Craig and Kummell, who had worked closely with Cowan, suggested *Panelopoly*. Then it was going to be *The $64,000 Panel* before the final name emerged. [10]

Although the imitation was popular, it never equaled the parent show. Part of the problem possibly was that it had contestants who competed. The audience may have been somewhat divided and the atmosphere less warm. Also there was no consolation prize for the loser. The first show got off badly when the master of ceremonies, Sonny Fox, made a serious mistake. O'Hanlon had wrongly identified the father of Desdemona as Polonius, rather than Brabantio, and Fox said this was correct. *The $64,000 Challenge* and Fox quickly apologized the next day to an outraged press and public, and O'Hanlon was allowed to return the next week and begin again. Despite the seemingly less appealing nature of *The $64,000 Challenge,* by the end of the 1955–56 television season, it had managed to best its parent format on occasion in the ratings. [11]

As was the case with the other EPI ventures into entertainment, *The $64,000 Challenge* was secretly controlled. In fact it was probably the most tightly controlled quiz show at this time because the producers had to contend with two contestants and thereby attempt to govern the winnings of two potentially unpredictable participants. The weekly meetings in Martin Revson's office now had a new program to discuss. Possibly because it proved to be not as popular as its predecessor, Revson's criticisms increased, and this in turn increased the efforts of the producers to mold the outcome of the quiz to what they conceived to be the sponsor's wishes.[12]

The third major big-money quiz program to emerge after *The $64,000 Question* during the first full season was *Do You Trust Your Wife?* a non-EPI package hosted by comedian Edgar Bergen and his puppet repertoire. This show had the remarkable good fortune to be given the time slot immediately following *The $64,000 Question* opposite *See It Now*. The weekly news outlet of Edward R. Murrow could not keep pace in the vicious ratings cycle and was relegated to Sunday afternoons. *Do You Trust Your Wife?* had much of the idea of the aborted *The Big Moment:* couples could win up to $100 per week for up to twenty years by having the husband or wife answer each question of varying categories. This quiz was the only one to originate from the West Coast and made much of the fact that it had managed to circumvent the huge tax bite that plagued winners on the other big-money quiz shows. Mr. and Mrs. Steve Rowland remained on the show for fourteen weeks, during its first season, thus winning $100 per week for fourteen years.[13]

Imitation of *The $64,000 Question* was not confined to U.S. television. A program in Brazil featured 45,000 cruzeiros as top prize. Great Britain had its equivalent quiz, as did Sweden. On Mexico's version, *The 64,000 Peso Question* (sponsored by Revlon), Jamie Olvera became the first contestant to reach the pinnacle by identifying two of the scouts of Hernando Cortes in his war against the Aztecs. The most famous overseas quiz program, however, belonged to Italian television: *Lascia o Raddoppia* (translated *Leave or Double* or, more colloquially, *Double or Nothing*), which had a top prize of 5,120,000 lire (approximately $8,500). *Lascia o Raddoppia* had a number of noteworthy occurrences. When contestant Maria Zocchi, also known as Miss Tuscany, whose category was cycling stopped at 2,500,000 lire she broke down on the show, crying that she could not risk any more money needed for her ailing mother. Ex-King Farouk of Egypt, who saw the show, promptly sent her the $4,000 difference between the amount she won and the amount she might have won. On another occasion the cleavage-conscious television camera refused to tip below the neckline of Maria Luisa Garoppa for fear of revealing her ample bustline, creating quite a furor among the viewers of 250,000 Italian television sets. Truly the big-money appeal and format of *The $64,000 Question* spread around the world, without regard to nationality or ideology. Even the anti-capitalism of the *Daily Worker* was captured by the allure of Cowan's creation: it had a $64,000 fund drive at the height of the quiz mania.[14]

Easier than imitating *The $64,000 Question* or, at least, less creative, would have been to purchase the show; and this was exactly what the rival networks of CBS tried to do, maneuvers that *Variety* labeled "unprecedented" in the history of television. The original contract with CBS was due to expire in January 1956. As late as August of the previous year, heads of both the National and American Broadcasting companies said they had neither interest nor plans for any big-money quiz shows. Their disclaimers were probably meant to conceal both their rating-based envy and their negotiations underway to buy the Cowan creation. NBC was encouraged to buy *The $64,000 Question* primarily by the advertising firm of Batten, Barton, Durstine, and Osborne whose client, the Armstrong Cork Company, had the Tuesday 10:00 P.M. time slot opposite the highest-rated program on television. The offer NBC made to Revlon was rumored to be around $2 million "cuffo" ($2 million worth of daytime exposure on the network). The offer also included a free prime-time slot (thirty minutes) for any other show that Revlon might care to sponsor.[15]

The situation was further complicated when Revlon became disenchanted with the advertising agency of Norman, Craig, and Kummell, which handled its account for *The $64,000 Question*. Charles Revson criticized adman Walter Craig, who had done as much as anyone in bringing Revlon and *The $64,000 Question* together, for agreeing to take the account of Speidel, cosponsor of *The Big Surprise*, the first rival imitation of *The $64,000 Question*. Revson viewed Craig's decision as a conflict of interest and dropped Norman, Craig, and Kummell. Both Charles and Martin Revson were angered at the appearance of *The Big Surprise* and never fully forgave Cowan and Carlin for creating it. The agency succeeding Norman, Craig, and Kummel was C.J. LaRoche and Company, which handled a portion of the Revlon account in other media. Then, ironically, in February 1956, the new agency Revlon hired to replace LaRoche for *The $64,000 Question* was Batten, Barton, Durstine, and Osborne. Revlon apparently saw no conflict in hiring the same agency that handled the program directly opposite its quiz. From the viewpoint of BBD&O, obtaining the Revlon account defused their desires and efforts to have *The $64,000 Question* removed from its Tuesday night roost onto a NBC slot. It was known that ABC made a comparable offer for the quiz, but neither network succeeded in obtaining the prize. As Louis Cowan belonged to CBS, so did *The $64,000 Question*.[16]

During the 1955–56 television season of *The $64,000 Question* as rivals began to proliferate, the progenitor of the big-money quizzes continued its unparalleled success. Although it dropped from its number one spot in the ratings on occasional weeks, *The $64,000 Question* was still the most popular show regularly shown on television. During the mid-1950s, there was a wider variety of television ratings systems than today with varying methods of survey research among them. Videodex, Incorporated, used almost 10,000 television diaries; the Pulse, Incorporated, conducted nearly 70,000 door-to-door interviews per week; Trendex, Incorporated, relied upon an average of 750 telephone interviews per each half-hour program; the American Research Bureau, Incorporated, used a selected 2,200 diaries; and A.C. Nielson Company, the most accurate rating service then and which has even further solidified that position today, used Audimeters, which were electronically connected to television sets to record what was being watched. In addition to using the most sophisticated research techniques, it used a carefully selected national sample of only 900 sets. Despite the variations of method among the services and the variations within their respective top ten listings, *The $64,000 Question* topped every rating by the end of the 1955–56 season.[17]

Nor did the fame of the show's successful contestants dwindle during the first full season. The second person to win the top amount, Dr. Joyce Brothers, was a psychologist who has been probably the only big-money quiz champion to go on to win something akin to permanent celebrity status, with numerous books and articles containing psychological advice on such matters as child rearing and love problems. When she first reached the interview stage with Koplin, she specified her knowledgeable categories as psychology and home economics. Koplin said she could not appear with such uninteresting topics, but that a female psychologist with a category in wrestling or boxing would have enough contrast possibly to merit an appearance. He initially dismissed Brothers with this advice, not expecting to see her again, but she came back several weeks later, after having memorized several encyclopedias of boxing, and claimed she was now an expert in the manly art. Skeptical of such memory power, Koplin proceeded to quiz her from a boxing reference and discovered another potential quiz winner so well versed in the chosen category that Joyce Brothers needed no coaching in the usual manner of the show. In fact, Koplin deliberately wrote rather difficult questions for her, but she amazed the producers and the viewing nation by winning $64,000.

Later in the season, jockey Billy Pearson also achieved the top amount in the incongruous category of art. On the night he won, his wife collapsed from the tension and spent a week in the hospital. Pearson's postquiz prizes included being the honored guest at the Kentucky Derby, a movie offer from his friend John Huston (the film was to be *Typee*, based on Herman Melville's novel, but it was never produced), and a proposed role in a television series beginning in fall 1957. [18]

Part of the reason for the popularity of the big-money quiz shows within the television industry was economic. Even with the large amounts of prize money, the quizzes were among the least expensive shows to produce: they used cheap sets; there were no actors to pay; and they were live. When *The $64,000 Question* was at the height of its first summer's success, it cost about $25,000 a week to produce, including prize money; in contrast a filmed program, such as *I Love Lucy* cost at least $35,000 per week. In spite of the rapid inflation in the cost of television time as the 1950s wore on, the quizzes remained inexpensive relative to the industry. For example, one year later the Revlon show averaged nearly $70,000 per week, including a weekly average of $13,500 to give out as winnings; *This Is Your Life* sponsored by a cosmetics rival of Revlon, the Hazel Bishop Company, cost almost $100,000 per show.[19]

Did the immense popularity of quiz shows indicate a newly found or latent appreciation of intelligence by Americans? The quiz craze occurred immediately after the heyday of McCarthyism and carried over to the Soviet launching of the first orbital satellite, Sputnik, in October 1957. If the McCarthy years of 1950–54 can be seen as a time of rampant anti-intellectualism, perhaps best expressed at the midway point during the 1952 presidential campaign when columnist Joseph Alsop coined the word *eggheads* for intellectual supporters of Adlai Stevenson, then the post Sputnik years perhaps revealed a period when the word *intellectual* had lost much of its opprobrium and intelligence achieved admiration.[20] The quizzes had their greatest appeal during the limbo' years between the extremes of anti-intellectualism and the post-Sputnik period of a reawakened concern for education and exhibited characteristics of both poles. The mid-1950s were years of a national easing of tensions. The Korean War was finally over, as was the most vituperative phase of the cold war at home, and America settled back into the recuperative first term of President Eisenhower.

To say that the popularity of the television quiz paved the way for the rejection of anti-intellectualism following the Sputnik launch in late 1957 is probably extreme, but those same millions of Americans who shuddered at the successful Soviet endeavor had been captivated only months before by a bright and amiable young college instructor, Charles Van Doren, as he struggled through weeks of answering, correctly, difficult questions of endless variety on the quiz program *Twenty-one*. Certainly Americans were being exposed to and entertained by a type of intelligence that may have consisted of little more than a succession of excellent memories, but the appearance of such television fare gave the populace an interest in knowledge, perhaps even an appreciation for it, however trivial, in preparation for the time when knowledge and its public support would turn serious after it was thrust into the renewed context of the cold war.

In spite of their popular demonstration of knowledge, quizzes were also profoundly anti-intellectual in one regard. The quiz champions were not the same kind of intelligentsia who received the scorn and wrath of McCarthyism. They were rarely professional people demonstrating their vocational expertise on the shows, although this was to change somewhat with the appearance of *Twenty-one* the following season. This newly televised knowledgeable hero was the common man, and his knowledge was, most frequently, avocational. His was the unexpected intellect or, as a typical critique read: "The giveaway show represents some sort of climax in the age of the common man. By no previous device... have the shoemaker, the school-teacher, the civil service clerk and other representatives of the breed been raised to such heights of distinction".[21]

In fact, however, many of the new so-called common celebrities were anything but ordinary folk. The educational levels of the contestants were, for the most part, hidden. Barney Arluck, the first contestant on *The Big Surprise*, was introduced as a policeman, but he was also a law school graduate, although that fact was kept as inconspicuous as possible. The other noted policeman contestant, Redmond O'Hanlon, was represented as an average person who knew Shakespeare, but in fact he was also a postgraduate student of English literature.[22]

The average American as intelligent and heroic—willing to take risks—personified by the successful quiz contestants, is a theme with a definite populist strain, expressing both antielitism and anti-intellectualism, as well as the more positive affirmation of the common man as basically wise. Psychologist Gerhart Wiebe, then an assistant to the president of CBS, analyzed the "empathy force" behind the quiz-show appeal: "We're all pretty much alike and we're all smart." Since the contestants were prototypical of the American televiewer, a "fantasy of equality" emerged. The average American became both famous and heroic through the "electronic proxy" of the quiz winner.[23] Perhaps rather than the popularity of intellect the enormous fascination with the quiz programs symbolized the democratization of intelligence for millions of Americans.

The quiz-show mania also reflected the traditional optimism in the American value system whereby a person, through luck and pluck, can achieve material wealth, quite literally overnight. Dan Wakefield, writing in the *Nation*, called the quizzes the "newest translation of the Great American Dream." Nor were the quiz shows alone in the reflection as the optimistic notion of the American dream that humble people can move rapidly to riches with the correct combination of circumstances certainly was being reinforced elsewhere in society in the mid-1950s; as sociologist W. Lloyd Warner wrote of the business sector: "Mobility to the top is not decreasing; in fact, for at least the last quarter century, it has been increasing." Historian John Brooks amplified that statement: "The famous Horatio Alger legend of rags-to-riches has become more, rather than less, factual than it was in Alger's time." Were it not for the deliberate withholding from the public of the adversity suffered by the contestants, first by Cowan, then later continued by EPI, the quiz shows would fit very nicely into the Horatio Alger niche in American social legend.[24]

Perhaps more valid than the view of the mid-1950s as a period of time closely bordered by an earlier anti-intellectualism and a later appreciation for intellect or as a time of incessant optimism is the picture of a relatively affluent time with a decided materialistic strain. This interpretation may present a more valid explanation of the extraordinary appeal of the big money quiz program. The primary interest in the quiz was not its possible affirmation of the average American as basically intelligent or its neo-Horatio Alger aspects but rather the money. Cultural critic Max Lerner saw both populistic and materialistic elements in the phenomenon as he described *The $64,000 Question*: "It is Huey Long's 'Every Man a King' put into TV language."[25] Another put it more cynically, after Charles Revson, the sponsor, stated: "We're trying to show the country that the little people are really very intelligent and knowledgeable. That's why the show *The $64,000 Question* has caught on— because of the little people." A friend was heard to say: "That's right Charles, It's the little people. Little people — and big money."[26] For the purpose of this study, however, the most important aspect of the success of *The $64,000 Question* was not the reasons for its appeal, however intriguing they might be, but the influence the show held for future programming: televised fraudulent quizzes that tarnished the participants, the sponsors, the networks, and, perhaps, the national character.

NOTES

1. John Crosby, "It Was New and We Were Very Innocent," *TV Guide*, September 22-28, 1973, p. 7.

2. U.S. Congress, House, Committee on Interstate and Foreign Commerce, *Investigation of Television Quiz Shows*, before a subcommittee of the Committee on Interstate and Foreign Commerce, House of Representatives, 86th Cong., 1st sess. 1959, Carlin testimony, pp. 791, 793, Koplin testimony, pp. 748-749, Martin Revson testimony, p. 803 (hereafter cited as *Investigation*).

3. Ibid., sworn statement of Abrams as part of Richard N. Goodwin testimony, pp. 849-850, Abrams testimony, pp. 980-981, 944-995, Carlin testimony, p. 792, Foreman testimony, pp. 912, 918, Koplin testimony, pp. 749-752, Martin Revson testimony, pp. 804, 830, 838, Webb testimony, pp. 852, 854-855, 858-859, 866.

4. *New York Times*, March 16, 1955, p. 48; *New York Journal-American*, August 16, 1955, p. 26; "The $64,000 Question," *Newsweek*, September 5, 1955, p. 45; *Variety*, March 16, 1955, p. 27.

5. "$64,000 Question," p. 45.

6. *New York Times*, August 23, 1955, p. 49, September 30, 1955, p. 53, December 11, 1955, p. 85; *Variety*, August 27, 1955, p. 27.

7. *New York Times*, August 23, 1955, p. 49; *Investigation*, sworn statement of Shirley Bernstein as part of Goodwin testimony, p. 922, Freedman testimony, pp. 211, 221-222, Koplin testimony, p. 743.

8. *New York Times*, August 23, 1955, p. 49, September 30, 1955, p. 53, October 9, 1955, p. 88, December 11, 1955, p. 85.

9. "The Big Money," *Time*, September 3, 1956, p. 38; *New York Times*, October 10, 1955, p. 53; *Investigation*, Koplin testimony, p. 766; "The Little Boy Blew It," *Newsweek*, April 16, 1956, p. 77; *Newsweek*, April 30, 1956, p. 78; *New York Times*, March 11, 1956, p. 87; "A Prodigy Rings the Bell," *Life*, May 7, 1956, pp. 88, 90.

10. *New York Times*, November 17, 1955, p. 71, October 19, 1955, p. 67, October 10, 1955, p. 52; *Broadcasting*, April 16, 1956, p. 19; "The Enormity of It," *Time*, September 19, 1955, p. 88; *New York Times*, April 9, 1956, p. 51; "Poor Loser," *Newsweek*, April 23, 1956, p. 58.

11. *New York Times*, April 9, 1956, p. 51; " 'Question' and Answer," *Newsweek*, July 23, 1956, p. 69; "Poor Loser," p. 58.

12. *Investigation*, Carlin testimony, p. 793, Koplin testimony, p. 745.

13. Fred W. Friendly, *Due to Circumstances Beyond Our Control*, (New York: Vintage Books, 1967), pp. 77, 85-86; "How They Got $74,000," *Newsweek*, July 23, 1956, p. 70; "Knowing Your Wife," *Newsweek*, January 9, 1956, p. 63; "$100 a Week for 20 Years," *Time*, December 19, 1955, p. 46.

14. *Daily Worker*, September 6, 1955, p. 1; "45-19-39," *Time*, September 10, 1956, pp. 95-96; "Quiz Crazy," *Time*, February 27, 1956, pp. 74-75; Daniel Seligman, "Revlon's Jackpot," *Fortune* (April 1956): 239; "The Swedish Shark," *Newsweek*, February 25, 1957, p. 66; "Tearjerker," *Time*, July 9, 1956, p. 40; William Weaver, "Letter from Rome," *Time*, July 9, 1956, p. 40; William Weaver, "Letter from Rome," *Nation*, June 2, 1956, pp. 478-479.

15. *New York Times*, September 21, 1955, p. 67; "Fort Knox or Bust," *Time*, August 22, 1955, p. 47; Seligman, "Revlon's Jackpot," pp. 239-240.

16. *New York Times*, September 21, 1955, p. 67; *Investigation*, Foreman testimony, p. 911, Koplin testimony, p. 749, Charles Revson testimony, p. 881, Webb testimony, p. 852.

17. "TV's Figures Won't Quite Add," *Business Week*, September 29, 1956, p. 45.

18. "The Artful Jockey," *Newsweek*, April 30, 1956, p. 78; *Investigation*, Koplin testimony, pp. 779 and 784; *Newsweek*, February 27, 1957, p. 65; *Time*, April 30, 1956, p. 90; "Winner Take All," *Newsweek*, December 19, 1955, pp. 44-45.

19. Seligman, "Revlon's Jackpot," p. 239; "The $64,000 Question," *Newsweek*, September 5, 1955, p. 44.

20. Richard Hofstadter, *Anti-Intellectualism in American Life* (New York: Vintage Books, 1962), pp. 3-19.

21. John Sharnik, "Giveaways: Little Men, Big Money," *House and Garden* (November 1956): 46.

22. *New York Times*, October 23, 1955, p. 53, June 22, 1955, p. 59.

23. *Nation*, April 28, 1956, p. 370.

24. John Brooks, *The Great Leap* (New York: Harper and Row, 1968), p. 59; Dan Wakefield, "The Fabulous Sweat Box," *Nation*, March 30, 1957, p. 269; Warner cited by John Brooks, *The Great Leap* (New York: Harper and Row, 1968), p. 59.

25. "The Enormity of It," *Time*, September 19, 1955, p. 88.

26. Richard Gehman, "How to Think Big," *Cosmopolitan* (December 1955): 77, 81.

3 | ENTER THE QUIZMASTERS: THE 1956-57 SEASON

As the first full television season following *The $64,000 Question* flickered to an end in June 1956, it was inevitable that the headstart enjoyed by Entertainment Productions, Incorporated, and their successful imitations, *The $64,000 Challenge* and *The Big Surprise*, as well as the popular non-EPI program *Do You Trust Your Wife?* would fade as more and more producers and independent packagers copied the big-money quiz formula for big ratings and bigger profits. One such production unit was Barry and Enright Productions headed by Jack Barry and Daniel Enright.

Barry, the intitial emcee for *The Big Surprise*, was the only half of the partnership that consistently appeared in front of the television camera. He was primarily an announcer who treasured his exposure on television (a friend and coworker characterized him "as a kindergarten egomaniac. He suffers the same as most people do who like to appear on television and be recognized on the streets"). He joined with Enright (whose real name was Enrenreich) in 1947 when the latter was program supervisor at radio station WOR in New York City. Enright's show business career goes back as far as that of Lou Cowan, starting in radio in 1939. Some of the shows Enright and Barry created were *You're on Your Own, Juvenile Jury* (similar to Cowan's *Quiz Kids*), and *Life Begins at Eighty*.[1]

In the middle of the 1955-56 television season, *Life Begins at Eighty* was canceled, leaving Barry and Enright with only one show on television, a children's cartoon show, *Winky Dink and You,* hosted by Barry. Enright secured a daytime quiz-show variation on one of the simplest of all games. The quiz was called *Tic Tac Dough,* modeled after the familiar tick-tack-toe in which two contestants played the game on a large board with nine squares, each with a labeled category and each X or O requiring a correct answer to the question for the particular square. As was the case with most other daytime quiz and game shows, the stakes were relatively small; only $100 was given for each game. A tie game forced the following game to be played for a greater amount. With *Tic Tac Dough* the potential for greater prize money was present. As an open-ended game, a contestant could remain on the quiz indefinitely.[2]

Albert Freedman, who had worked intermittently for Enright since early 1955, was hired away from *The Big Surprise* to produce *Tic Tac Dough.* This new quiz seemingly had a more formal apparatus by which applicants became contestants, for a fairly lengthy written examination was given to quiz aspirants. This process was immaterial, though, as Freedman soon managed to "interview" a high percentage of contestants and continued the same sort of coaching that he had witnessed on *The Big Surprise. Tic Tac Dough* premiered in July 1956, hosted by Jack Barry, and soon became a popular staple of daytime television.[3]

Barry and Enright's grandest creation was yet to surface. Since Dan Enright had found it fruitful to imitate the quiz format in the past, it was certain that he would attempt a big-money quiz show of his own. Taking the continuing-contestant, or "hangover" contestant, appeal of *The $64,000 Question* (a program device that actually went back to a 1945 radio quiz show, *Winner Take All*), and stretching it to an open-ended format as *Tic Tac Dough,* thus devising the potential for unlimited winnings added to enlarged funds, Enright created *Twenty-one,* a more complex variation on the card game twenty-one. Like *The $64,000 Challenge* it pitted one contestant against another in a dual isolation booth quiz. The object of the game was to get twenty-one points by correctly answering questions valued in difficulty from one to eleven points. Contestants did not choose their categories; over a hundred were represented at random in the quiz. Once the category was stated by the emcee, however, the contestant chose the number of points he wished to attempt to gain; if he answered a ten-point question and then an eleven-point question correctly, he would have the necessary twenty-one points.

A hypothetical game will illustrate the method. Contestant A is playing contestant B. In the first round A correctly answers a ten-point question, and B misses an eight-point question. In round two A again correctly answers a ten-point question, and contestant B correctly responds to an eleven-point query. Up to this time both players have been kept in their soundproof isolation booths, unaware of the other's progress. At the end of the second round, if neither one has reached twenty-one, the emcee would then ask both, at the same time, whether either one wanted to stop. Contestant A, believing that his twenty points, at the very worst, would tie his opponent, elects to stop the game. He would then win. Since there are nine points between his score and that of player B, contestant A would receive $500 for each of the nine points. If, however, neither contestant chose to stop after the second round, they would continue with another round. Now contestant A correctly answers the one-point question, giving him twenty-one points. At this point the emcee would tell contestant B that A had achieved twenty-one and that his only hope to remain in the game was to choose and correctly answer a ten-point question to tie A. Contestant A would be allowed to listen in on the progress of his opponent. If the contestants tied, another game would be necessary, and the point differential would be worth an extra $500 for each tie match. Consequently a series of tie games could put the stakes well into the tens of thousands of dollars.[4]

In March 1956, Barry and Enright filmed a rough rehearsal of *Twenty-one*. They showed the film to Pharmaceuticals, Incorporated, and its advertising agency, Edward Kletter Associates. Pharmaceuticals, Incorporated, headed by Matthew Rosenhouse, had sponsored most of the Barry and Enright packages in the past and would do so now. The two parties signed a contract in May agreeing that Pharmaceuticals, Incorporated, would pay Barry and Enright $15,000 per show and an additional $10,000 per week for prize money. The contract duration was twenty-six weeks, with renewable options every thirteen weeks thereafter. Pharmaceuticals made a variety of nonprescription drugs and sundries, such as Sominex sleeping aids, Aqua-Velva after-shave lotion, and Conte shampoo; their most famous product was (and still is) Geritol, an iron tonic for "tired blood." Enright secured a spot on the fall television schedule with NBC. Like virtually all other quiz shows that followed in the path of *The $64,000 Question*, *Twenty-one* started as an independent production; the network supervised only what are called "below-the-line" elements in the show, (such as the props, cameras, and technicians, which the producers paid for). "Above-the-line" features—talent, script, production, and direction—remained entirely under the supervision of the independent producer.[5]

Twenty-one made its debut Wednesday, September 12, 1956, in the 10:30 to 11:00 evening slot. The initial producer was Howard Merrill, with Enright as supervisor-producer and Jack Barry as the master of ceremonies. The first contestants "seemed to stumble to victory" according to *Variety*, and Enright quickly sensed that some form of contestant control was necessary to produce a more exciting contest. Showmanship would have to take precedence over honesty. The coaching begun on *Tic Tac Dough* and instituted on *Twenty-one* by Enright was more direct, crasser, and more thoroughly deceitful than anything practiced by Mert Koplin and EPI. The only subtlety about Dan Enright was his uncanny ability to decide and choose which contestants would submit to his deceptions.[6]

What *Twenty-one* needed to excite the viewing public, reasoned Enright, was a big winner, and he thought he had one in Richard Jackman, a struggling writer from Oneonta, New York, who had appeared briefly on *Tic Tac Dough* in September. To Jackman *Tic Tac Dough* was completely honest; he had received no coaching by Freedman and lost rather quickly. In late September Barry and Enright asked him if he would like to take the examination for *Twenty-one*. It was a massive test with 363 questions in approximately 105 categories, but Jackman scored well enough that he was asked to appear on the show. Before his appearance on October 3, he was called into Enright's office for what was called a practice session to help the contestant familiarize himself with the format and ease his nervousness.

Enright had a large file of cards on his desk with questions on one side and answers on the other, and he spent the next two to three hours going through them with Jackman. Enright told Jackman to request a variety of questions of differing points to help in gauging the relative difficulty of the questions. Just prior to his appearance Enright nervously told Jackman, "You are in a position to destroy my career." Jackman said he did not understand what Enright was talking about. Enright replied something to the effect, "You will." On his big night in the isolation booth and to his astonishment, Richard Jackman's questions on *Twenty-one* were exactly the same as those from the batch of file cards in what he had thought was to be an innocent practice session. He breezed through the evening, somewhat dazed, defeating three opponents seventeen to six, twenty-one to eight, and nineteen to seven, amassing $24,500 in winnings.

The next day when Jackman told Enright that he could not continue on such a rigged program, Enright asked him to reconsider. Jackman flew to Buffalo, related his experience to his mother, and decided to refuse the money he had won unethically. The following Monday Enright tried to persuade him to stay on the show, saying that the reaction had been so good to his appearance that he could continue to play and win to the point where he would be guaranteed $100 per week for the rest of his life. Jackman still declined the offer and wanted no part of his winnings, but after much urging by Enright, he finally accepted a check for $15,000. Enright also convinced him to appear on the next show to "bow out" or publicly state that he had decided not to risk any more of his prize money, thereby formally ending his brief run on *Twenty-one*. Had Jackman not appeared, it would have seemed rather strange to the viewing audience and forced Enright into an embarrassing explanation. Thus Richard Jackman was not "game" enough for the plans of Dan Enright, who would have to find another candidate to be the first continuing champion of *Twenty-one*.[7]

On the evening that *Twenty-one* premiered, an ex-soldier working his way through City College of New York, Herbert M. Stempel, watched the quiz from his Forest Hills home. Stempel was unimpressed by the questions. He thought he could answer practically every one from the continually changing categories, and he told his wife so. On September 27 he wrote a letter to the quiz show requesting an opportunity to appear. A few days later, Stempel was called and told to come to Manhattan to take the examination for the show. The day after his three and one-half hour test, Herbert was contacted by producer Howard Merrill and told to come to the office of the quiz owners, Barry and Enright. There the twenty-nine-year-old collegian met Enright and was told that he had scored 251 correct on the test, the highest of all applicants up to that time. Also present at the meeting were Barry, Robert Noah, cocreator and, for a while, executive producer of *Twenty-one*, and some public relations men, Al Davis and Art Franklin, employed by Barry and Enright. Enright saw a potential champion in the young man, but he had to be sure. The executives informally quizzed Stempel on a wide variety of esoteric questions, ranging from naming the capital of Nepal to giving the width dimension of a football field goalpost, and then conducted an extensive interview into Stempel's background to determine whether he was a suitable contestant.

On the night of October 16, Enright telephoned Stempel and asked him to come over to his office immediately. Richard Jackman had left the show the previous week, and the contestants facing each other on *Twenty-one* were so dull-witted and boring that they had yet to garner any points between them. Enright thought something had to be done to enliven the show, and perhaps Stempel could help. Stempel, however, was unable to leave his house because he was babysitting. Undaunted, Enright drove to the Forest Hills home. He took with him an attaché case from which he pulled out all of his category cards and asked Stempel questions sequentially from one to eleven in each category. Stempel assumed that this was a rehearsal for the time when he might be asked to appear as a contestant. He answered the bulk of the questions offered him, and Enright helped on the rest.[8]

Then the creator of *Twenty-one* leaned back and asked, "How would you like to win $25,000?" Stempel was stunned and did not answer. His thoughts grew hazy as Enright mumbled something to the effect that this could happen if he cooperated. Enright then told him that he must appear on the show the following evening and instructed him to choose the two nine-point questions and then stop. Stempel's reaction was: "I had been a poor boy all my life, and I was sort of overjoyed, and I took it for granted this was the way things were run on these programs. At first I had not realized when I first applied but then I was sort of taken aback. I was stunned. I didn't know what to say . . . I told him I would do it."[9]

Enright had found his first big winner. Only matters of detail needed to be worked out. He asked to see Stempel's wardrobe and picked out an ill-fitting double-breasted suit that had belonged to Stempel's deceased father-in-law and a blue shirt with a frayed collar. Enright wanted to created an image of a penniless ex-GI working his way through college for the next *Twenty-one* champion. In reality Stempel's wife's family was quite wealthy, and the couple had never suffered financially, a fact hidden from the television audience. Enright instructed Stempel to get a short haircut and wear a loudly ticking wristwatch on the program. The wristwatch, he reasoned, would increase the tense atmosphere of the isolation booth if the ticking were picked up by the microphone. At about that time, Stempel's wife, Toby, came home and Enright left, leaving Herbert to tell his wife about their impending fortune.

The next afternoon Stempel reported to studio 6B for a rehearsal on how to behave that evening. Enright showed him how to bite his lip and how to pat, not smear, his brow to give the effect of overwhelming tension. Enright told him to wait five seconds, pause, stutter, and say "Nine points, please. I'll take nine points." Nothing was left to chance. Every sigh, motion, and word uttered by Herbert Stempel on *Twenty-one* was prearranged by the show's mastermind. That evening, after two hapless contestants completed their fifth straight zero-zero tie and were ushered off the program by a new rule devised by Enright, Stempel stepped into his isolation booth, took the two nine-point questions he had heard that afternoon, and defeated accountant Maurice Pelubet eighteen to zero. Even the air conditioning in the booth was turned off to make the contestants sweat. For his four-minute performance Herbert was $9,000 richer.

Week after week the CCNY student bowled over opponents and swelled his winnings to over $50,000 on television's newest quiz. Every Tuesday afternoon and just before showtime, Herb Stempel and Dan Enright rehearsed. Stempel's opponents were usually unaided. In November Enright brought over Al Freedman from *Tic Tac Dough* to be the producer of record for *Twenty-one*, replacing Howard Merrill. Freedman and Enright would work well together, and the new producer eventually took over most of the contestant coaching chores. Freedman had little contact with Stempel, however; all he did was the legitimate and normal coaching of repartée between contestant and master of ceremonies. Remembering the answers to the questions was easy for Stempel: "The actual stage directions were the most difficult things because everything had to be done exactly. Woe betide you if you did not do it as had been planned by Mr. Enright."[10] While becoming one of the newest celebrities on television, Stempel was also receiving training as the most unknown actor on the screen.

In enticing contestants to agree to their deceptive means, Freedman and Enright's appeal was not solely limited to the pecuniary. Altruism, self-promotion, and public relations were among the other responsive chords they hit with contestants. They left no emotional angle untried in their cajoling. Rose Leibbrand, one of Stempel's opponents, was persuaded that her appearance would bring publicity to and promote the cause of the organization of which she was then executive director, the National Federation of Business and Professional Women's Clubs. In her initial interview with Enright and Freedman she recalled, "They kept asking me about my ethics in regard to finances. My attitude toward handling money or my attitude toward finances. The question was so subtle that I cannot remember it. I was very much puzzled and I apparently gave all the wrong answers." Leibbrand definitely was not going to be a big winner on *Twenty-one*, merely a colorful extroverted contestant to be used as a one-shot opponent of the CCNY student with the photographic memory. She was familiarized with the quiz by Freedman in her dressing room just prior to going on the air and told that these practice questions were just that— that different questions would be used on the air. Freedman provided the answers to any questions she did not know. He told her to "ham it up" and pretend ignorance upon initially hearing the questions. Then, according to Leibbrand, Freedman instructed her not to bid for more than seven- or eight-point questions "or else!" although Freedman later vehemently denied that he had ever threatened her. After she chose the lower-valued questions and dutifully lost to Stempel, Leibbrand was furious that the 175,000 members of her organization had been notified to watch such a fraudulent program. Apparently her fury did not last long enough to provoke action, however; she never informed the president of the National Federation of Business and Professional Women's Clubs of the behind-the-scenes activities of *Twenty-one* or anyone else until the legal processes called upon her over two years later. [11]

As Herb Stempel rolled down the road to riches, both he and his quiz mentor began to see rough spots along the path. About the fifth week Stempel was on, Enright informed his rather disappointed contestant that he could not keep all the money he had won because of budgetary reasons. Nonetheless the new champion would be guaranteed a high amount even though he could theoretically lose it all according to the rules of the contest. (A long series of ties with an eventual loss could wipe out a very large amount of prize money.) Enright, in fact, told Stempel to sign an agreement to that effect; if he refused, he would quickly find himself losing on *Twenty-one*. Stempel signed the contract, which was neither notarized nor witnessed by anyone else:

Dear Sir: In order to protect my winnings, I hereby agree to the following setlement. On sums between $40,000 and $60,000, I will take $40,000. On sums between $60,000 and $80,000, I will take $50,000. On sums between $80,000 and $100,000, I will take $60,000. I believe in sums over $100,000 I will take $60,000 also, with the proviso that you make good to me all sums up to $40,000.

If Stempel won a great deal of money, he was not going to get it all.

At about this time, another unsettling event occurred. It was a usual Tuesday afternoon rehearsal, and Enright was asking

Stempel questions from his card file that would be used on the next night's performance. When Jack Barry poked his head into his partner's office, Enright quickly grabbed up his cards and shoved them into his drawer. Stempel was incredulous. He had assumed that the emcee knew about the coaching and asked Enright, "Dan, doesn't Jack know about this?" Frantic, the supervisor muttered, "Mind your own business and pay attention to your lessons." Surprisingly there was no evidence that Barry was aware of any of the details of production for *Twenty-one* or any other program that his partner created. Indeed very few knew about the shenanigans—not Matt Rosenhouse nor anyone else at Pharmaceuticals, Incorporated, and not Edward Kletter and the advertising agency for the show. Unlike the relationship between EPI and Revlon, Enright and Freedman operated more independently and with more self-assurance. Meetings with the sponsor were infrequent. For Dan Enright there was no need for implicit sponsor approval for what he was doing, real or imaginary, as had been the case at EPI.[12]

The budgetary problem that Enright mentioned to Stempel was a problem only to the producers, not the sponsor. According to the contract, Pharmaceuticals contributed $10,000 per week for prize money. If the average weekly winnings were less than that amount, the difference would have been refunded to the drug company at the end of the first twenty-six telecasts and every thirteen weeks thereafter. If the prize money exceeded $10,000 per week, however, the additional funds were stipulated to come from the pockets of the producers. Therefore part of the reason for Enright to manipulate the quiz destinies of his contestants was to stay as close to his budgetary outlay as possible. With the concerted efforts of Freedman and Enright to control the outcomes of the matches on *Twenty-one*, the weekly amount of winnings paid out averaged only between $500 and $750 over $10,000 per telecast during the entire two-year run of the quiz. The sponsor would have been much more concerned had it been known that it had a refund coming, but with Barry and Enright contributing slightly beyond the $10,000, there was never any financial cause for Pharmaceuticals to investigate the working of the show.[13]

Stempel was possibly the most troublesome contestant ever

to confront a big-money quiz show, as Dan Enright discovered in the months ahead, but even in October and November 1956, the creator of *Twenty-one* was becoming dissatisfied with the quiz show's most successful winner in its brief history. The ratings were not particularly impressive. While Stempel was in the midst of his winning streak, both of the $64,000 quizzes were in the top-ten rated programs by Nielsen and Trendex, but not the unlimited quiz, *Twenty-one*. Freedman and Enright were searching for a more attractive champion to replace him. They soon found one: Charles Lincoln Van Doren.[14]

As the quintessential contestant of the big-money quiz shows and one of the most meteoric folk heroes of the 1950s, Van Doren's life deserves some elaboration. Born in 1927, he was the product of one of America's most renowned literary families. His mother, Dorothy, was at one time an editor of the *Nation* and a novelist as well. His uncle, Carl, was a distinguished historian who had won a Pulitzer Prize for his biography of Benjamin Franklin. His father was perhaps the brightest jewel of all in the glittering family. Mark Van Doren, also a Pulitzer Prize winner (in poetry) and author of a near-definitive work on Nathaniel Hawthorne, was considered one of the finest literary critics in the nation, as well as being one of the great teachers in higher education. The intellectual stimulus for Charles Van Doren did not come solely from his family, extraordinary as it was. His childhood and adolescence were punctuated with such frequent household guests as Joseph Wood Krutch, Franklin P. Adams, Mortimer J. Adler, Clifton Fadiman, Morris L. Ernst, and Sinclair Lewis. The neighbor to his father's 150-acre farm in Connecticut was James Thurber.[15]

Impressive as his informal education was, Charles Van Doren also excelled in traditional academia. He attended the select Manhattan High School of Music and Art where he studied clarinet to the point of such expertise that he was nearly at the concert level. Young Charles entered college still considering music as a career, but his interests soon changed to more philosophical pursuits. He attended St. John's College in Annapolis, Maryland, famed for its "great books" course for undergraduates, an educational approach synonymous with the old friend of the family, Mortimer Adler. While in college Van

Doren demonstrated a flair for acting. James Thurber was so impressed with his acting skill in a 1947 amateur performance of his own play, *The Male Animal*, that he tried to persuade Charles to pursue the career professionally. Upon entering graduate school at Columbia University, Van Doren's interests and talents shifted to science; he wanted to be an astronomer. In 1949, he received a master's degree in mathematics; his thesis was "An Introduction to Inversive Geometry."

Finally his goals seemed to stabilize somewhat as he turned in the direction of his father's work. Van Doren became a candidate for the degree of doctor of philosophy in English and in 1951 won a fellowship to Cambridge University, where he researched the life and writings of the eighteenth-century poet William Cowper, the eventual subject of his dissertation. While abroad Van Doren briefly attended the Sorbonne and underwent a period of critical self-examination in which he was particularly bothered by the fact that he was following in his father's literary footsteps. He even started writing a novel, which contained patricide. He returned home in the mid-1950s and embraced teaching as his life's work. His first close contact with the television industry was begun during the two and one-half years spent as a researcher for Clifton Fadiman's many projects, including the programs *Down You Go* and *Conversation*. Van Doren was the assistant editor to Fadiman's anthology, *The American Treasury*. With historian Ralph Roske he coauthored *Lincoln's Commando*, a biography of the Civil War naval commander William B. Cushing. In 1956 Van Doren received seventy-five dollars from the United States Information Agency for writing a short pamphlet, *What Is American Culture?* Eventually he secured a predoctoral instructorship in English at Columbia, also the academic residence of his father. Columbia President Grayson Kirk labeled the younger Van Doren "an able and exciting teacher."[16]

Charles Van Doren seemed to settle down in the halls of Columbia. He moved into a small Greenwich Village apartment and truly enjoyed his teaching. One thing he did desire, however, was to be financially independent from his family. The approximately $4,500 per year Columbia University paid him helped, but certainly it was not much above an adequate income. A casual friend suggested to him that he try to get on the new quiz show *Tic Tac Dough*. Van Doren did not even own a television set and was only vaguely aware of the show. Nonetheless he wandered downtown one day to Barry and Enright's office and took the 100-question test for *Tic Tac Dough*. He was also given the longer examination for *Twenty-one* although he was unaware of its purpose. Leaving several hours later, he met Albert Freedman in the hall. Van Doren had met Freedman socially on a few occasions previously but had no knowledge as to his occupation. They chatted briefly, and the young instructor told the television producer that he had applied to the daytime quiz to which his friend had directed him. The following week Van Doren was notified that he had been selected as a contestant for *Twenty-one*, a show he had never heard of. Informed that he was much too intelligent to play *Tic Tac Dough*, Van Doren agreed to try for the bigger money. He explained later in an interview: "I thought I was happy. It wasn't much money, but I'm a bachelor living alone. I'd written a couple of books and had a few more planned. I thought I had my next four years planned. But you know these are the Eisenhower years; there's money lying around everywhere. I wasn't aware of it." For two straight telecasts in November he stood waiting in the wings as a standby contestant before he finally got the chance to face Herbert Stempel on November 27, 1956.[17]

Two days prior to his appearance, Freedman called him over to his apartment. There the producer told Van Doren that the current champion on *Twenty-one*, Stempel, was unbeatable, unpopular, and detrimental to the show. Then Freedman asked Van Doren, as a personal favor to the producer, whether he would agree to an arrangement whereby he would tie Stempel several times to increase the entertainment value of the show. Van Doren replied that he would prefer to compete honestly, but Freedman reiterated that this was impossible because Stempel was unbeatable and *Twenty-one* was first and foremost entertainment, and such arrangements were common practice on television. Van Doren still hesitated, but the producer added that by beating Stempel and becoming a winner on the contest, he would be doing a great service to teachers. With that lure

Charles agreed, and the two men met the next day to go over the questions that would be used on the first appearance of the young instructor. [18]

When Albert Freedman joined *Twenty-one*, he assumed all of the duties of coaching contestants and prearranging the outcomes of the matches. The usual method, as Enright and Freedman planned it, was for one of the two contestants to be coached while the other one would play the quiz honestly, unaware of the collusion. His duties did not surprise him: "By the time I came to *Twenty-one* . . . I knew I had to put on a show, produce a show, that would have a great deal of entertainment value, a show that people would enjoy watching, really enjoy watching. And I knew by that time that at certain periods, at certain times, control was necessary of a degree." For Freedman, obviously, *Twenty-one* was more of a show than a quiz. Since Dan Enright had been working with Stempel, the show's first big winner, he continued to assist him even after Freedman arrived on the set. Freedman had little contact with the "high strung human Univac" (as Enright later called Stempel).

Van Doren and Stempel first faced each other on *Twenty-one* on November 28, 1956, and played three exciting tie games. The contrast between the two collegians was striking: Van Doren, the tall, handsome, young Ivy Leaguer with the engaging smile and manner versus the stout Jewish student from CCNY. The charismatic Van Doren was on his way to becoming an idol.

Stempel had to be told that he would eventually lose to the Columbia instructor, but Enright waited until the day before their second telecast together to tell him (December 4). Stempel was upset even though he knew that he would have to leave the quiz eventually. Much of Stempel's anguish, he later related, was personal; he despised Van Doren and envied all the advantages he had enjoyed. The press had built up the duel as a contest between CCNY and Columbia, and Stempel begged Enright to let him play against Van Doren fairly. The decision had been made, however, and Stempel had to go. He was never told explicitly that Van Doren was receiving aid, but he suspected as much, since Enright told him that he would tie Van Doren in the first game on December 5 and lose the second one eighteen to ten. Stempel was particularly irritated that Enright instructed him to miss a question that called for identifying the Academy Award-winning picture of 1955, *Marty*, in his first game with Van Doren for the following evening. *Marty* was one of his favorite films.

To assuage the agitated and money-conscious Stempel, Enright held out the inducement of possible future employment with Barry and Enright as research consultant at $250 per week, as well as a possible appearance on *The Steve Allen Show*. Stempel bitterly resigned himself to the fact that his days of fame and fortune were over. Even his offer to refund part of his winnings to play Van Doren legitimately was refused. The end of Herb Stempel on *Twenty-one* sparked the beginning of an emotional release for the troubled ex-GI.[20]

The afternoon of December 4, after meeting with Enright, Stempel informed his friend, Dr. Nathan Brody, "Tomorrow I take a dive." He explained that he would tie the first game at twenty-one points each and lose $20,000 in the second round. As in a tawdry boxing hoax, Enright had managed his controls to the extent of having a contestant take a dive rather than merely helping contestants do well, the practice at EPI. Stempel also told his tale to his druggist, his barber, his maid for the evenings he was on television, and Enright's publicity man, Al Davis. Davis had been forewarned by the *Twenty-one* supervisor that Stempel seemed to be emotionally unstable. Davis, in turn, told his partner, Art Franklin. Stempel felt particularly close to Franklin and eventually confronted and complained to him also.

Stempel told both men about $18,500 that Enright had given him some weeks before. The money was an advance toward his winnings which theoretically he could have lost had the quiz been fair. Enright admitted advancing money to the contestant on probable winnings but denied to his two public relations advisers that he had coached Stempel. The advertising agency for the show had earlier been notified of the advance, but Edward Kletter did not think it an overly unusual move, since he imagined it to be a small amount. Herb also told reporter Dave Gelman of the *New York Post* what his score would be on the upcoming match with Van Doren, but Gelman did not reveal the extraordinary prediction by the strange young man until early in 1957.[21]

The night Herb Stempel dreaded quickly arrived.

BARRY. Good evening. I'm Jack Barry. Tonight here on "Twenty-one" Herbert Stempel, our 29-year-old GI college student can win $111,500, the highest amount of money ever to be won on television. But to do this he's risking much of the money he has won thus far. So right now let's meet our first two players, as Geritol, America's No. 1 tonic, presents "Twenty-one."

ANNOUNCER. From New York City, Mr. Charles Van Doren, and, returning with $69,500 from Forest Hills, N.Y., Mr. Herbert Stempel.

BARRY. Gentlemen, welcome back to "Twenty-one." Your two smiling faces here tonight after that hectic battle you were involved in last week—I'm sure we're in for tremendous excitement here on the program. How are you tonight, Mr. Van Doren?

VAN DOREN. I'm all right.

BARRY. You're OK? and Herb, you've got your $69,500 riding here at stake. How do you feel. OK?

STEMPEL. I'm fine, thank you.

BARRY. Good enough. Herb, there's been some question raised as to whether or not you knew, before going into this game, that should there be tie games occur as they have, that so much more of your money would be risked—I mean, for instance, right now we're going to be playing for $2,000 a point. Were you aware that this would, would happen, could happen?

STEMPEL. Sure I was, Mr. Barry. I knew it all along since I've been in the game to start with, and as a matter of fact I have played several tied games, one with Dr. Carballo and—

BARRY. That's right, you did—

STEMPEL. And also with Miss—Miss Strong—

BARRY. Uh-huh.

STEMPEL. And I know I'm putting an awful lot of money on the line. I'm certainly risking an awful lot of money, but by the same token I could win a lot of money, too, which is also very important.

BARRY. Yes, indeed you can. You can win or lose a lot. All I wanted to make clear was that you knew certainly that this could possibly happen. You had no way to know that it would happen, but that it could possibly happen, as it did with Dr. Carballo?

STEMPEL. That is right, Mr. Barry.

BARRY. Right, Herb, and I hope we've cleared that up for some of the viewers who have wondered about it, and if you two fellows are ready, may I caution you once again that tonight it'll be the biggest game we've ever played here on the program—$2,000 a point. Be very, very careful before you answer—take your time, and the very, very best of luck to both of you.

Neither player inside the studio can hear anything until I turn their studios on with switches which I control right here in front of me, nor can they see anybody in the television studio audience because of the way the lights are constructed. Can you hear me, Mr. Van Doren?

VAN DOREN. Yes, I can.

BARRY. Very good; I have your studio on. Your studio's on, Herb. Can you hear me?

STEMPEL. Yes, I can.

BARRY. All right. Now we're going to go on trying to get 21—I'll be back to you in just a moment, Herb.

Now, Mr. Van Doren, I guess you know pretty well from last week how to play this game—you gotta try to score 21 points, you do it by answering questions that have a point value from 1 to 11. The high point questions are much more difficult than the lower point questions, and you'll tell me how much you know about the category by grading yourself from 1 to 11. The first category, the Civil War. How much do you know about it—you tell us from 1 to 11.

VAN DOREN. That's an awful big subject. Uh, I'll try for 8 points.

BARRY. For 8 points, because of a disagreement with his commanding general, Ulysses Grant was virtually placed under arrest for a brief time early in 1862. Who was the commanding general of the Union Army at that time?

VAN DOREN. Oh, yes, uh—I know his name. Halleck, General H. W. Halleck.

BARRY. You're right—you have 8 points. Herb Stempel, $69,500 is at stake, at $2,000 a point. Of course the winner will get the difference at the end of this match in your scores at $2,000 a point. The category is the Civil War. How many points do you want?

STEMPEL. I'll try 9.

BARRY. For 9 points, because he did not sanction secession, this man was the only southerner who refused to leave the United States Senate when his State seceded from the Union in June of 1861. Name him and the State he represented.

STEMPEL. Andrew Johnson of Tennessee.

BARRY. You're right—you have 9 points. Mr. Van Doren, you have 8 points. The category is boxing. How many points do you want, from 1 to 11.

VAN DOREN. I'm not sure I should do this—uh, I'll try for nine points.

BARRY. For 9 points, name the three heavyweight champions immediately preceding Joe Louis.

VAN DOREN. Well, uh, Louis defeated James J. Braddock, and before Braddock was Max Baer, and before Baer was either Max Schmeling or Primo Carnera. Let's see—uh—I believe it's Schmeling. Was it Schmeling?

BARRY. No, I'm sorry, it was Primo Carnera. I'm sorry, you lose 9 points. That's—you don't go below zero, we put you back to zero, and better luck on the next round.

Herb Stempel, you have 9 points, the category is boxing. How many do you want to try for?

STEMPEL. Seven.

BARRY. For 7 points, one of the most famous promoters in boxing history, the man who promoted the first million dollar gate, is largely responsible for prize fights being staged out of doors. Name this man.

STEMPEL. Tex Rickard.

BARRY. Right. You now have 16 points. Gentlemen, I want to caution you not to speak now because this is the one point when you can be heard. This is the spot you know before we've reached 21 when you get a chance to stop the game. If either of you want to stop the game you can do so, but I caution you not to do it, particularly if at $2,000 a point, unless you really think you are leading at this point. If either of you stops the game whoever has the higher score at this point will win $2,000 a point for the difference in your scores. If neither of you wanta stop, we'll then continue on to 21. I'm going to give you some time to think it over. [Click of the studios being turned off.]

If either player stops the game now, Herb Stempel, who is leading by 16 points, at $2,000 a point, will win $32,000 more, bringing him up to $101,500. But he doesn't know it, because they do not know each other's scores. Let's see what happens. [Click of studios being turned on.]

If either of you want to stop the game, you must tell me so right now. No—neither of you? Well, gentlemen, I'm ah—I think I need a breather more than you do, so suppose we take time out here for just a second while I talk to the people and then we'll continue on with our game of "Twenty-one." Please don't talk because your studios are both on the air.

All right, gentlemen, we're going on now to "Twenty-one." Herb, I'll be back to you in just a moment. Mr. Van Doren, you have no points at the present. The category is "movies and movie stars." How many points do you want from 1 to 11?

VAN DOREN. I think I should take about 7, but I just can't risk it—uh, I'll try for 10 points.

BARRY. For 10 points, one of the tough questions—in 1954 the Oscar for the best supporting actress, best director, and best story and screenplay writer all went to people who had worked in the film "On the Waterfront." Name these people.

VAN DOREN. Well, the director was Elia Kazan.

BARRY. That's right.

VAN DOREN. And the writer was ah—ah—Schulberg.

BARRY. Right.

VAN DOREN. Budd Schulberg.

BARRY. And the best supporting actress?

VAN DOREN. Uh, well, the only woman I can remember in that picture was the one who played opposite Brando, but I would have thought that she would have got the best actress award. But if she's the only one I can remember—let's see—she was that lovely frail girl—Eva Saint—uh, Eva Marie Saint.

BARRY. Right. You have 10 points. Herb Stempel, you have 16 points. The category is movies and movie stars. How many points do you want to try for, from 1 to 11?

STEMPEL. I'll try 5.

BARRY. Which would give you 21 points if you guess this right and you will be the winner again. Because this is a critical moment, if you need some extra time you can have it. You asked—let me make sure again, you asked for 5 points. All right. What motion picture won the academy award for 1955? Do you need some extra time to think about it?

STEMPEL. Ah—I sure do.

BARRY. I'll tell you when your time is up. Your time is up, Herb Stempel. For 5 points which would give you 21, what motion picture won the Academy Award for 1955?

STEMPEL (mumbling). I don't remember. I don't remember.

BARRY. You don't want to take a guess at it? If not I'll have to call it wrong, Herb.

STEMPEL. "On the Waterfront?"

BARRRY. No, I'm sorry, the answer is "Marty." "Marty"—you lose 5 points which puts you back down to 11—better luck on the next round. Mr. Van Doren, you have 10 points. The category—explorers, explorers. How many points do you want to try for?

VAN DOREN. I'm going to go all the way to 21—I mean. I mean try for 11 points.

BARRY. You want to try to get to 21 by 11—by answering an 11-point question?

VAN DOREN. That's right.

BARRY. All right. If you answer this you will have 21, but you'll still have to wait for Herb Stempel to get another crack at it, and you can have some extra time if you need it. Here is your question—Pizarro—(spelling) P-i-z-a-r-r-o—was an early Spanish explorer who discovered and conquered an advanced civilization. Tell us the civilization he discovered, the country this civilization was in, and the leader of the civilization at the time of the conquest. Would you like time to think it over?

VAN DOREN. As much as you can spare.

BARRY. I'll tell you when your time is up. Tell us the civilization he discovered, first of all, if you can, or take it any other way you want.

VAN DOREN. Pizarro discovered the Incas.

BARRY. Right.

VAN DOREN. And the Incas lived in Peru.

BARRY. You're right. And the leader of the civilization, which would give you 21 points if you get this right.

VAN DOREN. (mumbling)—but he had a brother, Huascar—the man who had a room full of gold—I guess, I guess that Atahaulpa was the leader of the Incas at the time of the conquest.

BARRY. That's your answer—Atahaulpa?

VAN DOREN. That's right.

BARRY. Then you score 21 points! Mr. Van Doren, you have the desired number of points—21—but Herb Stempel still has to get a chance at it—now, I'm going to allow you to listen in, so please do not speak. Herb Stempel, you have 11 points. The category—"Explorers." How many points do you want to try for from 1 to 11?

STEMPEL. I'll try 10.

BARRY. You're gonna try to go 21?

STEMPEL. Yes.

BARRY. I can tell you now that your opponent has already scored 21 points. If you answer this next question correctly, you'll have 21 and we'll have another tie, which means we'll have to play another game at $2,500 a point. If you miss, of course, he will win, and I'm not even going to bother to figure it up 'cause it's quite gigantic. Here is your question and take your time. You can have some extra time if you need it. Four great voyages were made by Christopher Columbus, and many different places were among his discoveries. Tell us on which voyage, the first, second, third or fourth, each of the following places were discovered: the Virgin Islands, Martinino or Santa Lucia, Hispaniola or Haiti and South America. Do you need some time to think this over, Herb Stempel?

STEMPEL. I sure do.

BARRY. I'll tell you when your time is up. Your time is up Herb—for 10 points which will either give you 21 or put you back down to about 1 point. Uh, four great voyages were made by Columbus, different places were among his discoveries, tell us on which voyage, the first, second, third, or fourth, each of the following places was discovered. Want to take a crack at the

Virgin Islands?

STEMPEL. Uh, I'll try, uh, Hispaniola.

BARRY. All right.

STEMPEL. That was on the first voyage.

BARRY. You're right.

STEMPEL. South America was on the third voyage.

BARRY. That's right for the second part.

STEMPEL. Now what are the other two now?

BARRY. Martinino or Santa Lucia and the Virgin Islands.

STEMPEL. Martinino is on the fourth voyage.

BARRY. That is right—and the Virgin Islands?

STEMPEL. Therefore the Virgin Islands must be the second.

BARRY. You're right, and you have 21 points. Gentlemen—gentlemen—it happened—it happened again. You both have 21 points; there is a tie. As you know, in the case of a tie we play another game, the stakes go up—we're gonna play in just a moment for $2,500 a point. I can't even figure out how much this is, but one of you could win either $50,000 or somewhere around there, win or lose, and I think at this point—first of all I want to say congratulations to both of you—I don't care who wins or who loses—you guys really know your onions. I want to—they really do—we're going to, we're going to take a moment out here now for you to settle down to get into this which will be an even bigger game than the other and while you relax a bit, and we all do, I'm going to call on my good friend Bob Sheppard with some important and helpful news for anyone who is suffering from common rheumatic- and arthritic-like pains. Bob.

[Commercial.]

BARRY. Before we go on I would like to say that all of the questions that are used on "Twenty-one" have been authenticated for their accuracy and the order of their difficulty by the editorial board of the Encyclopedia Britannica. Fellows, you all set? Mr. Van Doren, Herb Stempel, $2,500 a point. Take it easy on this—be very careful. I'll get back to you in a moment, Herb.

All right, Mr. Van Doren, the first category—"Newspapers." How many points do you want from 1 to 11?

VAN DOREN. I'll try 8 points.

BARRY. For 8 points, the grandsons of Joseph Medill, two of

the most successful journalists in the country from 1914 on, were the owners and managers of the Chicago Tribune and the New York Daily News. Who are they?

VAN DOREN. Well, the Chicago Tribune—that would be Colonel Robert R. McCormick.

BARRY. You're right.

VAN DOREN. And the Daily News, wouldn't that be Patterson, Joseph Patterson?

BARRY. It would be, and you have 8 points.

Herb Stempel, with your $69,500 still at stake, although now at $2,500 a point, the category is "Newspapers." How many do you want to try for?

STEMPEL. I'll try 11.

BARRY. The toughest question of them all. One of the most revered names in American journalism is that of a Kansas newspaper publisher who died in 1944. Tell us this man's name, the name of his newspaper, and the title of the editorial he wrote which made him and his paper nationally known.

STEMPEL. The name of the editor is William Allen White.

BARRY. That is right.

STEMPEL. His paper was the Emporia Gazette.

BARRY. That is right. Finally, for 11 points.

STEMPEL. I'll have to think a little bit about the third.

BARRY. Herb, you can take a little time—you go right ahead.

It's the title of the editorial we want which he wrote. It made his paper nationally famous, and well known.

STEMPEL. I don't know.

BARRY. No idea?

STEMPEL. Just a moment—(mumble).

BARRY. I beg your pardon?

STEMPEL. Just won't help to guess, I don't know.

BARRY. I'm afraid I'm going to have to give it to you then, Herb. The editorial, the title was "What's the Matter with Kansas?" I'm sorry you don't answer—you don't lose any points, but you stay at zero. Better luck on the next round.

Mr. Van Doren, you have eight points. The category "Kings." K-i-n-g-s. How many points do you want?

VAN DOREN. I'll try for 10 points.

BARRY. For 10 points; it's well known that some of Henry the

Eighth's six wives fared better than others. He divorced his first wife, Catherine of Aragon, married his sixth, Catherine Parr, just a few years before he died. Name the second, third, fourth and fifth wives of Henry the Eighth and describe their fates.

VAN DOREN. Oh, my goodness. You want me to name the second, third, fourth, and fifth wives and what happened to all of them?

BARRY. That's right.

VAN DOREN. I'll have to think a minute. Ah—Catherine—you mentioned Catherine of Aragon—she was the first one. Now the second one was, aah—Anne Boleyn.

BARRY. That's right.

VAN DOREN. Uh, now the third—the third was Jane Seymour—

BARRY. Right.

VAN DOREN. And I believe she died a natural death—she died in childbirth—uh—

BARRY. That is right.

VAN DOREN. After the birth of the future Edward the Sixth. Now the third—the fourth now—

BARRY. Right.

VAN DOREN. Uh, let's see—two Annes—Anne of Cleves.

BARRY. Right.

VAN DOREN. And I don't think he beheaded her—no, uh, did he divorce her?

BARRY. You'll have to tell me rather than—

VAN DOREN. He—divorced her.

BARRY. He did. You're right. Finally, the fifth.

VAN DOREN. The fifth—one more—uh, one more. Oh. I think that Henry the Eighth married three, three Catherines. Now—

BARRY. We mentioned Catherine of Aragon. Who was the other Catherine?

VAN DOREN. The sixth wife—uh, Catherine Parr—was that the sixth one?

BARRY. Yeah.

VAN DOREN. Catherine of Aragon, Catherine Parr—Catherine Howard.

BARRY. Right. And what happened to her?

VAN DOREN. Yes, what happened to her—considering Henry the Eighth he probably divorced her (mumbling) he—he divorced his—did he behead Catherine Howard?

BARRY. He did. You've got 18 points.

Herb Stempel, you have no points—the category is "Kings" K-i-n-g-s. How many points do you want from 1 to 11?

STEMPEL. I'll try 10. 10.

BARRY. Ten points. It is well known that some of Henry the Eighth's six wives fared better than others. He divorced his first wife, Catherine of Aragon, married his sixth, Catherine Parr, just a few years before he died. Name the second, third, fourth and fifth wives of Henry the Eighth and describe their fates.

STEMPEL. Second, third, fourth, and fifth?

BARRY. Right. And describe their fates.

STEMPEL. Anne Boleyn was the second—

BARRY. Right.

STEMPEL. Jane Seymour was the third—

BARRY. That is right.

STEMPEL. Anne of Cleves was the fourth.

BARRY. Right again.

STEMPEL. And Catherine Howard was the fifth.

BARRY. You're right—you've got all the names, now can you describe their fate.

STEMPEL. Well, they all died.

BARRY. Well—Herb, I'm going to have to ask you how they died.

STEMPEL. I knew what you meant, Mr.—I knew what you meant Mr. Barry, I was just making a little fun—

BARRY. First, Anne Boleyn—

STEMPEL. Anne Boleyn—executed.

BARRY. Right. Jane Seymour.

STEMPEL. I'm not sure about her—

BARRY. Want to go on to Anne of Cleves?

STEMPEL. Yes.

BARRY. All right.

STEMPEL. Anne of Cleves—divorced.

BARRY. Right. Catherine Howard.

STEMPEL. Catherine Howard—executed.

BARRY. Right. And finally, back to Jane Seymour.

STEMPEL. Died in childbirth.

BARRY. You're right. You have 10 points. Gentlemen, may I caution you now not to divulge your scores because you can hear each other. We're at the point now when you get a chance to stop the game—if either of you stops the game, whoever has the high score wins. So be very, very careful—I'm going to give you some time and I'll tell you when your time is up.

If either player stops the game right now, Mr. Van Doren, who is 8 points ahead at $2,500 a point, will win back $20,000 from Herb Stempel. But he doesn't know, because they don't know each other's scores. Let's see what happens.

If either of you want to stop the game you must tell me so right now.

VAN DOREN. I'll stop.

BARRY. Then you win $20,000. Congratulations, Mr. Van Doren. You deserve congratulations and while I'm saying that I want to say by golly you've had a tremendous run here, Herb, you had $69,500 when you started, you lost $20,000—you're still going to go home with $49,500, which is a big sum. Herb, in the few brief moments we have, what are you going to do with your dough?

STEMPEL. Well, Mr. Barry, this came so suddenly—the first thing I want to do is outfit my family, and I, I would also like to make a small contribution to the City College fund to repay the people of the city of New York for the free education which they have given me, then I'm going to guard the rest of my money, put it in a bank and—I—would also like to thank you and the members of your staff for all the kindness and the courtesy which you've extended to me.

BARRY. Herb, I want to say one thing—we may have a lot of contestants in the future, but I doubt that anybody will ever display the knowledge, the fighting spirit, and the courage that you have on this program. We, your friends, all the students at CCNY, I'm certain are just as proud of you as we are and deservedly so. Thank you for being a wonderful contestant—Herb Stempel, ladies and gentlemen—

Well, he went home with $49,500—you've got $20,000 right now Charles Van Doren, come back next week—tell us whether you want to continue playing or quit. Our congratulations for a wonderful victory. Goodnight to Charles Van Doren, ladies and gentlemen.

Friends, we don't have much time. Remember Geritol and Geritol, Jr. Goodnight everybody—see you next week. Thank you.

(Commercial)

(Closing music—NBC chimes.)[22]

Thus Van Doren triumphed and was launched on a spectacular celebrity career. As Herbert Stempel left his isolation booth, he overheard someone say backstage, "Now we have a clean-cut intellectual as champion instead of a freak with a sponge memory." Dan Enright thought he had seen the last of his disheartened and bothersome ex-contestant. For Van Doren the road ahead looked rosy indeed. There were a few problems to be settled between himself and his quiz coach, Freedman. The producer initially did not like Van Doren's speaking style and had to work at teaching the young instructor how to pause, skip parts of the question, and answer in a manner calculated to squeeze the maximum amount of tension from the process. Freedman actually gave Van Doren a script to memorize.[23]

Just before the Columbia instructor made his television debut, Freedman orally guaranteed him $1,000 for his services. This amount had grown to $8,000 prior to the December 5 program. After that telecast the winnings soared for the most famed folk hero of the isolation booths. Van Doren had no idea that he would achieve such celebrity status. He was stunned. His saturation of the airways extended over fifteen telecasts of *Twenty-one* over a period of time covering several weeks more than that (the quiz was occasionally preempted by network specials). He was not limited to the mere four weeks of exposure that the winners of *The $64,000 Question* were. Several times during the course of his long run, though, conscience pangs struck the young intellectual. He asked Freedman more than once to be relieved of his quiz duties, but the answer was always "not at this time"; a series of exciting tie games would have to be arranged. Just before Christmas 1956 Van Doren told the producer that he could not continue on the show at his present salary from Columbia because he was unable to collect any of his money until he was beaten or quit. As the masters behind *Twenty-one's* scenes did for Herb Stempel, they also advanced Van Doren $5,000 on his winnings. The now-famous instructor later rationalized his decision to stay on the show: "I was almost able to convince myself that it did not matter what I was doing because it was having such a good effect on the national attitude to teachers, education, and the intellectual life."[24]

Here was a new hero, a genuine intellectual star on the video horizon. He was receiving two thousand letters per week, including some from as far away as Basutoland. Reportedly one out of every four of those letters came from a teacher, a parent, or a student thanking Van Doren for the worthwhile image he projected toward education and the value of studying. In a hyperbolic bit of public relations, Freedman said to the world, "He is the modern equivalent of the Renaissance man, . . . he's what almost every woman watching wants her husband to be like." Van Doren, in fact, received an estimated five hundred marriage proposals in the mail. As the weeks rolled on, he continued to bowl over opponents and his fortune grew. By mid-January 1957, he had passed the $100,000 mark in winnings. By his tenth telecast he had won $122,000. By the program of February 19, he had accumulated $143,000, the greatest single amount won on one quiz show.[25]

Charles Van Doren was the most talked-about young man to arrive on the American cultural scene since Elvis Presley, with whom he was frequently compared as a better example for American youth to idolize. Engaging, successful, and handsome, Van Doren was called by television critic Janet Kern of the *Chicago American* "so likable that he has come to be a 'friend' whose weekly visits the whole family eagerly anticipates." *Time* magazine honored him as the first and only quiz contestant to receive a cover story; it marveled, "Just by being himself, he has enabled a giveaway show, the crassest of low-brow entertainment, to whip up a doting mass audience for a new kind of TV idol—of all things, an egghead." Had Charles Van Doren signified the end of anti-intellectualism in America? Not likely, but the same optimistic notions about innate American intelligence and the possibility that the Horatio Alger tales were more than just myth surfaced with Van Doren on the nation's mental landscape despite the fact that big-money quiz shows were by then nearly two years old. It was not so much a love of learning with Van Doren and the American people, but fascination with material success, as *Commonweal* cogently observed: "Americans have always venerated the fact, and the quiz show has merely underlined this aspect of our culture. Further, these facts are materially useful: they earn money . . . In the Amercian tradition, they are respected for this material value, not in any sense as knowledge for the sake of knowledge." Charles Van Doren was a bright young man who used his wits in the most dramatic American way possible: to amass a quick fortune.[26]

What much of the public did not notice about *Twenty-one* was that this show did not promote the common man as did the $64,000 quizzes and *The Big Surprise*. There was no exploitation of people with mundane occupations and paradoxical categories because *Twenty-one* was not limited by topics for its questions. Nor would one find many cobblers or grandmothers on *Twenty-one*. Generally the contestants were from a much higher educational level. No other big-money quiz made more use of attorneys, teachers, professional students, and college-educated persons. Enright and Freedman, on this most thoroughly controlled of quiz shows, were not seeking contestants with personality but people with poise.[27] Another aspect largely unnoticed by the press about *Twenty-one* was the extraordinary lack of geographical distribution of its contestants. With the exceptions of Richard Jackman, from Oneonta, New York, and Harold Craig, a college-educated dairy farmer from upstate New York, and the final two contestants, from Los Angeles, every contestant of the quiz on the seventy-two weeks it was on the air was from the New York City area. On a program where control was crucial, it was imperative that participants be readily available during the week for preparation.[28]

Twenty-one prospered with Van Doren. During his long run on the show, after the first eighteen telecasts of the quiz, *Twenty-one* was moved from Wednesday nights to Monday evenings opposite what was probably the most popular television program of the 1950s, *I Love Lucy*. NBC took a chance going against CBS in that manner, and the gamble seemed to pay off. Although it never topped *I Love Lucy*, by March *Twenty-one* had a very respectable 34.7 Trendex rating and was the first NBC effort to show any sort of promise against the insurmountable *Lucy* in the ratings race. Actually it was difficult to be precise about the ratings of *Twenty-one*, because it was usually pre-empted in the first week of the month when the network broad-cast a special program. Because Trendex and American Re-search Bureau rated television shows only during the first week of any month, *Twenty-one* rarely made the top-ten-rated shows when, in all probability, it may have deserved such a rating for the latter part of the month. Nonetheless rumors were begin-ning to surface that NBC was willing to buy *Twenty-one* out-right, as well as all other Barry and Enright packages, for $1 million or more.[29]

Finally a plan was devised to relieve the anxious Van Doren of his winning streak. An attractive and willing opponent was found; a series of exciting tie games was arranged; and the young teacher was freed of his mental burden. On February 25, 1957, Van Doren was tied by an attorney (a Columbia Univer-sity graduate), Vivienne Nearing, for the second straight week. At that time Freedman told Van Doren that he would only have to appear on two more shows. The next Monday, however, *Twenty-one* was preempted, so Van Doren had only one remain-ing performance. On March 11, the attractive lawyer who lived only four blocks from Van Doren in Greenwich Village defeated the "wizard of quiz" when he was unable to identify the king of Belgium. He answered "Leopold" instead of "Baudouin" in a multipart question. Nearing, like Stempel and Van Doren, needed a behind-the-scenes monetary inducement to stay on the show and continue her deceitful ways; hers was $10,000.[30]

Although Charles Van Doren was gone from *Twenty-one*, he was not gone from television memory, for the post-winnings life of publicity descended upon him as it had upon earlier winners. His prize money shrank from a high of $143,000 to $129,000 after the several ties with Nearing, which was still a single quiz-show record. The actual amount for the young scholar was more on the order of $28,000 after federal and state income taxes of over $100,000. After he left the show, life moved quickly for Van Doren. He was the honored speaker at the thirty-third annual convention of the Columbia Scholastic Press Association. At about this time, the biography he coauthored with Ralph Roske was published and received favorable reviews. In mid-April he married Geraldine Ann Bernstein, a young woman he had employed in February to answer his fan mail. Perhaps the greatest honor of all was his assured future in television. Days before he married, NBC signed him to a five-year contract for approximately $50,000 per year. His duties were rather unclear. He was listed as a programming consultant, and it was speculated that he might have something to do with educational programs. Then it was rumored that Van Doren might be used as a panelist on a future NBC quiz show. All that was certain was that the network could not let such a charismatic and now-familiar face drift away unpurchased.[31]

Getting Van Doren off *Twenty-one* was a minor problem for Dan Enright compared to the return of Herb Stempel. In February 1957 Dave Gelman of the *New York Post* called Stempel back about his quiz-show tip, and Herbert spilled out the entire tale of his times with *Twenty-one*. Gelman may have been impressed, but the libel lawyer for the paper was not and advised against printing the story. His advice was followed. After the rebuff from the *Post*, Stempel's anguish increased. By this time he was undergoing psychiatric treatment as a result of his being on *Twenty-one*. Part of his problem was financial. Most of his $49,000 (before tax) winnings had been spent. He had given a considerable amount to an ex-convict acquaintance to set up an illegal gambling operation in Florida, which promised great wealth; he had lent $2,500 to a freelance writer who promised to do a profile on Stempel for a national magazine; and both he and his wife had spent freely.

On March 7 he went to seek financial aid from his old friend and quiz coach, Dan Enright. The producer felt threatened when Stempel intimated that he would expose all of the *Twenty-one* machinations unless he was given more money or a job. Enright promised a job with Barry and Enright upon Stempel's graduation from CCNY in June. To combat what he thought was a blackmail attempt by Stempel, Enright persuaded the troubled young man to sign a document saying that he had not received any aid whatsoever on *Twenty-one* and held out the lure of a panelist's position on a "possible" future program. In addition to the false statement he had Stempel sign, the creator of *Twenty-one* secretly tape-recorded the conversation he had with Stempel on March 7, 1957, as possible future security for his position should Stempel try any extortion again. Enright also offered to pay the cost of Stempel's increased psychiatric visits. He then informed his publicity men, Al Davis and Art Franklin, of the blackmail attempt and told them to deny the "fix" story should any reporter hear of it.

Much of Stempel's malaise was Van Doren and his accompanying fame. He deeply resented that Enright had not put him in that position. In one conversation with Enright on March 10, Stempel asked if the producer could set up a charity match between him and Van Doren at the CCNY campus around the time of graduation. Stempel had already done a few charity contests at his college since leaving the show. Enright replied that Van Doren had no wish to do any more quiz efforts, but if Vivienne Nearing were still on the show at that time, she would probably participate. Stempel was startled. Inadvertently Enright had told him that Nearing would soon beat Van Doren. The next day Stempel withdrew $5,000 from his savings account and placed a bet on the female attorney with his favorite bookie at two-to-one odds; he won $10,000 when Nearing accomplished the television upset of the season.[32]

In his eagerness for fame and fortune and with all his willingness to talk about his troubles with *Twenty-one*, Herb Stempel never talked to any NBC officials. Nor did he ever say anything to the man behind the money used by Barry and Enright, Matt Rosenhouse, the sponsor, a man who certainly would have put an end to *Twenty-one* had he known its true nature.[33]

With Herbert Stempel temporarily appeased, Dan Enright could go back to his main television show and help Al Freedman plan strategies for more stable contestants. Nearing was soon defeated by a medical research consultant, Hank Bloomgarden, who also defeated Vassar College President Henry Noble McCracken on the same program. Bloomgarden was an exemplary contestant on *Twenty-one* . He had been inveigled into quiz cheating by altruistic appeal; his appearance on the show week after week enabled the National Association for Mental Health to receive worthwhile publicity, which he hoped would have a favorable impact on contributions for the organization. For Bloomgarden, Enright and Freedman decided to arrange the longest-running series of tie games in the show's history, thereby increasing the televised tension and, they hoped, the ratings. The candidate they selected to oppose Bloomgarden later turned out to be possibly the most damaging contestant to the infra-structure of the fraudulent television quiz shows, James Snodgrass. [34]

Snodgrass's entry onto the show in many ways resembled that of Van Doren's. He was a struggling artist who lived in Greenwich Village. Having returned from a trip to Europe in March 1957, out of work, and hard pressed for money, a friend suggested that he apply to be a contestant on *Tic Tac Dough*. Snodgrass took the test and was notified within a week that he had done so well on it that he should try the *Twenty-one* examination. After doing well enough on that test to catch the attention of Freedman and Enright, he became a standby contestant in mid-April. Although that status did not always guarantee appearing on the air, he faced Bloomgarden on April 22. A few days previously, Freedman had assured the young man that all the coaching he was receiving was merely for the sake of the viewers' entertainment and was being done all the time. Freedman told Snodgrass to wear an off-white shirt and to have his teeth cleaned, also for entertainment's sake.

The day after his first bout with Bloomgarden, Freedman informed Snodgrass of the series of tie matches predetermined for the two men. The producer was slightly dissatisfied, however, with the style and timing of the young artist, and he rehearsed the answers Snodgrass was to recite by using a stopwatch. He told Snodgrass that he was scheduled to lose on the May 20 program after the duel with Bloomgarden had pushed the stakes up to $3,000 per point. Snodgrass was not so much bothered about being written out of the quiz as being asked to miss a question about his favorite poet, Emily Dickinson. He was told to identify incorrectly the author of the lines, "Hope is the thing with feathers that perches in the soul," as Ralph

Waldo Emerson. Snodgrass was peeved. Three days before what was supposed to be his final appearance on *Twenty-one*, he wrote a letter detailing all the questions and answers for him on the upcoming show, as well as his instructions to miss. He stated that he would not "take the dive" and would answer the Dickinson part of the question correctly. He addressed the letter to himself and mailed it by registered mail on May 17, 1957. He had used the mails in a similar fashion twice before to protect his writings from possible plagiarism without resorting to the more expensive process of copyrighting. Snodgrass explained his action: "It was just something that I knew maybe some day — that maybe I would have to prove, that I would perhaps say something and I would be called to task for it, and I would have to be able to prove it. I don't know. I just did this to protect myself." In one of the more prophetic acts in television annals, Snodgrass would later discover he had done far more than protect himself.[35]

The May 20 *Twenty-one* was played with several interesting developments (see appendix 1). During the commercial break after Snodgrass shocked Freedman by answering, "Emily Dickinson" instead of "Emerson," both the producer and Enright took the extraordinary step of coming onstage to his isolation booth to investigate. They asked Snodgrass if he felt well. Jack Barry, seeing that something was amiss, asked him on the air whether he was able to continue with the next game, played at a record $3,500 per point. Snodgrass had no intention of quitting despite the consternation of Enright and Freedman, but the following match almost proved his undoing in circumstances totally unplanned by the producers. In the second round of questions, both Bloomgarden and Snodgrass picked the eleven-point, and most difficult, question. They were asked to name the five groups of vertebrae in the human spinal column. Bloomgarden correctly listed sacral, lumbar, thoracic, cervical, and coccyx. Snodgrass, however, began his answer with "sacrum" instead of "sacral," identifying the bone itself rather than the type of group. The answer required adjectives instead of nouns. The young artist lost by twenty-one points, giving his opponent $73,500 for the evening.

Almost immediately after the program had ended, the studio

started receiving hundreds of telephone calls from physicians across the country complaining that if Snodgrass was wrong for naming the bone group in noun form instead of adjectivally, then Bloomgarden was also incorrect; he had said "coccyx," a noun, instead of "coccygeal." The pressure on Barry and Enright mounted over the next few days; even Dr. Morris Fishbein, the former editor of the *Journal of the American Medical Association*, complained to the show. *Encyclopaedia Britannica* verified that it had indeed been inconsistent in listing the groups, and a rematch between Snodgrass and Bloomgarden was announced. The game would start again at $3,500 per point, and Bloomgarden was guaranteed the $52,500 he had going into what was seemingly his last battle with Snodgrass.

Immediately after the May 20 telecast, Freedman, unaware of the small swelling storm over the medical technicality, went to Snodgrass's dressing room and, according to Snodgrass's later testimony, screamed that he was ruined because of Snodgrass's intentional refusal to lose as originally planned. Now that he had lost by twenty-one points at $3,500 per point instead of the prearranged lesser amount, the show had exceeded its budget and could be financially ruined. Freedman denied this conversation, and it does seem to be a rather odd occurrence because, unlike Enright, Freedman had no financial stake in the quiz show and rarely concerned himself with its budgetary workings, although there is also no apparent reason why Snodgrass would make up such a story.[36]

The medical question mistake, though, saved the show from having to pay out $73,500 in one evening because the rematch afforded Enright and Freedman the opportunity to control the final outcome of Snodgrass versus Bloomgarden at something closer than twenty-one to zero, thus recouping some of their financial loss. Freedman no longer trusted Snodgrass and only partially aided him for his final appearance on June 3. He was given the questions and answers for the first game and for the last round of the second game. It was clear to Snodgrass at what point of the contest he would be on his own, but he still hoped to defeat Bloomgarden. He failed, however, to name the prime minister of Ghana and left the show with only $4,000 for his seven-week bout on *Twenty-one*, while Hank Bloomgarden became one of the big winners on the quiz with $92,500.[37]

Barry and Enright ended their first season of *Twenty-one* on a jubilant note despite the troubles with Snodgrass. On May 2, 1957, NBC bought all the assets of Barry and Enright Productions, Incorporated, which included other programs besides *Twenty-one*, for a reported $4 million. The actual figure, $2 million, was never disclosed to the press; it was the usual policy of networks neither to confirm nor deny the reported larger amount. As part of the contract, Barry and Enright continued to be the production unit for the quiz, but the sponsor, Pharmaceuticals, Incorporated, paid all monies directly to NBC. After the $2 million was recouped by the network in profits, there would have been a fifty-fifty sharing of all future profits with Barry and Enright. NBC had purchased *Twenty-one* because it was the first program in the network's history to make any ratings inroads against what was then (and again) the top-rated show in television, *I Love Lucy*. After the first twenty-six weeks of *Twenty-one*, the contract with Pharmaceuticals came up for optional renewal; theoretically the quiz might have been sold to another sponsor at that time and possibly even to another network. NBC was not going to let such a situation develop.[38]

The 1956-57 television season was not totally dominated by *Twenty-one* in the quiz-show genre, although it was probably the most interesting of its type, on camera and off. At EPI the two $64,000 quizzes and *The Big Surprise* progressed basically as they had the previous season. Early in the season *The $64,000 Question* remained the most-watched show on television until it was gradually overtaken by *I Love Lucy*. In fact, at the season's start the top-five-rated programs on television, according to Trendex, were all quiz or game shows: *The $64,000 Question*, *The $64,000 Challenge*, *Do You Trust Your Wife?*, *What's My Line?*, and *I've Got a Secret*. Matters seemed to run more routinely at EPI this particular season in some regards. BBD&O was the advertising agency of record for Revlon and its two $64,000 quizzes. It was certainly destined to last longer than most others had with the demanding Revson brothers. The weekly meetings with producer, sponsor, and ad men present continued, as did the stated inferences of Martin Revson and the controls practiced by Steve Carlin and Mert Koplin. BBD&O's silent position throughout, according to its executive vice-president, Robert Foreman was that the producers "had certain controls which they could exercise. Beyond that, it was never discussed."

The meetings continued to be extraordinarily implicit, at least to those who wished to interpret them in that way. The only fault of BBD&O, from the viewpoint of Revlon, was hiring Al Ward, a rather cynical assistant whose job was to write memorandums for the weekly EPI-Revlon meetings. Then he circulated the notes of what he thought had been decided at the sessions within a few days to those who had been present. A very good example of an Al Ward memorandum follows below, one of the few written records of those meetings:

CONFIDENTIAL NOTES
BATTEN, BARTON, DURSTINE & OSBORN, INC.
MEETING OF MARCH 15, 1957

From Albert Ward to M. Revson, G. Abrams, B. Mandel,
H. Fleischman, S. Carlin, B. Foreman.

1. The contestants for the Tuesday, March 19, "Question" show will be:
Robert Strom, "Science."
Commander Stafford, "American Literature."
Kate Lloyd, "Men's Fashions."
2. It was decided there was a definite need for "64,000 question" to have more losers.
3. There will be a reexplanation of the prize plateaus in the new rules.
4. There will be some kind of visual illustration of the new plateaus.

1. The contestants for the Sunday, March 17, "Challenge" show will be:
Teddy Nadler versus Dr. Ranney, "Civil War."
Mrs. Lowell Thomas, Jr., "Geography."
Count Lukawiecki versus Grace Iapergola, "Hot Rods."

2. Discussion of change of format for "Challenge."
   (a) EPI met with Y. and R.
   (b) We will kinescope the new format Sunday, March 24.
3. It was decided that the rule which tells the champion whether or not the challenger won or lost, will not be worried about because the new rules will encompass this problem.

Everybody at the meeting was against dropping to the next lower money plateaus when both champion and challenger lose.

EPI will have their discussion and give us some resolution next week.

Steve Carlin rereviewed the rules as applied to the "Challenge" format.

4. Tom Noonan was discussed as a possible replacement for Hal March during his vacation.[39]

Most of the memorandum is fairly mundane, but item 2 is exemplary of the inferences of Martin Revson translated into seemingly direct orders from the sponsor. Although Revson probably only strongly wished that the quiz had more losers, his words were interpreted as "a definite need" to produce losers. Upon receiving this particular memo, Mert Koplin dutifully selected several contestants whom he knew were not very well informed in their categories with the belief that they would probably lose at the lower levels of the quiz.

Ward's duties were eventually terminated when one memorandum was found to be too explicit. In it he stated Revson's desire that the outcome of a match on *The $64,000 Challenge* occur as the executive hoped. After the actual quiz produced the written outcome, Martin Revson was furious that his informal comments in the weekly meetings could be so damagingly transformed into production directives and ordered that Ward cease writing memorandums.

Revson's actions against Ward can be interpreted in two different ways. As he later testified, Revson stopped the circulating memorandums after it became evident to him that his comments at the weekly meetings carried unintentional power. To Martin Revson, Steve Carlin was always the man in charge at the sessions. He, not the sponsor, was the tough personality. If sponsor complicity was the case, however, as Carlin and Koplin maintained, Revson's quashing of Ward's notes could be interpreted as destroying evidence when he discovered his wishes were being recorded too explicitly.[40]

Of all the EPI quiz shows, *The $64,000 Challenge* bore the brunt of Revson's criticisms, although it maintained healthy ratings throughout the season and Revlon only cosponsored it. Revson continually complained about all details of the programs and questioned Carlin's showmanship. Sometimes his advertising adviser, George Abrams, joined in the criticisms. Mert Koplin continued to produce the show, along with the other two EPI big-money quizzes, and attempted constantly to enliven the quiz for the pleasure of Martin Revson. Early in the season a celebrity dual between actors Vincent Price and Edward G. Robinson in the category of art was one of television's top draws. The final match drew an enormous audience of approximately 55 million people. *The $64,000 Challenge* also had the advantage of being able to pick from previous winners from *The $64,000 Question* and *The Big Surprise*. All participants on any EPI quiz had to sign a release agreeing not to appear on any competing quiz show without the approval of the EPI directors. The only quizzes that chosen winners were able to return to were other EPI sweepstakes. From *The Big Surprise* stock-market prodigy Lenny Ross came to *The $64,000 Challenge* in early 1957 to defeat a series of challengers and amass a combined total of $164,000 for both quiz shows, a record at the time for conglomerate quiz winnings. *The $64,000 Question* sent over jockey Billy Pearson late in the season to win on *The $64,000 Challenge*. The biggest success on the two contestant quiz was Teddy Nadler, the most-discussed contestant of the 1956–57 season next to Charles Van Doren and, in some ways, a more fascinating character.[41]

Nadler was a forty-seven-year-old, seventy-dollar-per-week supply clerk in St. Louis who had quit school at the age of thirteen. The son of a Romanian cobbler, Nadler was gruff, ungrammatical, and somewhat crude, but he possessed the most photographic memory of all of the quiz-show contestants who had surfaced on television. Nadler stated that he had not read a book or newspaper since 1940 but claimed to remember everything he had read prior to that time. It took him five letters to *The $64,000 Challenge* to get to the interview stage, at which a large part of EPI's staff of sixty-six people questioned him. They were skeptical of someone whose education had ceased at the eighth grade, and Nadler's "earthy accent" almost got him rejected. But, Koplin recognized a natural "human almanac of information" when he saw one. Like some of the other big winners for EPI, Teddy Nadler received no hints or help in any form other than the tailoring of categories. He fit the mold Koplin had once described as the obscure person whose head was filled with innumerable minutiae ready to spew forth at the first opportunity.

Nadler first appeared as a challenger on the quiz late in 1956 but so astounded the producers with his variety of knowledge that he was shortly challenging all comers on topics of wide diversity. He appeared on *The $64,000 Challenge* thirty-eight different times, well ahead of Van Doren's tenure at *Twenty-one*. Nadler's reign was not continuous, however; he would be brought on for a few weeks in a burst of memory display, put off the show for a while, then returned. He did not always win, but in his strong categories he was unbeatable. By April 1957, immediately after the height of the Van Doren attention, he had defeated political scientist Austin Ranney in the category of the Civil War, saloonkeeper Toots Shor in baseball, and the wife of Lowell Thomas, Jr. in geography. Nadler was an irritating contestant who frequently overshot his answers with added uncalled-for information or unnecessarily completed the answers of his opponents. In one poll he was disliked by 70 percent of the viewers, yet EPI continued to bring him back. Perhaps they had found the ultimate "common man" for the big-money quiz show. Nadler was especially strong in the subjects of history and geography. He claimed to know the name of every island on earth and the name of most battles fought in Western civilizaton. His prodigious memory caused the Nevada State Hospital to request the right to study his brain and enable the ulcer-ridden man to win $152,000, a single quiz show record that topped Van Doren. Said Nadler of himself: "I'm not like Van Doren who is educated and appeals to the ladies because of his looks. I'm ugly and I'm a nitwit, except for my memory." The big-money quiz had found its perfect contestant in the totally nonanalytical mind of Ted Nadler.[42]

The parent quiz, *The $64,000 Question*, also fared well during the 1956-57 season even though it finally relinquished its number-one roost. It also occasionally altered its usual pattern of production in an effort to boost ratings. For weeks early in the season, *The $64,000 Question* advertised that "a mysterious world famous guest" would arrive to appear. After the buildup, it turned out to be Randolph Churchill, Winston's rather boring son, and, to the embarrassment of all concerned, he miserably flubbed his question at the $128 plateau. Hal March invited him back for another try, but Carlin was furious at the failure of his promotional gimmick and overruled the master of ceremonies.[43]

Since the $64,000 on the quiz could be achieved in only four weeks, *The $64,000 Question* was more limited than *Twenty-one* or *The $64,000 Challenge* in its ability to cultivate interest in a contestant whose stay was so short. The solution in obtaining a contestant of greater longevity was solved by Revlon's president, Charles Revson, in one of his rare appearances at the weekly meetings in his brother's office. He suggested that the quiz expand its prize limit, adding $32,000 plateaus beyond the first $64,000 up to a possible $256,000, four times the amount of the original maximum. His suggestion was immediately adopted at the height of the Van Doren pinnacle. The first contestant eligible for the grand amount was another of EPI's natural and unaided prodigies, Robert Strom.[44]

Strom, a ten-year-old, had begun reading and writing at the age of three and touch typing one year later. A fifth-grader from the Bronx, young Robert's category was science, which meant that he frequently had multiple questions in mathematics, chemistry, physics, astronomy, and electronics, all of which he answered correctly. He chose to go for Revson's higher option after winning $64,000, and week after week he amazed the viewing nation as he drew complex mathematical formulas and baffling astronomical sky charts on the window of his isolation booth to answer his questions. Finally, acceding to his parents' wishes, Robert Strom stopped after $192,000 on the first—and now expanded—big money quiz. Strom had topped them all;

his amount was a record for a single show or combined program. His final question (or questions) for $192,000 was to identify scientists of achievement in frequency modulation, analytical geometry, and radioactivity; then he was given a diagram of a summer sky and asked to identify seven constellations and their first-magnitude stars; next he had to identify a complex electronic formula for resonant frequency, and finally name the discoverers of the laws governing the behavior of gases. At the time when Strom was demonstrating his quiz wizardry, *Life* magazine was so distrubed at what it saw that it described quiz shows as "injurious" to the young viewers whose values might be misguided by money.[45]

The third of the established EPI big-money quizzes, *The Big Surprise*, did not have as good a season as the other two and quietly left the air in May 1957. At that point Koplin's key assistant on *The Big Surprise*, Shirley Bernstein, joined the staff of *The $64,000 Challenge* to concentrate solely on *The $64,000 Question*. The new producer of *The $64,000 Challenge* became Ed Jurist although Bernstein was gradually to take over his position.[46]

Do You Trust Your Wife?, held over from the previous year, managed to top its first-year record for winning by a couple. Erik and Helena Gude were able to maintain a winning streak of twenty-two consecutive weeks on the program, which won them $100 per week for twenty-two years. *Do You Trust Your Wife?* constituted the most refined tax dodge of the quiz shows, although with the addition of the new $256,000 potential to *The $64,000 Question*, a similar scheme was devised. Revlon attorney Adrian DeWind established a lessened tax burden for winners on *The $64,000 Question* who went beyond $64,000 by paying such amounts over a period of three years. The arrangement enabled Robert Strom to keep over $80,000 that normally would have gone to the Internal Revenue Service.[47]

With over one year to prepare since the coming of *The $64,000 Question*, the 1956–57 television season saw a proliferation of new quiz shows. *Tic Tac Dough* was one of the first to come on the screen in the preseason or summer of 1956. This Barry and Enright production had thrived on daytime television. When

Albert Freedman left the show as producer in November 1956, he was replaced by Howard Davis Felsher, who continued collusion with contestants. Occasionally Felsher only instructed contestants which categories to select. More rarely, as in the example of sixteen-year-old Kirsten Falke, he gave contestants the question cards to memorize. *Tic Tac Dough* was more loosely controlled than the richer *Twenty-one*. A much smaller percentage of the contestants were aided on *Tic Tac Dough*, at least when it remained on daytime television, but whatever aid Felsher deemed necessary for the betterment of the quiz's entertainment value, he always had to clear it first with the mastermind, Dan Enright.[48]

With the notable exception of *Twenty-one*, most of the big-money quiz shows that appeared during the 1956–57 season led a troubled existence. Before *The $64,000 Question*, ABC's *Break the Bank*, hosted by the indefatigable Bert Parks, had had the biggest money on television as its prize: $12,000. With the rapid inflation of prize offerings *Break the Bank* was left behind until it announced at the start of the season that it was going to be the first quarter-of-a-million-dollar quiz show and rename itself *Break the $250,000 Bank*. This quiz was the classic example of the flawed thinking that money was the only key to the success of *The $64,000 Question*. *Break the $250,000 Bank* was a disaster in the ratings. First, its long-time sponsor, Dodge, left the newly inflated version, leaving Lanolin Plus as the sole sponsor. Within a few months, it was replaced on the air by a less costly game show, *Hold That Note*, a guessing game similar to *Name That Tune*. *Break the $250,000 Bank* failed to notice that the saturation point in big-money quiz shows had possibly been reached.

"It's noteworthy," commented John Lardner on the quiz-show stakes, "that the dosage has been increased from time to time, as with drugs in the outside world, to keep up with adjustments in the public's appetite." Though commenting, not disinterestedly, on his own show, *The $64,000 Question*, an executive from BBD&O made a telling point: "Everyone assumed that money was the *Question's* big hook. Had that been true *Break the $250,000 Bank* would've had a rating four times higher than the *Question*. Actually, its rating was only a third of the *Question's* and it died quickly. The wrong ingredient was copied."[49]

If more was the "wrong ingredient," then it might be doubted whether the enormous popularity of Louis Cowan's biggest creation was due primarily to the materialism of the American public. That *The $64,000 Question* was the first of the big-money television quiz shows may have been a major cause for the following it drew. By fall 1956, the television screen was possibly becoming satiated with money, and it was not enough to dispense riches without displaying the personalities of the money winners, real or devised, and staging a clever game in itself. *Twenty-one* was interesting beyond merely the asking and answering of questions. Dan Enright once said in this regard, "Money has become a cheap commodity... The Game's the thing. Our's is a good one."[50]

A longer-lasting effort than *Break the $250,000 Bank* in the big-money quizzes by ABC was *Treasure Hunt* which premiered in September 1956. Scarcely a quiz, this program pitted a male contestant against a female in a brief session of relatively simple questions enabling one of them to go on to the basic part of the show—choosing one of fifty "treasure chests," one of which contained $25,000. *Treasure Hunt* was the only big-money program with a structure for winning based purely on luck. As the president of ABC Robert Kintner said, "We are more interested in giving away entertainment." The introductory questions prior to the basic guessing game bulk of the show were deliberately chosen from a number of questions correctly answered by the contestants in a preshow warmup. The producer of *Treasure Hunt*, Bud Granoff, explained that this was done to encourage the correct picking of a chest, which was the whole appeal of the show, although convivial host Jan Murray helped somewhat in that regard. As for the type of contestant sought, Granoff said, "Charles Van Doren couldn't get on this show," and in another article the refreshingly blunt producer stated, "We don't cater to geniuses and freaks." Soon after the debut of *Treasure Hunt*, Robert Kintner left the network he had helped make competitive with the older two and became the new president of NBC. *Treasure Hunt* would follow him to the new network, but not until the following season.[51]

Other attempts into the big-money field were CBS's *High Finance*, which left the air within two months, and *Giant Step*, which did not last long either but demonstrated EPI's continuing fascination with children as contestants, the quiz was limited to children and awarded material benefits such as typewriters and college scholarships rather than any direct monetary winnings. The show was good training for producer Jurist, who later took over from Koplin on *The $64,000 Challenge* and then left EPI for another quiz show, *Dotto*.

The Price Is Right, which quietly premiered in November 1956 on daytime television, blossomed into one of the biggest successes of the following season. Like *Treasure Hunt*, it was more of a guessing game than a quiz show. A panel of contestants had to guess the price of items placed before them—such as television sets, freezers, and fur coats. The contestants who came closest to the listed retail price of the article without going over it would win the item. *The Price Is Right*, hosted by Bill Cullen, was created and produced by the masters of game shows, Mark Goodson and Bill Todman, and proved to be a healthy antidote to the surfeit of dollars on the television screen. Probably more than any other show on television, *The Price Is Right* was calculated to do what all commercial television programming is designed to do: to encourage the American consumption ethos. No other quiz sparked greater interest in the process of buying and consuming. *The Price Is Right* offered merchandise, the ultimate use of money to most viewers. Mark Goodson summed up the appeal of his new program best of all: "Money on television has become just a lot of numbers, but an icebox is still an icebox."[52]

The proposed quiz shows that almost got on the air but ultimately did not were the most outlandish of all and demonstrated that even television has limits to its bad taste. Revlon's attempt at the cosmetic quiz was *The Most Beautiful Girl in the World*, an incredible bit of nonsense that would have combined the elements of a beauty contest, a big-money quiz show, and the good-deed-service orientation of *The Big Surprise*. It was devised by Joe Cates, the first producer of *The $64,000 Question*, and his assistant, Elroy Schwartz. Thrice postponed,

The Most Beautiful Girl in the World first had sponsor problems and then emcee problems because the Revson brothers wanted Hal March to host the show. Finally (and fortunately) the proposed pageant was aborted in November 1956. The ultimate in bad taste for the 1956–57 season, though, belonged to a quiz show proposed by Walt Framer, creator of *Strike It Rich* and *The Big Payoff* and target of Louis Cowan as paragon of "those awful microscope-on-misery-programs." Framer's latest heart-throbbing quiz was to have been *Behind Closed Doors*, which would have provided a winning prize of free psychiatric care to those "contestants" who needed it.[53]

The 1956–57 season saw the first public surfacings that the big-money quiz programs were not the straightforward contests of knowledge that they appeared to be on the screen. Prior to Herbert Stempel's efforts to get people to listen to and believe him that his appearance on *Twenty-one* was rigged, the first and most serious allegation had occurred in December 1956. Dale Logue, a contestant on *The Big Surprise*, missed her question at the $10,000 plateau. She claimed it was the same question as one she had missed in what she was asked in a warmup session prior to going on the air. She hired an attorney and sued the producers of the EPI quiz for $103,000, claiming she was deliberately "sacked." Carlin publicly called her charge "ridiculous," but Logue's lawyer brought the case to the attention of the Federal Trade Commission. The FTC began an investigation at the lower staff levels, although it doubted that it had any jurisdiction in the matter since it was usually assumed that while the FTC could regulate advertising, it had little control over what went on television or radio between the commercials. The investigation was very slow and consisted of little more than the FTC's getting ex parte statements from the producers as well as their assurances that *The Big Surprise* was not false and deceptive. What went on between the FTC and *The Big Surprise* was not a full investigation at all and was closed at the staff level in May 1958, long after the quiz had left the air. The complaint never reached the FTC chairman or any higher levels. At the news of Dale Logue's charge, Martin Revson asked EPI's directors, Harry Fleischmann and Steve Carlin, if there was any truth to the story and received denials that any controls existed on

The Big Surprise. Amazingly the incident was nearly devoid of press coverage.[54]

During the 1956–57 season, two articles in national magazines, one in *Time* in April 1957, the other in *Look* in August raised the question that the quiz shows might be fixed. The *Time* article, "The $60 Million Question", (the $60 million coming from the combined amount spent by all networks on quiz shows), began by asking, "Are the quiz shows rigged?" It was a bold question at the time and the article answered: "The producers of many shows control the outcome as closely as they dare—without collusion with contestants, yet far more effectively than most viewers suspect." *Time* obviously had not discovered the rampant collusion on *Twenty-one* and, in fact, seemed rather impressed by the fact that the Enright productions, unlike most other quizzes, required a written examination. The article focused mainly on the EPI quiz shows. Without naming sources, *Time* described the basic method that Mert Koplin used in subtly and informally drawing out a potential or certain contestant's expertise and then framing the questions accordingly. It mentioned that Marine Captain Richard McCutchen won the first $64,000 question in his specialty, French cuisine—he was weaker in Chinese and Italian cooking—and that Gino Prato was deliberately given questions in Italian opera, his strength, rather than in French or German opera. It quoted McCutchen as saying, "I think they pretty well establish your limits," and Paddy Keough as describing his screening, "About six fellows with baseball record books questioned me about 75 minutes. They must have asked me about 150 questions." Clearly the intent of "The $60 Million Question" was to show that the most popular of all television fare was carefully controlled to maximize the entertainment value of the quiz. Much of what it reported was not really news: that the repartée between contestant and emcee was rehearsed; that the Manufacturers Trust Company's vault used on *The $64,000 Question*, guarded by Ben Feit, was open to someone, presumably the producers, for the purpose of depositing the questions; and that program rules had been arbitrarily changed to allow such popular contestants as Robert Strom and Ted Nadler to continue for weeks more. It mentioned the plight of Dale Logue in brief and quoted another contestant from the then-cancelled *The Big Surprise*, Nils T. Granlund, saying that he, too, received questions on the quiz that he had previously heard in the warm-up session. As for Charles Van Doren, the *Time* article said the young scholar "feels certain that no questions were form-fitted to his phenomenal mind."[55]

The *Look* article, "Are TV Quiz Shows Fixed?" began by discussing the Logue incident but formed no conclusions. It was more suspicious and critical of *Twenty-one* than *Time* was, stating that there was some matching of categories from the show's written test with contestants. It pointed out, for example, that Van Doren had missed all questions in the category of babies on the test and therefore received none from that topic as a contestant. Of the 108 categories in the written preshow exam Enright volunteered the information that usually about sixteen were picked for each contestant. *Look* quoted Bill Ladd, the television editor for the *Louisville Courier-Journal*, who was one of the few people in the country who contended that Van Doren purposely missed his final question on *Twenty-one* (Who is king of the Belgians?) because, to Ladd, it seemed to be an easy question. Beyond that, the article tended to overuse the word *control* to the point of confusion. It divided quiz and game shows into the categories of "spontaneous," "controlled," and "partially controlled." The only two spontaneous programs *Look* discovered in its investigation were *Two for the Money*, a low-budget quiz hosted by Herb Shriner, and *Name That Tune*.[56] The article was wrong about the latter. The tunes identified by contestants on the show had been previously hummed to them without giving the titles during sessions prior to telecast. *Name That Tune* also provided its contestants with a thirty second clock in the preshow session to train them for quick identification. None of this was known to the public.[57]

"Are TV Quiz Shows Fixed?" incorrectly labeled *The $64,000 Question* as more controlled than *The $64,000 Challenge*, putting the latter quiz in the "partially controlled" category. The article maintained that since one of the contestants on *The $64,000 Challenge* had to be a former winner from either *The Big Surprise* or *The $64,000 Question*, then the questions were naturally more difficult and, to *Look*'s logic, more difficult to prearrange. The article further reasoned that a quiz with two contestants was undoubtedly harder to manage than a quiz with only one. *Look* called no quiz shows dishonest but singled out *Treasure Hunt* as the most controlled of all because it chose questions from a trove given to contestants before airtime. The article also provided the ultimate answer from a quiz show producer to the later investigation and to *Look* on the question at the time, "Are TV Quiz Shows Fixed?" The artless Bud Granoff of *Treasure Hunt* ended all discussion by saying, "If a sponsor wants to give away loot, it's his own business how he does it."

Both pieces of journalism were among the first to ask whether the outcomes of some big-money quiz shows were predetermined by producer control. They went below the surface and discovered that principles of showmanship sometimes overrode ostensibly honest intelligence contests. Yet neither article went deep enough to unearth the more unethical practice of collusion, the prearranged performance between producer and the fully aware contestant. The most corrupt quiz, *Twenty-one*, was not their target. Perhaps captured by the charisma of Van Doren or convinced that nonspecialized knowledge would have been next to impossible to try to control within a framework of questions, the *Time* and *Look* articles failed in their ultimate purpose. From hindsight, one might have hoped that, at the very least, they would have prompted some minimal investigation. Incredibly, neither article was ever read by or brought to the attention of network presidents, Robert Kintner and Frank Stanton, men presumably in a position to inquire further about the working of quiz shows. As both men later testified, these initial exposés simply passed beneath their view.[58]

One final attempt to publicize the belief that quiz shows were using questionable, if not dishonest, methods of control came from television reporter Harriet Van Horne in the *New York World-Telegram and Sun* in spring 1957 between the appearance of the *Time* and *Look* pieces. In a series of four articles she explored the inner workings of the quizzes quite thoroughly. From her sources, she stated: "Some of the cynics and the contestants who didn't make it say a lot of rehearsal goes on behind closed doors, that, contestants are given hundreds of 'practice questions' and that some of them, with slight variations in wording, later turn up on the show." Van Horne also related Dale Logue's charge and the story of Nils T. Granlund from *The Big Surprise*, who died a few days after the article was published. The most damning statement came from her interview with Joe Cates, the first producer of *The $64,000 Question* who had since gone to NBC: "The questions are controlled. That is necessary from the point of showmanship. The men who assess the contestant's field of knowledge are usually the men who mark out the field from which the question is to be drawn."[59]

These emerging glimmers of truth about the big-money quiz shows appeared to have virtually no effect on the continued practices of deception. The break would not come with journalistic investigation but from a disgruntled applicant to a quiz show. The series in the *New York World-Telegram and Sun* captured only the attention of Martin Revson, who asked Steve Carlin and Harry Fleischmann if there was any truth to Cates's remarks; the EPI executives again offered their complete denials of any wrongdoing. At about this time William Ewald of the United Press conducted an investigation similar to Van Horne's and discovered no evidence of unethical practices, an outcome that helped to alleviate Revson's apprehension. Although some stated truths about the quizzes had surfaced during the season, the truths that could not be ignored nor explained away would have to wait another year.[60]

NOTES

1. U.S., Congress, House, Committee on Interstate and Foreign Commerce, *Investigation of Television Quiz Shows*, before a subcommittee of the Committee on Interstate and Foreign Commerce, House of Representatives, 86th Cong., 1st sess., 1959, Enright testimony, p. 450, Franklin testimony, p. 152 (hereafter cited as *Investigation*); "Meeting of Minds," *Time*, September 15, 1958, p. 47; *New York Times*, February 17, 1957, sec. 2, p. 13.

2. *Broadcasting*, August 6, 1956, p. 14; *Variety*, June 27, 1956, p. 22, July 11, 1956, p. 31.

3. *Investigation*, Freedman testimony, pp. 211, 214, and 221; *Variety*, June 27, 1956, p. 22.

4. [Lester Bernstein], "The Wizard of Quiz," *Time*, February 11, 1957, p. 44; *New York Times*, December 1, 1957, sec. 6, p. 90.

5. *Investigation*, Enright testimony, p. 246, Fisher testimony, p. 445, Kletter testimony, pp. 155–156, 165, 167.

6. Ibid. Enright testimony, pp. 224, 262, Freedman testimony, pp. 217–219; *Variety*, September 19, 1956, p. 46.

7. "Are TV Quiz Shows Fixed?" *Look*, August 20, 1957, p. 45; *Investigation*, Enright testimony, pp. 245, 258, Jackman testimony, including a transcribed kinescope of *Twenty-one* for October 3, 1956, pp. 117–118, 120–130.

8. Alfred Bester, "Life Among the Giveaway Programs," *Holiday*, May, 1957, p. 116; *Investigation*, Enright testimony, pp. 245, 258, Stempel testimony, pp. 23–25.

9. *Investigation*, Stempel testimony, pp. 25–26.

10. Ibid., Enright testimony, pp. 245, 258, Stempel testimony, pp. 22–23, 26–29; "Meeting of Minds," p. 47.

11. *Investigation*, Freedman testimony, pp. 230, 232, 243, Leibbrand testimony, 111–115.

12. Ibid., Enright testimony, p. 248, Freedman testimony, p. 240, Kletter testimony, p. 161, Stempel testimony, pp. 27, 30, 32.

13. Ibid., Enright testimony, pp. 254–255, Kletter testimony, pp. 156, 176, 183, Stempel testimony, p. 30.

14. *Variety*, October 17, 1956, p. 27, November 7, 1956, p. 25.

15. [Bernstein], "Wizard," pp. 44–46.

16. Ibid., pp. 45–46, 49; "Know-It-All," *Newsweek*, January 28, 1957, p. 60; Charles Poole, review of *Lincoln's Commando*, by Charles Van Doren and Ralph J. Roske, *New York Times*, April 18, 1957, p. 27; *Time*, April 22, 1957, p. 47.

17. [Bernstein], "Wizard," p. 49; Van Doren interviewed and quoted in Bester, "Life," p. 115; "Getting Rich on TV," *Newsweek*, March 25, 1957, pp. 64–65; "Know-It-All," p. 60; *Investigation*, Van Doren testimony, pp. 624–625.

18. *Investigation*, testimony of Van Doren, p. 625.

19. Ibid., Enright testimony, pp. 257–258, Freedman testimony, pp. 212–213, 215, 217–218; "TV Quiz Business Is Itself Quizzed About Fix Charges," *Life*, September 15, 1958, pp. 22–23.

20. *Investigation*, Stempel testimony, pp. 31, 35–36.

21. Ibid., Brody testimony, p. 44, Davis testimony, pp. 94–95, 106, 108, Franklin testimony, pp. 134, 136, Kletter testimony, p. 158, Stempel testimony, pp. 36, 43, 51–52.

22. Ibid., transcribed kinescope of *Twenty-one* for December 5, 1956, as part of Stempel testimony, pp. 37–43.

23. Richard Gehman, "The Real Meaning of Intelligence," *Cosmopolitan* (September 1957); 28; Richard N. Goodwin, *Life*, November 16, 1959, p. 30; *Investigation*, Van Doren testimony, p. 625.

24. *Investigation*, Enright testimony, p. 255, Van Doren testimony, pp. 625–627.

25. [Bernstein], "Wizard," pp. 11, 44–46, 49–50; "Getting Rich on TV," p. 63; *New York Times*, January 22, 1957, p. 59, January 29, 1957, p. 63, February 19, 1957, p. 63; "On Getting Rich Quick," *Newsweek*, February 11, 1957, p. 74; "Whither Charley?" *Time*, March 25, 1957, p. 50.

26. Kern cited by [Bernstein], "Wizard," p. 44; "The American Dream," *Commonweal*, February 22, 1957, pp. 523, 525.

27. Goodwin, *Life*, p. 30.

28. *Investigation*, Stempel testimony, p. 50.

29. *New York Times*, October 17, 1958, p. 58; *Investigation*, Ervin testimony, including a letter from Ervin to Robert W. Lishman, November 2, 1959, pp. 195, 197; *New York Times*, March 3, 1957, sec. 2, p. 11; "When Winners Pay," *Newsweek*, April 1, 1957, p. 10.

30. "Challenger," *Time*, March 11, 1957, p. 51; *Investigation*, Enright testimony, p. 256; *New York Times*, February 19, 1957, p. 63, February 26, 1957, p. 59, March 12, 1957, p. 67; *Investigation*, Van Doren testimony, pp. 626–627.

31. *New York Times*, March 13, 1957, p. 63, April 18, 1957, p. 31; Jay Monaghan, review of *Lincoln's Commando*, by Charles Van Doren and Ralph J. Roske, *New York Times*, April 21, 1957, sec. 7, p. 10, March 16, 1975, p. 12, April 18, 1957, p. 27, April 13, 1957, p. 39; *Time*, April 22, 1957, p. 47.

32. *Investigation*, Davis testimony, p. 97; "If You Ask Questions . . . ," *Newsweek*, September 15, 1958, p. 62; "Meeting of Minds," p. 47; *Investigation*, Stempel testimony, pp. 47–48, 51–52, 56.

33. *Investigation*, Stempel testimony, p. 54.

34. "Battle of the Bones," *Time*, June 3, 1957, p. 68; *Investigation*, Freedman testimony, p. 243; *New York Times*, March 26, 1957, p. 67; *Investigation*, transcribed kinescope of *Twenty-one* for May 13, 1957, as part of Snodgrass testimony, p. 65.

35. *Investigation*, Snodgrass testimony, including a transcribed kinescope of *Twenty-one* for May 20, 1957, pp. 59–62, 71–76, 78, 91.

36. *New York Times*, May 23, 1957, p. 67, May 28, 1957, p. 67; "Battle of the Bones," p. 68; *Investigation*, Freedman testimony, pp. 219, 231, Snodgrass testimony, pp. 78–85.

37. *New York Times*, June 4, 1957, p. 71; *Investigation*, Snodgrass testimony, pp. 85–86; "Telling Tales on '21,' " *Newsweek*, October 6, 1958, p. 52.

38. *Investigation*, Ervin testimony, including letter to Lishman, pp. 186, 195, 197, 207, 209.

39. Ibid., Foreman testimony, p. 912, confidential notes exhibit in Koplin testimony, p. 760, Martin Revson testimony, including a memorandum from Albert Ward to Robert Foreman, June 8, 1955, pp.

816, 818–819; *Variety*, August 15, 1956, p. 25, October 31, 1956, p. 23.

40. *Investigation*, Abrams testimony, p. 983, Koplin testimony, including exhibit, pp. 760, 782, Martin Revson testimony, p. 845.

41. Ibid., Carlin testimony, p. 793, Cohn testimony, p. 681, Koplin testimony, pp. 750–752; *New York Times*, October 22, 1956, p. 53, October 29, 1956, p. 35, February 11, 1957, p. 53, July 8, 1957, p. 45, November 4, 1956, sec. 2, p. 11.

42. *New York Times*, February 17, 1957, sec. 6, p. 25; "Getting Rich on TV," p. 64; Betty Hoffman, "Famous Overnight," *Ladies' Home Journal* (November 1957): 161, 163–164, 190, 192–193; "Human Almanac," *Time*, March 18, 1957, pp. 63–64; *Investigation*, Koplin testimony, p. 761; John Lardner, "The Ear and the Overshoot," *New Yorker*, August 9, 1958, pp. 70–72; "Portrait of a Winner," *Newsweek*, April 15, 1957, p. 70.

43. "$128 Bust," *Time*, October 1, 1956, p. 70.

44. *New York Times*, March 13, 1957, p. 63; *Investigation*, Martin Revson testimony, p. 821; "Whither Charley?" p: 50.

45. "The Misuses of Money," *Life*, March 25, 1957, p. 42; *New York Times*, April 10, 1957, p. 67, April 17, 1957, p. 63, April 24, 1957, p. 67; "Whither Charley?" p. 50.

46. *Investigation*, Bernstein statement, pp. 922–923, Koplin testimony, p. 742.

47. *New York Times*, March 13, 1957, p. 63, April 28, 1957, sec. 3, p. 1; "Getting Rich on TV," p. 64; *Wall Street Journal*, December 4, 1973, p. 16.

48. *Investigation*, Falke testimony, pp. 336–338, 341, Felsher testimony, pp. 405–408, 427.

49. BBD&O executive Herminio Traviesas quoted in Stanley Frank, "Television's Desperate Numbers Game," *Saturday Evening Post*, December 7, 1957, p. 150; "Fun and Games," *Time*, January 21, 1957, p. 40; "How to Get on a TV Quiz Show," *Changing Times*, June, 1956, p. 46; John Lardner, "Life Around the Booths," *New Yorker*, November 30, 1957, p. 147; "On Getting Rich Quick," p. 74; Jess Stearn, "How to Win a Quiz Show," *American Mercury* (August 1957): 38; *Variety*, August 8, 1956, p. 23, September 12, 1956, p. 23.

50. *New York Times*, December 1, 1957, Section 6, p. 93; Lardner, "Life Around the Booths," pp. 149–150.

51. "Are TV Quiz Shows Fixed?" p. 46; "The Big Money," p. 37; "Fun and Games," p. 40; "Getting Rich on TV," p. 63; *New York Times*, February 16, 1958, sec. 2, p. 12; *Variety*, September 12, 1956, p. 26.

52. "The Big Money," p. 37; *New York Times*, December 1, 1957, p. 94; "Fun and Games," p. 40; *Investigation*, Jurist testimony, p. 315, Koplin testimony, p. 742; *Variety*, November 14, 1956, pp. 29, 39,

November 28, 1956, p. 25.

53. Bester, "Life Among the Giveaway Programs," p. 174; "The Big Money," p. 37; *New York Journal-American*, July 19, 1955, p. 9; *Variety*, August 15, 1956, pp. 25, 44, November 14, 1956, p. 26, November 28, 1956, p. 25.

54. "Are TV Quiz Shows Fixed?" p. 45; *Investigation*, Babcock testimony, p. 565; Kintner testimony, including a letter from Kintner to Oren Harris, October 12, 1959, pp. 548–549, 558, Martin Revson testimony, p. 821; "The $60 Million Question," *Time*, April 22, 1957, p. 82.

55. "The $60 Million Question," pp. 78, 80, 82.

56. "Are TV Quiz Shows Fixed?" pp. 45–47.

57. *Investigation*, Fisher testimony, pp. 435, 438–439.

58. Ibid., Kintner testimony, p. 1043, Stanton testimony, pp. 1094, 1097.

59. *New York World-Telegram and Sun*, April 17, 1957, p. 25, April 18, 1957, p. 21, April 19, 1957, p. 17, April 20, 1957, p. 3, April 22, 1957, p. 19.

60. *Investigation*, Abrams testimony, p. 998, Martin Revson testimony, p. 882. Meyer Weinberg in *TV in America* (New York: Ballantine Books, 1962), p. 4, the only work in this subject of comparable scope to this monograph, aptly described the 1956–57 television season as the "Year of Reassurance."

4 | THE QUIZ CHARADE ENDS: THE 1957–58 SEASON

The very essence of the quiz program's appeal lies in its implied representation of honesty. Were it generally understood that these programs do not present honest tests of the contestants' knowledge and intellectual skills, they would be utterly ineffectual in acquiring the public's "time." [1]
—District Attorney Frank Hogan

The 1957–58 season held hope for Herb Stempel. After all Dan Enright had promised him a job. After he graduated from CCNY in June 1957, Stempel went back to his mentor for supposed employment with Barry and Enright. The executive producer, who had dreaded the reappearance of the ex-GI, told him that all Barry and Enright shows had been sold to NBC and he was thus unable to do any hiring—the matter was out of his control. Stempel knew when he was being put off. Later, after he discovered that Enright still maintained production control, he stormed back to the producer. This time Enright told him that he had tried to get him a job but was overruled by the network. He said that he had submitted a list of thirty names for a rotating panel for a new quiz, *Hi-Lo*, to NBC and the network had rejected three of the names, one of them Stempel's.

Stempel's anger built that summer. In early September he called Jack O'Brian, the freewheeling television critic for the *New York Journal-American*, and told him his story about *Twenty-one*. The newspaper decided not to publish the story without further proof for fear of libel, but it did ask Enright about the tale. Enright immediately called Stempel and offered him a job as a panelist on the final week of the summer quiz, *Hi-Lo*. Herbert refused the offer. The point had passed where the creator of *Twenty -one* could mollify or defuse its first "star." Controls no longer worked on Herbert Stempel.

By the fall of 1957, then, Stempel had contacted two newspapers about the deceptions on *Twenty-one*, and both had refused to print his story. The *New York Post*, though, was still intrigued by the tale. In September 1957, soon after Enright had been confronted by the *New York Journal-American*, Paul Sand of the *New York Post* called Art Franklin of Barry and Enright and told him that the *Post* was still interested in the Stempel story and was assigning five reporters to it to investigate. Franklin himself did not believe the story but did not deny its authenticity to the reporter; his public relations experience had taught him that such a denial could have been interpreted as an admission of guilt. He calmly explained to Sand that he had heard of the charge by the former contestant and so had the *Journal-American* which had declined to print the story.

At the same time, someone on the *Journal American* staff learned of the Stempel tip to Jack O'Brian and called a press representative at NBC, Ellis Moore, warning him to "prepare for the storm." Moore frantically called for a meeting; present were Moore and Sydney Eiges, vice-president in charge of press for NBC, Franklin and Al Davis, and Enright. The purpose of the gathering was to decide what to do about the story Stempel was spreading. NBC made no initial effort to determine whether the story was true. Enright recalled that no one even asked him. Art Franklin later described the session to congressional counsel Robert Lishman:

LISHMAN: At that meeting did Mr. Enright deny to anybody that he had given assistance to Mr. Stempel?
FRANKLIN: It never came up. It was just automatically assumed by everybody there that Herb Stempel was a raving lunatic.... The people from NBC did not seem to know what was going on but I was used to that. I dealt with them for many years before.
LISHMAN: Was there a discussion there as to what steps

should be taken to keep the story from breaking in the news-papers?

FRANKLIN: No; because NBC was so terrified about the possi-bility of this all being true that they sort of kept their hands as clean as possible by "kicking it under the carpet."

Franklin had this to say about the network role at the begin-nings of the hint of scandal: "Well, it struck me then as sort of a situation where a husband may suspect a wife, but he loves her too much to ever want to really know, you know. NBC loved Barry and Enright in those days." The meeting ended with Franklin's suggestion that the best action to take was no action at all.

Syd Eiges gave a verbal report of the meeting to Thomas Ervin, vice-president and general attorney for NBC. But Ervin was still unsatisfied and called for another conference with En-right. On September 20 Eiges, Ervin, and his assistant, Ben Raub, met with Enright and his lawyer, Irving Cohen. There Enright brought out the proof that Herbert Stempel was indeed deranged and had tried to blackmail him. Enright told Ervin that he had secretly tape-recorded the blackmail threat at the March 7 meeting with Stempel but did not play the tape. He also showed the NBC attorney the following statement, which he persuaded Stempel to sign:

I do hereby state and declare to whomever may be now or in the future concerned that Dan Enright, producer of Barry and Enright Productions, has never in any way shape nor form gi-ven, imparted or suggested to me any questions or answers connected with the program *Twenty-One.*

(signed)
Herbert Stempel

That was proof enough for Tom Ervin and NBC, but what about the press? Eiges called the *Journal-American* and requested that the newspaper talk with NBC before printing any of the Stem-pel story because there was "another side to it." Three days later, the *Journal American* called Eiges and said his request was unnecessary; the paper had decided not to print the story without more significant corroborating evidence. The *New York Post* also declined to print any story about the "alleged" fixing on *Twenty-one*. Dan Enright had weathered another Stempel storm. As for NBC, it was made aware finally of Herb Stempel's charge, but preferred to rest on Enright's word and not think about the problem.[2]

NBC still had not decided what to do with its newest star, Charles Van Doren, at the start of the 1957–58 season, but by the summer of 1958, his future seemed best suited to the network's morning *Today* show. Van Doren got along well with the program's host, Dave Garroway, and had first appeared on his show *Wide Wide World* before being hired as a summer replacement for Garroway. Early in the season Van Doren had written a lengthy article for *Life* publicly devaluing much of his life as a quiz celebrity. He related none of the truth of his rigged performances but concluded that what he had done was not to be considered heroic or good for education's image. At the end of the article, he wrote:

An educated man, then, and a quiz show contestant are moving rather rapidly in opposite directions. The world of the educated man is full of mysteries. It is foggy and dark; with lots of unlighted passages leading off to no one knows where. The more educated he is the more passages he discovers.... Opposed to the dim uncertainty of the world of the educated man is the bright little circle of light in which the quiz show contestant basks in his isolation booth. All is certainty there. One need not worry or be distressed. Only those questions are asked which have answers, and then only if the answers are available, on a card held in the M.C.'s hand. Probably fireflies, flitting about in the spring twilight, are as sure of their little circles of luminescence as the contestant is of his.

But, he added, "I'm going to keep all of that money though!"[3] Only Van Doren agonized over the revealing substance behind his prose. To the public, he was still the egghead as hero.

The star of *Twenty-one* for the 1957–58 season was a young woman, Elfrida Von Nardroff. Like Van Doren, she was a graduate student at Columbia University, working toward her doctorate in psychology, and her father was on the physics faculty. She was also personnel manager at the American Institute of Certified Public Accountants. For twenty-one exciting weeks she toiled on the quiz, and, with Albert Freedman's expert coaching, she rolled up a brief record for quiz winnings on a single show, $220,500. She received only $43,000 after taxes but happily left the show to begin her dissertation in experimental psychology and said: "I don't agree with people who say the quiz shows are debasement of American cultural life. They are just one side of it and a lively one at that."[4]

Over at EPI *The $64,000 Challenge* continued to be troublesome, although there were a few bright moments. Teddy Nadler returned for a second season to increase his winnings beyond those of Elfrida Von Nardroff to the phenomenal total of $264,000, the all-time record. Robert Strom came over from *The $64,000 Question* of the previous season to win over $50,000 more for the combined two-quiz total of $242,600. In September 1957 Reverend Charles E. "Stoney" Jackson, Jr., of Tullahoma, Tennessee, was invited to appear on *The $64,000 Challenge* in the near future. He had appeared on *The $64,000 Question* the prior television season in early 1957 and had won $16,000. His category was great lovers, and he had left the quiz show feeling that it was totally honest with no questionable practices in his experience. In fact Koplin had screened him so carefully on the older quiz that the minister was truly unaware, he said later, that the many facts brought out during his preprogram interview were ever used on the air. For *The $64,000 Challenge* Jackson was introduced only at the end of a show in late September and was then told that his actual appearance would be delayed several weeks while Dr. Joyce Brothers opposed a series of boxers. Jackson finally participated on December 29. A couple of days before, he was interviewed by Shirley Bernstein, who lacked Mert Koplin's finesse and turned the session into a question-and-answer screening. To one question she asked, "Do you know who wrote a poem about a couple where one lover had to swim to meet the other?" Jackson replied that that would have to be about Hero and Leander and that "[Christopher] Marlowe and [George] Chapman wrote it. Chapman finished it up." When he could not come up with the name of the author of a similar poem in the nineteenth century, Bernstein gave him the answer: Thomas Hood. When Jackson stood in his isolation booth for the first time on *The $64,000 Challenge*, the same question about Hero and Leander with the Thomas Hood answer was given to his opponent, who missed it. When he received the same question, he was tempted to blurt out that he had received the answer before but held back and won $4,000. Stoney Jackson was most upset at what had happened to him; he refused to return to the show and initially refused the check.

He immediately sent a telegram to *Time* magazine saying that he had been given an answer on the quiz. He never heard from *Time*. He also went to the *New York Times* and told the story, but it would not publish the story without more proof. Had Jackson been aware of the interest of the *New York Journal-American* or the *New York Post* in the subject of quiz-show fraud, the story might have been printed. When Jackson returned home, the *Nashville Tennessean* declined to print his outrage; neither did his hometown twice-weekly paper for which he wrote the sports column. As Herbert Stempel had discovered earlier, Stoney Jackson was learning the frustration in trying to convince people that he had participated, unknowingly, in a fraud in front of millions of televiewers. In early 1958 Jackson told all his parishioners and fellow ministers of the deceit, but few were shocked. Unable to convince even his own congregation of the immorality involved in his quiz-show appearance, he gave up trying to convince anybody, and the fraudulence continued on its unpublicized path.[5]

By the time of Reverend Jackson's appearance, Shirley Bernstein was the producer of *The $64,000 Challenge*. Revlon, however, refused to have a woman listed in such a high position of responsibility; instead, Steve Carlin was listed as executive producer in the credits and Bernstein was put down as associate producer (no producer was listed). On March 23, 1958, Wilton J. Springer faced Arthur Cohn, Jr., in the category of theater. Just hours before showtime, both men were in the studio waiting to go on the air. Bernstein approached Cohn and told him to send Springer into her office, saying, "I want to give him some warm-up questions"; she added, looking at Cohn, "You don't look nervous." Cohn did as he was told and went to sit out in the orchestra pit with his wife and aunt. A short while later

Springer came back, rather worried, and said to Cohn, "They're going into secondary leads in plays," and gave the example of the character of Maggie Cutler in *The Man Who Came to Dinner*. Springer was frantic because he did not know many secondary leads. Cohn's wife speculated, "Isn't it funny that you got warm-up questions and not my husband?" Cohn sat puzzled and waited to go on the quiz. That evening Springer defeated Arthur Cohn, and among the several questions asked was the Maggie Cutler example Springer had received.

Cohn was upset that he had been duped. He felt cheated and after the show, about midnight, called up Bernstein, angrily demanding to know why he had not been given a warm-up session as Springer had. Bernstein pleaded ignorance of the situation until Cohn told her that Springer had talked to him immediately upon leaving her office. He knew about the sample question about Maggie Cutler, and so did his wife and aunt. Bernstein could only express amazement at the coincidence of having the same warm-up question reappear on the air. Cohn bristled at the flimsy reaction and derisively said, "Sleep well tonight, Miss Bernstein."

Bernstein did not sleep at all that night, fearful that the game was, quite literally, over. The next morning she talked to Springer and asked him to call Cohn and tell him not to say anything to anyone about the incident. Springer replied that he would do what he could, but he never called Cohn. On the same day, meanwhile, Cohn went to see his friend, George Abrams of Revlon, with whom he had done business. He met that day with Abrams and his assistant, Bill Mandel, and told them what had happened on their quiz show. Abrams was truly shocked. For the first time he was aware that something beyond the mere "tough" or "easy" questions was being used to control contestants. He believed Cohn but still thought that the use of the question might have been coincidental and urged him to accept the $250 consolation prize that he had refused the night before. Cohn finally had them direct the check to a charity. Abrams also wanted Cohn to go to Thomas K. Fisher, vice-president and general attorney for CBS, and tell him the story, but Cohn was becoming increasingly reluctant to become involved in any sort of accusatory process. He was then an unemployed advertising agent who wanted to get back into the industry some day and reasoned that any publicity he started would ruin his chances toward that end.

Abrams's suspicion about EPI was aroused. He called Carlin and Fleischmann the same day with the news of the Cohn-Springer match on *The $64,000 Challenge*. The producers explained that not all contestants were given warm-up sessions because some appeared calm enough not to need them. They called the reappearance of the Maggie Cutler question an incredible coincidence because the producer was never fully sure which questions from the large file would appear on the air. It did not take much to convince Abrams that the entire affair had been an accident. Nonetheless Revlon's advertising representative told his employer, Charles Revson, what had happened in connection with the Cohn-Springer match and explained how he had been assured that it was a bad coincidence and probably would never occur again. Revson appeared disinterested and had few questions. When he asked Abrams if he were satisfied with the producers' assurances, Abrams replied that he was. Revson later testified that this meeting with Abrams never occurred and that he did not learn of the Cohn-Springer mismatch until August of that year.

Arthur Cohn persisted. He sent letters to twenty-five friends describing what had happened to him on *The $64,000 Challenge*. A few days latter Bernstein called Cohn and said she was most upset at the "coincidence" and pleaded with the ex-advertising man not to spread his story. Abrams met Carlin a couple of days later, and the executive producer volunteered to talk to Cohn, but Abrams persuaded him not to do that because Cohn was too upset. Cohn had decided not to press his case, and Shirley Bernstein slept better. With all the mounting close calls that EPI and Barry and Enright endured that their deceptions might have unraveled before the public eye, it was ironic that the break finally came from a quiz outside the sphere of either.[6]

The 1957–58 season saw the greatest proliferation of quiz and game shows in television history, many of them lower-budgeted game and panel programs sparked, in part, by the popularity of *The $64,000 Question* and its offspring. By end of season twenty-two network quiz or game shows were on the air. They comprised 18 percent of NBC's overall programming, with forty-seven half-hour periods filled by them per week. They included *Haggis Baggis, Play Your Hunch, Anybody Can Win, Pick a Winner,* and *Number Please.* Particularly popular were the televised variations of the game of bingo, such as *Bingo at Home, Lucky Partners,* and *Wingo,* a local show from New York City. Many of the new games gave away not money but, like *The Price Is Right,* merchandise to home viewers, much to the dismay of most critics. Saying, "Money alone has lost its lure," Jack Gould explained the new trend:

> Viewers are weary of watching others win; they want something for themselves. After ten years the carnival concessionaires are descending on TV.... Television's creative bankruptcy in day to day programming could not be more vividly illustrated.... The renewed emphasis on giveaways, particularly with the added feature of giving money or prizes to home viewers rather than studio participants, is symptomatic of the recession's influences on TV programming.[7]

Gould was correct. America was enduring its most severe recession since World War II in that strange television season, and nowhere was the appeal of the home giveaway more apparent than in the program that had premiered the previous season, *The Price Is Right.* The price-guessing panel quiz grew during its second season and secured a weekly half-hour on prime time. The show quickly zoomed into the top ten. The home participant expansion sent 80 million postcards per week to New York City post offices, and the Postal Department in Washington, D.C., reported a 300 percent increase in postcards received nationwide. The postcards seemed to be an extension of the ratings system to the shows' producers. The responses certainly meant that the shows were in touch with their viewers, as well as affording a recession-weary public the chance to win merchandise or money.

The recession undoubtedly triggered the increase in home-participating quiz and game shows, but the rush of sponsors, or more importantly prize donors, to such shows also fostered their growth. *The Price Is Right* and its imitators always announced the manufacturer of the gift they displayed on the show before giving it to the winner. These free endorsements, or "plugs," became the hallmark of daytime television and the bane of most critics. The Ohio Tappan Company gave away $230,000 worth of ranges that season, which averaged out to spending 42¢ per 1,000 viewers, a ratio much cheaper than a normal commercial. Philco Corporation called *The Price Is Right* "a genuine free commercial." Some companies refused to jump onto the "plugola" (as it came to be called) bandwagon of advertising, notably General Electric and Sunbeam in the appliance field and also Lanvin Perfume. Lanvin's president Edouard Cournaud said, "If you give away too much too often, it loses its value." Plugola, however, was the new advertising technique of the day, and television writer Dale Wasserman described the state of the medium: "As that once promising baby, television, moves straight from infancy to senility."[8]

Quiz shows had become such a staple in the television industry that unanticipated demands were created for them. One enterprising woman, Diane Lawson, successfully created and operated a contestant selection firm. Lawson and Lawson, hired by several quiz producers, scouted the streets for potential contestants. Like *The $64,000 Question*, many later shows sought a general type of contestant. *Haggis Baggis* instructed Lawson and Lawson to look for "potential hams and extroverts" to enliven its style. One contestant scout described the "ideal daytime quiz couple" as "from Indiana. The boy is 26, the girl 24; they are white and Protestant and they have two kids." The one problem Diane Lawson ominously noted in her occupation was that "people tend to change like Jekyll into Hyde the minute they win 25 bucks. They go kind of nuts with that carrot in front of 'em. They'll win something and boom! All the things you picked 'em for go out the window. All they're thinking about is the damned money."[9]

Female contestants, in particular, were in short supply. By mid-season, 1957–58, only 44 of the 114 contestants who had appeared on *The $64,000 Question* were women, and only 3 of the 11 top winners were female. The ratio was even worse for *The $64,000 Challenge*, and on *Twenty-one* a mere 20 of the show's 73 contestants were women, less than one third; all but one of those was a career woman. Barry and Enright even sent scouts to California to seek out potential female contestants.

Livingston Welch, chairman of the Department of Philosophy and Psychology at Hunter College, explained the shortage by saying that women have few hobbies, therefore less avocational knowledge or interests. John Lardner simplified the supposed problem: "Women as a group are less tolerant of nonsense than men are."[10]

Of the new quiz shows that came forth during the 1957–58 season, *Dotto* was one of the most successful. It premiered on January 6, 1958, on daytime CBS television and soon became the highest-rated daytime show. *Dotto* was a quiz show based upon the children's game of connecting dots. The quiz had two opposing contestants who strived to connect dots comprising a famous face by answering questions. Each face contained fifty dots, and the contestants were given the choice of attempting five-, eight-, or ten-dot questions. A correct answer connected the corresponding dots. When the famous face was finally identified by one of the contestants, each unconnected dot was worth $20.[11]

Dotto was packaged by the production organization of Marjeff, Incorporated, a subsidiary of the veteran independent television-producing firm of Frank Cooper Associates. The initial sales agent for the program was Sy Fischer, who also became program supervisor. It was Fischer who hired Edward Jurist to product *Dotto*. An EPI veteran, Jurist had begun his career as a producer on *Quiz Kids*, the first notable Louis Cowan creation, before coming to this latest in the series of fraudulent quiz shows. Assisting Jurist were associate producer Art Henley and director Jerome Shurr; his key aide was associate producer Stan Green, the counterpart of Mert Koplin for the new quiz. Green, through the direction of Jurist, was the primary person responsible for coaching contestants. Jurist reasoned that *Dotto* would require stricter controls than those he had known while working on *The $64,000 Challenge* because *Dotto* asked general-knowledge questions, as did *Twenty-one*, rather than the specialized and easier-to-control knowledge of the $64,000 quiz shows. Jurist also wanted many of the contestants of *Dotto* to have several series of tie games, thereby increasing the monetary excitement of the quiz.[12]

Unlike some quiz shows, *Dotto* culled its contestants directly

from the studio audience, although always for a program at
least one week later. Jurist also employed Diane Lawson to
search for potential contestants, on occasion directing her to
seek out the "All-American look." The usual procedure was to
gather twenty or thirty potential contestants from the studio
audience after each daily show and informally interview them
immediately after the quiz in the same studio building. Jurist,
Shurr, Henley, Green, and sometimes Lawson normally attended these sessions. The possible contestants were given a
brief written test and a test asking them to identify dot-
connected caricatures. When the potential contestants were
weeded down to four or five after the test, Stan Green screened
them. Before that, Jurist would hold a planning session to determine who to choose. He was much more casual about his
deceptions than Dan Enright or EPI were and included a larger
number of participants in the riggings. Jurist described the procedure for planning *Dotto:*

> We sat down in committee and said, gee, I don't like her any more.
> Let us dump her. Gee, she is great. Tomorrow let us have a contestant
> of 35 points (meaning the person would correctly name the caricature
> with 35 of the 50 dots connected) and a 25 and try for a tie of 20 on the
> second one.
>
> Then the artist would be there and I would say—I had established a
> pattern of recognition with him or them so that when I said 35 he knew
> that only the last five—in other words, it didn't matter whether the
> picture was 25, or 35, or 45 [meaning when it was identifiable]. . . . Our
> purpose was entertainment of a longer and a shorter game and a tie
> and a continued tie and the mounting excitement. That is what we
> were really scheduling. We were scheduling the entertainment. [13]

The *Dotto* artist, Eric Lieber, worked closely with the producer.
He met every day with Jurist and Green to confirm the controls
on his drawings of people and to decide at what point in the
dot-connecting process the caricature would become readily
identified by most people. Sometimes a contestant would be
told what face hid behind the dots, and at other times it would
be presumed that the contestant would identify the face at the
appropriate time. Lieber later testified that over 90 percent of
everything he conceived for *Dotto* was predetermined in the

above manner.[14]

Jurist instructed Green in the "playback" method of coaching contestants, which he had learned while at EPI: "Primary procedure was to find out what people knew and frame questions accordingly. The second procedure, to inculcate is a word I like to use, the people with information you thought that they ought to have in such a way that they ideally were not aware you were doing it." Unfortunately for Ed Jurist and *Dotto*, Green was not a good screener; in fact, he was rather sloppy. Antoinette DuBarry Hillman, a contestant on *Dotto* in February 1958, described her session with Green:

He would say, for instance, what do you know about baseball. Then you would say what? he would say, well, who has a home run record, and you would say Babe Ruth. Then he would ask a couple of other questions about baseball.... Then he would say, how would you recognize Mickey Mouse? You would say he has little bitty ears and a button nose and so forth. Actually the first day I was on the show he did throw me a curve and I think quite inadvertently, because he asked me in the preliminary thing how I would recognize Victor Borge. We went through this bit. Then when I got on the show and was answering the questions, I got my first clue [for the emerging dot connections] and it was Danish. I didn't think too much about that. Then the second clue was a musician. How many Danish musicians do you know? I couldn't believe it was possibly the man he mentioned because I thought this was all very upright.... Some of the questions sounded a little familiar to me, but I thought they were being kind. It was my first day around. Finally I had to give in and say Victor Borge. I was right and I won. When I went off stage I popped over to Mr. Green and started to thank him, and he said hush, hush, hush. From then we played the whole thing like a solemn minuet, like everybody bowing and smiling and taking you back and forth and pretending nothing at all was going on. We would have these little talks, but never came clean with each other. We got very cozy. Nice man and everything else. We pretended nothing else was done.

After several days of winning, Hillman was finally told to go on the air with no coaching. She lost but managed to retain $1,460.[15]

Dotto was sponsored by the Colgate-Palmolive Company through its advertising agency, Ted Bates and Company, one of the most successful agencies in television. *Dotto* was such a successful television property that it went on nighttime television on July 1, 1958, on NBC. It was most unusual for a different network to purchase a prime-time option on a show already on another network, but such was the case with *Dotto*, which was a further indication of its popularity. In summer 1958, the quiz continued its daytime run on CBS and was featured on Tuesday nights on NBC. Colgate-Palmolive was the sponsor for both, and Edward Jurist the producer for both shows. He did, however, hire Gil Cates to be associate producer for the nighttime version. Cates managed the contestants and their preparation and, like Green during the day, was not subtle in his coaching. Contestant David Huschle, who had been on five consecutive days in February, appeared on nighttime *Dotto* for three weeks in July; Cates gave Huschle all the questions and answers he would receive, as well as identification of all the connecting-dot pictures he would have to guess, except for the final caricature.[16]

The master of ceremonies for *Dotto*, Jack Narz, knew nothing of the backstage deception. All Narz knew was that, in addition to the three questions he had for connections of five, eight, and ten dots, there was a fourth question, called the "kicker," which he would ask instead of the ten-dot question when signaled to do so by Jurist. The producer would touch his head when he wanted the very difficult kicker asked. Narz knew that this question promoted tie matches and was rarely used to eliminate contestants.[17]

On May 20, 1958, before NBC secured a portion of *Dotto*, an event occurred that, more than any other, helped bring about the end of the fraudulent television quiz shows. Edward Hilgemeier, Jr., a part-time night club comedian, part-time bartender, part-time valet and butler, and contestant on six previous quiz or games shows, waited as a standby contestant for *Dotto* in the Forty-seventh Street studio of the quiz. He sat in the dressing room with the two contestants about to go on the air, the champion Marie Winn, a student at Columbia College, and the challenger, Yeffe Kimball (Slatin). Associate producer Art Henley came by and took away Kimball and another contestant for instruction in the repartée with the emcee, leaving

Hilgemeier alone with Winn. As he sat there, he noticed the woman writing intently in a notebook. She said nothing to Hilgemeier except that she had already won over five hundred dollars and expected to win more. When the other people came back and everybody was led off to a rehearsal area, with Hilgemeier trailing along, his suspicions were first aroused by the great familiarity and friendliness between Marie Winn and the staff of *Dotto*. Finally the quiz was on, and Winn quickly defeated Yeffe Kimball (see appendix 2). As Hilgemeier stood in the wings watching the quiz, he felt as if the answers Marie Winn was giving were "on the tip of her tongue before the question was completed." He wandered back to the dressing room and looked at Winn's notebook, where he found a page with names written on it:

Bing Crosby—
Barry Fitzgerald—Abbie Players
Donald Duck—3 Nephews
Dagwood—Mr. Dithers
Short Stories—hemingway—
Zhukhov
Alexanders Ragtime Band.
Band Played On.
MacNamaras Band.
Johnsons Polar Garden.
Sewards Folly.

May 20, 1958.

Hilgemeier had just heard Winn give some of these answers and presumed the others were answers for future quizzes. He ripped out several pages from the notebook and returned to stageside, where he met Yeffe Kimball coming off, who had just lost. He said to Kimball, "This is a fixed show." He took her to the dressing room and showed her the notebook and the pages he had torn out. Not really sure what to do, the couple unobtrusively left the studio while Marie Winn was still performing on *Dotto*.[18]

Kimball wanted to sue the program, so she and Hilgemeier went to her attorney, Arthur Seiff, later that same afternoon. In the meantime they had photostatic copies made of the notes Hilgemeier had found. Seiff directed them to another lawyer, Sidney Hoffman, who told Hilgemeier not to appear on *Dotto,* and instructed the couple to come to his office within a couple of days. That evening Hilgemeier and Kimball went to the offices of *Dotto* in the Hotel Woodstock to confront the producers. They were first met by Stan Green, who acted appalled by their story. Green wanted to see the original notebook pages, but Hilgemeier refused, showing him only a photostatic copy. Then Ed Jurist arrived and immediately separated the couple and heard each one's version. He expressed amazement that a contestant had received answers to questions later asked on the air. The producer incorrectly assumed that Hilgemeier wanted to be on the show and offered him an appearance on *Dotto* or the soon-to-be-aired nighttime version if Hilgemeier remained silent. Jurist had no intention of keeping this offer but hoped to pacify a potentially troublesome person. To Jurist's surprise the young man said he was not interested in appearing on *Dotto* and left the office with Kimball.[19]

The next day television viewers of *Dotto* were informed that Marie Winn was ill and could not reappear on the show until she recovered. In fact she never returned. The following day, May 22, Hilgemeier and Kimball finally met with Sidney Hoffman. The lawyer was interested in the case and hoped to settle the matter out of court with *Dotto*. Kimball and Hilgemeier signed a contingency agreement that gave him one-third of all financial remuneration he could extract from Frank Cooper Associates. He also took the original notebook pages. About ten days later he telephoned Hilgemeier and told him that Frank Cooper Associates had offered him $500 and $2,000 for Yeffe Kimball if they signed a release promising not to sue. Hilgemeier refused the offer and told Hoffman that a large portion of his income depended on television quiz- and game-show appearances and that he was not going to jeopardize his reputation for $500. Hoffman advised him to settle at that time or his career would suffer, but the unemployed actor still refused. Later the offer went to $750, and Hoffman told Hilgemeier that Kimball had settled her dispute. On June 18 he went to Hoffman's office, was told that Kimball had received

$4,000 from the owners of *Dotto* to avoid a legal suit, and that they were prepared to give Hilgemeier $1,000 for the same purpose. Hilgemeier still refused and said that he should get just as much as Yeffe Kimball, even though he had not been a contestant on the quiz and thus deprived of possible winnings through Marie Winn's foreknowledge. Hilgemeier also told Ed Jurist that he should get as much as Kimball got.[20]

The powers behind *Dotto* were nervous. Sy Fischer instructed Jurist to send Hilgemeier to him. On July 11 Fischer said to the young man, "We'll give you $1,500 and that's it." Fischer also called Hilgemeier a blackmailer and threatened to call the police. Hilgemeier agreed to the amount, and Fischer told him he could collect it from Walter Schier, the attorney for Frank Cooper Associates. By this time Hilgemeier had befriended a reporter, Jack O'Grady of the *New York Post*, who was intrigued by the young actor's tale but would not print anything without sufficient proof. O'Grady accompanied Hilgemeier to Schier's office but was not allowed to follow him in. Schier gave Hilgemeier three documents, which he signed: a general release promising not to sue and accepting the money in lieu of being a contestant; a statement attesting to the fact that he was not represented by counsel; and a statement saying that, after a thorough investigation into the matter, he was satisfied that there was no fraudulence on *Dotto*. Schier also refused to give Hilgemeier any copies of the documents he had signed but did hand over the $1,500.

The disparity between Kimball's $4,000 settlement and his own $1,500 still bothered Eddie Hilgemeier, and in the next few weeks he deliberately set out to punish the people behind *Dotto*. He ceased going to Sidney Hoffman for legal advice after the lawyer had turned over Winn's original notebook pages to the show's producers. He now retained Irving Tannebaum as counsel and on July 25 drew up an affidavit describing everything that had happened to him in connection with *Dotto*, including his acceptance of the hush money. On July 31, with Hilgemeier's approval, Jack O'Grady delivered a copy of the affidavit to the office of the Federal Communications Commission. Incredibly the initial FCC response was basic disinterest, but the agency did begin a leisurely investigation, which took a full twelve days. On August 11, the FCC merely confirmed the information on Hilgemeier's affidavit.[21]

Events really began to turn against *Dotto* on August 7 when Hilgemeier left a copy of his affivdavit at the advertising department of Colgate-Palmolive. He also left a statement intimating that he wanted an additional $2,500 to equalize his settlement with that of Yeffe Kimball. Colgate was astounded and the following morning called its advertising agency, Ted Bates and Company, and told them of the former standby contestant's claims. The program managers of Ted Bates, James Damon and Christian Walsh, who were frequently on the set of *Dotto*, had seen or heard nothing questionable. Ted Bates's vice-president and former vice-president in charge of programming for NBC, Richard Pinkham, in turn quickly contacted CBS and told them of the allegations. By noon on August 8, the news had reached the desk of the new president of the CBS Television Network Division of less than five months, Louis G. Cowan. Cowan acted without hesitation and directed his vice-president and general attorney, Thomas K. Fisher, to investigate *Dotto*. That evening a meeting was held at the offices of Frank Cooper Associates. Present from the Marjeff production unit for *Dotto* were Ed Jurist, Sy Fischer, Jerome Shurr, Frank Cooper, and Walter Schier; from CBS came Fisher and an assistant; and from Ted Bates was counsel Mike Frothingham. Most conspicuous at the meeting was a frightened Marie Winn. Jurist and Sy Fischer denied that any answers were ever given prematurely on *Dotto* but did admit to giving the $1,500 to Hilgemeier in an effort to stem off unfavorable publicity from what he called an obvious blackmailer. Winn was the focal point of questions from CBS and Ted Bates. Tom Fisher and Frothingham interviewed her for about an hour with Schier present. Prior to this meeting the Marjeff people, at the suggestion of contestant scout and party to the fraud, Diane Lawson, devised a story for Marie Winn whereby she would maintain that she wrote those items in her notebook after she had appeared on *Dotto* to aid her in describing her effort to her sister in Philadelphia, who did not have a television set. Winn agreed and tried to keep to her story during her interview with Fisher and Frothingham, but her performance was not convincing, as Tom Fisher's report attested:

When asked when she first realized the page from her notebook was missing she said she did not know it until just now. When asked about writing her sister to tell her about the show, she said she had not written because her sister had called her that evening. She kept her composure throughout the interview but at times hesitated several seconds before answering questions and... mentioned that she felt she was being imposed upon and that she had no obligation to come in.... Frank Cooper's people had previously advised Ted Bates that she had told them someone representing himself as a reporter had called on her Thursday inquiring about this matter. Jurist stated... shortly after Hilgemeier had made his complaint... on May 20 and at that time she stated that she had written the answers down after the show was over. It is clear, therefore, that in certain respects she lied to us—to wit, when she said she had not talked to anyone connected with Cooper Associates prior to Friday evening about the matter; when she said she did not know the page was missing from her notebook until Friday night; and when she said that she had not received a call from a purported newspaperman concerning the matter.

It is my conclusion based on the attitude of Miss Winn, the known untruths in her statements... plus the pointlessness of her need, as she states, of writing down answers after the show was over, coupled with the writing of names not appearing on the May 20 show (appearing May 21?) that Miss Winn was fed the information prior to the time she went on camera.

The problem then resolves down to: (a) Who fed her the information, and (b) whether it was an aberration or in the regular course of the program production.[22]

On Monday afternoon, August 11, Fisher and Frothingham viewed the May 19, 20, and 21 kinescopes for *Dotto*, which confirmed their suspicions that some of the information on Winn's notebook page were answers to questions on the following day's program. Associate producer Art Henley was also interviewed that day and denied the pattern of fixing. Another round of denials from the *Dotto* personnel followed the next day. On Wednesday the network executive and the advertising agency lawyer interviewed Hilgemeier and were generally impressed by his account of the events. Also on that day the FCC finally notified CBS of the allegations surrounding *Dotto*, to which the network replied that it had been investigating for five days. The FCC said it would like a report within two weeks, and CBS agreed to do its best to comply. At about the same time Hilgemeier told Jurist that he was going to break his story to the newspapers, but Jurist persuaded him to see Sy Fischer once more before doing anything rash. Fischer again offered Hilgemeier another $1,500 for his silence, but the young man refused. As he left Fischer called him a blackmailer and picked up the telephone, threatening to call the police and have him arrested for extortion. Hilgemeier told Jack O'Grady of the new offer, and the reporter persuaded the young man to go back the next day and take the money, saying that the money would be further proof of the program's corruption. Hilgemeier obliged and gave the money to O'Grady.[23]

Finally on August 15 the Marjeff-*Dotto* cover-up caved in, and Frank Cooper himself went to Colgate-Palmolive, with representatives from CBS and Ted Bates and Company present, and admitted that *Dotto* had been a largely controlled quiz show and admitted that many contestants had been coached. Cooper explained that such procedures were not new to television; as Tom Fisher related, "members of his staff have 'inherited' their knowledge from other shows in which they have participated." In what became an increasingly common justification for the deceptions in the months ahead, Cooper maintained that what had occurred on *Dotto* was common knowledge and practice throughout the television industry. CBS and Colgate-Palmolive nevertheless cancelled *Dotto* effective August 18, 1958. The parties concerned in the *Dotto* debacle, including the network, hoped there would be no publicity. Frank Cooper Associates hoped to buy Hilgemeier's silence even when it became probable that the quiz would be cancelled by the sponsor and network. CBS turned over all of its information to NBC, which carried prime-time *Dotto*. The news of the cancellation that first hit the press on August 16 carried only cryptic references to possible wrongdoing on the show. Richard Pinkham of Ted Bates offered no comment, nor did Ed Jurist or anyone connected with Frank Cooper Associates. *Top Dollar* from EPI, which never had any sort of controls in its production, replaced *Dotto*, and an attempt to portray the fall of just another quiz show was given to the press.[24]

The rumors persisted, however, as the story was circulated

that the FCC was looking into the matter. As was its customary practice in the early stages of any complaint investigations, the agency issued no comments. By this time Hilgemeier and O'Grady had also sent the affidavit to the district attorney's office for New York County, and on August 25 it became public knowledge that the district attorney was investigating *Dotto*. The events surrounding the brief description of Eddie Hilgemeier's story were described in print, but the young actor's name was still not released. On August 26 Hubbell Robinson, Jr., executive vice-president in charge of television programming for CBS and the man who had brought Louis Cowan to the network, announced that an investigation by the network had failed to turn up any "improper procedures" of programs on the air (*Dotto* was then conveniently off the air). To his credit, however, Robinson did note that the networks were unequipped to conduct an inquiry necessary for determining truth, since practically all quiz shows were produced independently of the networks.[25]

The significance of the *Dotto* cancellation and the meager publicity following was that they sparked the search for the truth behind the big-money quizzes. The *Dotto* news prompted other persons from other programs to attempt again to make believers out of previous journalistic nonbelievers. Herbert Stempel's story was finally accepted, and on August 28, 1958, both the *New York Journal-American* and the *New York World-Telegram and Sun* carried his saga: he had been told to lose to Charles Van Doren by *Twenty-one's* mastermind, Dan Enright.[26]

The shocked Enright launched a counterattack against the hapless Stempel. Barry and Enright immediately filed a civil libel suit against the *World-Telegram and Sun*, the first paper to mention specific names. They also asked to meet with the district attorney. The day the story broke, NBC, which now owned Barry and Enright Productions, called for a meeting with the representatives of *Twenty-one*, which was about to begin its third season on television. The NBC meeting was attended by Ken Bilby, vice-president in charge of advertising and public relations for the network, Tom Ervin, NBC's general counsel, and Sydney Eiges, NBC's vice-president in charge of press.

With Dan Enright were his lawyer, Irving Cohen, and his public relations men, Al Davis and Art Franklin. Privately Enright confessed to Franklin that he had fixed Stempel's appearance but swore that this had been the only rigging on the entire run of the show. NBC wanted more than mere indignation from Barry and Enright to counter Stempel's story. Bilby thought that the libel suit was a good idea, but NBC declined to join in the suit. In addition to the false statement Enright had Stempel sign on March 7, 1957, and which NBC had seen the previous fall, Enright brought out a fact only Ervin had known and which he hoped would be the ultimate proof of his innocence: his surreptitiously made tape recording of the March 7, 1957, meeting with Stempel.[27]

For NBC, which wanted to believe the successful producer, the tape recording was sufficient proof that Stempel was a blackmailer. Enright could not play the tape at the meeting because it was in a bank that was not open at that time. All agreed the tape should be made public soon. NBC issued the following statement that same day:

The charges made by Herbert Stempel against the show *Twenty-one* first came to our attention over a year ago. At the time we made an investigation and found them to be utterly baseless and untrue. We were completely convinced of the integrity of *Twenty-one* as a program and of the integrity of its producers, Barry and Enright.

At the time these charges were first brought to our attention and shortly thereafter, two major New York newspapers made thorough investigations of them and apparently concluded, as we did, that they had no basis in fact. As a result they printed nothing.[28]

Everyone at the meeting agreed that the tape recording should be turned over to the district attorney's office, which Enright did the following Friday.

The quiz-show accusers, Stempel and Hilgemeier, appeared to be on the defensive for a brief time. Hank Bloomgarden publicly denied receiving any aid on *Twenty-one*. So did Charles Van Doren, and Elfrida Von Nardroff offered, "It is inconceivable that they could have been fixed." The district attorney who had overall authority for the investigation was one of the great trial lawyers of the century, Frank S. Hogan, who was the Democratic candidate for the U.S. Senate against

Kenneth B. Keating that fall. He delegated the actual day-to-day investigation to one of his seventy-five assistant district attorneys, the very able Joseph Stone, who was aided by Melvin Stein and another attorney, as well as six additional nonlawyer investigators. In the first couple of weeks after *Dotto* was cancelled, Hogan and Stone were not sure what, if any, crime had been committed. If any producers had fixed quizzes using the sponsor's money without its knowledge, larceny might be a charge. Certainly after Enright accused Stempel of extortion, that was a crime to be investigated. Even after the Stempel story broke, Hogan said, "It is unfair to say now that this is a burgeoning scandal."[29]

By the end of August, Stone was calling in ex-contestants for questioning. Only the defunct *Dotto* and the more portentous *Twenty-one* were under investigation at this time. Because the district attorney had been called into the matter and there were hints that a grand jury might be convened, frenzied activity at the offices of Barry and Enright was taking place. Edwin Slote, the attorney for Art Franklin, advised Al Davis and Dan Enright to lie before the district attorney and to commit perjury if a grand jury was called. But Davis and even Enright were hesitant to accept such advice. For his client, Franklin, Slote suggested that he flee to the Cocos Islands, which he believed, incorrectly, were free from U.S. extradition. Franklin also wisely declined the lawyer's advice.[30]

On August 29 Enright met with Joseph Stone and executive assistant district attorney David Worgan and showed them Stempel's supposed disclaimer and played the tape for them. On September 2, at a news conference after several days' publicity in which Barry and Enright related tales of attempted blackmail by Stempel, they played the tape recording, which Enright hoped would prove that he had engaged in no fixing:[31]

ENRIGHT: There are certain stages we are going to discuss today.... I'm not going to disclose what the stages are, because I don't want to hold out any bait or anything like... I want you to write a piece of paper now to the effect that contrary to what you have said in the past, or written in the past, Dan Enright has at no time disclosed questions, answers, points, anything like it.

STEMPEL: I'll be glad to.

[Stempel writes the disclaimer. Enright tells that his lawyer recommended going to the district attorney about Stempel's blackmail, but that Enright declined because he did not want to "destroy" Herb.]

STEMPEL: May I say a few things before we continue? I'll admit I flipped. . . . I said to myself just now, I says, ahhh, Dan gave me a damn good break . . . and I came off with $50,000. . . . Unfortunately, I piddled it away through my own stupidity, and my wife's influence, etcetera. And also the whole thing. Let me tell you the whole thing in gist.

[Stempel explains giving money for the gambling syndicate.]

ENRIGHT: Herb, don't you realize that in backing a syndicate it's an illegal thing?

STEMPLE: Yes, yes, yes. I've already realized that. . . . The guy is a real murderer. . . . Frankly, I'm physically afraid of this guy. . . . He came up to the house. He talked to Toby* * * * *

[More admonition from Enright.]

ENRIGHT: I want to get a psychiatrist for you.

STEMPEL: I already have one.

ENRIGHT: No sir, I want you to go to a psychiatrist five days a week, not twice. Herb, to expedite yourself. . . . We will foot the cost. . . .

[More insistence on psychiatric help from Enright follows and the producer offers the lure of a possible panel show with Stempel on it.]

ENRIGHT: If we utilize you . . . you'll appear once a show, every day on the air. . . . We'll cut to your face; you'll say a few words; you'll be referred to by name when the occasion arises. . . . We recognize that, Herb . . we are in part responsible for your emotional upsets . . . because we opened that door for you. . . . If at any time, at any time, Herb, you're sitting at home in the evening and something starts to gnaw you.

STEMPEL: Call you up.

ENRIGHT: Call me up. . . . And if you need assurance, honest assurance. . . . Any time you have any gnawing feeling . . . just call me up.

[Stempel explains his bills, particularly on his car.]

ENRIGHT: Why don't you give up the car? What does it represent to you?

STEMPEL: I can't exactly explain it. . . . I had a beat-up old car that was hardly running, and now I've finally got myself a nice-looking car. It's not a Negro attitude or anything* * * *

[Stempel talks about his wife.]

STEMPEL: Let me explain the whole thing, Dan. . . . I felt here was a guy Van Doren that had a fancy name, Ivy League education, parents all his life, and I had just the opposite, the hard way up. . . . Here was my sort of own mental delusion that all this should have been coming to me. . . .

ENRIGHT: The world is a cruel world, and fate plays a greater part in all such things. . . . I don't know whether I can cope with life or not. But I don't think you can at this stage, Herb. And I say we have help.

STEMPEL: I'm perfectly willing to need help.

[Enright suggests that Stempel reduce if he is going to be a future panelist.]

STEMPEL: How can I? I'm down to 179 pounds. . . . I'm doing it in preparation . . . 'cause when I go on, I want to look like a gentleman, not a little, short, squat guy like I looked on *Twenty-one.*

[At this point the tape ran out.][32]

Stempel admitted that some of the conversation had taken place but emphatically claimed that Enright had altered the tape recording to reveal himself favorably. On September 3 Enright finally disclosed that he had advanced Stempel the $18,500, which the former contestant hoped would make his plight more believable. Said Stempel: "See, the show has to be phony, or I wouldn't have got the dough. Why, I could have lost everything, and Enright would have been out $17,000." Enright explained the advance as a way to pacify an unstable mind. The early days of the scandal were difficult for Stempel. *Time* called him "hardly a confidence-inspiring witness." On the September 8 show of *Twenty-one,* the master of ceremonies made the following statement to rebuff Stempel:

This is Jack Barry. Before the show starts there is something I must say to all of you. I am talking about the stories that you have read attacking my partner, Dan Enright, and me. All I want to say is this. The stories are wholly untrue. I repeat, they are wholly untrue. At no time has any contestant ever been given advance information about any questions ever used on this program. It has been a terrible experience to have to combat the unfounded charges that have been flying at us, but we do consider ourselves lucky in one respect. So many of you have expressed your faith in us and our program. A wise man once said that the truth will win out. I know that it will for we have not betrayed your trust in us. We never will.

To the best of Barry's knowledge, what he said was true, but the credibility of the pronouncement was short-lived. [33]

It was not long before the young actor and the CCNY graduate were joined by others in affirming that the quiz shows were rigged. By the end of the first week in September Joseph Stone had called in over thirty ex-contestants of *Dotto*, and several subsequently began declaring that they also had been aided on the program. One was Regan Leydenfrost, who described the association between her warm-up and her actual appearance on *Dotto*: "Anyone would have been an idiot not to have been able to give the anwers." Until September 6 the quizmasters of EPI had been untouched by the talk of fixed shows, but on that day the Reverend Charles "Stoney" Jackson finally got his disgust with *The $64,000 Challenge* into newsprint. [34]

Jackson's story that he had received a preprogram question on the air when he appeared on *The $64,000 Challenge* brought EPI, the most successful quiz group, under suspicion. Even before the Jackson story broke, though, the people at EPI were undergoing questioning. After Stempel's charge became public on August 28 and the slowly emerging quiz scandal had snared a different quiz, Revlon called a meeting to discuss the Cohn-Springer incident. The sponsor wanted more than vague assurances from Steve Carlin that the rigged match had been coincidental. In one regard the examination was moot, because by the summer of 1958, Revlon was no longer a cosponsor of *The $64,000 Challenge*. P. Lorillard was the sole sponsor. In fact the tobacco company also sponsored half of *The $64,000 Question*. Even more consequential was the fact that in June it was announced that *The $64,000 Challenge* would leave the air in September because of its faltering ratings. There was always the possibility, however, that the formerly successful show might be purchased by another network. Thus even though Revlon no longer sponsored the quiz, it was enough concerned as an ex-sponsor to try to stem off unfavorable publicity should the Cohn-Springer incident become known.

No Revson brother attended the Revlon-EPI meeting of late August to discuss the Cohn-Springer match. They sent as representatives George Abrams and William Jaffe, the company's attorney. From EPI Carlin, Fleischmann, and Leonard Steible, the lawyer for the organization, were present. Later, when congressional counsel Robert W. Lishman questioned Steve Carlin about the meeting, Carlin's answers showed either that he believed Revlon knew about the deceptions on his quizzes or, more likely, that the producers continually covered up their controls and tried to implicate the sponsor when the scandal finally broke:

LISHMAN: What did you discuss at that meeting?

CARLIN: They wanted to know how it happened. In regard to that, I attempted to explain it and I was not completely candid.

LISHMAN: If they knew you were controlling the show, why were you not candid?

CARLIN: Well, I don't know how to describe this, but you get yourself involved in a sort of psychological game, Mr. Lishman, in which everybody seems to know but no one is willing to admit, or no one is willing to ask, or if they know they don't want to confirm it. We just kept playing the psychological game.[35]

No sooner had Revlon's worries about the Cohn-Springer incident been calmed again by Carlin than the Stoney Jackson story broke, slightly more than a week later. When the reverend's revelations came out, William Jaffe, on instructions from Charles Revson, called up George Abrams, Revlon's advertising director, and told him there should be a meeting with CBS and EPI. Abrams then called Lennie and Newell, P. Lorillard's advertising agency, and told them that the Jackson story was the second such incident on *The $64,000 Challenge* and described the Cohn-Springer rigging to them. Abrams now knew that Carlin had lied when he said that the Cohn-Springer match had been the only irregularity on the quiz. At the same time, and totally unrelated to the quiz show, Martin Revson bitterly departed from Revlon in a stock dispute with his brother. Harry Fleischmann cornered Jaffee and told him not to press too hard in his investigation, but it was too late; the irrevocable hook of scandal had caught EPI, and the various uncontrollable forces of investigation now came crashing down.

On the Saturday that Stoney Jackson's story hit the press, CBS met with EPI, with Revlon and P. Lorillard attending. Throughout much of the meeting Tom Fisher of CBS was on the telephone with Jackson. Shirley Bernstein denied giving the reverend helpful tips for his quiz appearance, and the rest of the EPI officials were evasive with the network as to how the incident might have occurred. NBC had just purchased rights to *The $64,000 Challenge*, and EPI wanted the quiz to continue on the air after the end of its option with CBS. P. Lorillard and its agency, Lennie and Newell, were far from convinced that the show should be aired again. Nonetheless the officials decided to allow the quiz to go on the following evening because of a lack of sufficient evidence of deliberate rigging. It was to be the last performance of *The $64,000 Challenge*. P. Lorillard had had enough bad publicity and bad ratings, and the quiz was dropped off the air September 12. NBC and a new sponsor chose not to put it back on.[37]

That same day Frank Hogan announced that he would ask Judge Mitchell J. Schweitzer, an old classmate of his from Columbia University Law School, of the court of general sessions of New York County to empanel a grand jury for the sole purpose of investigating the quiz shows to "determine whether the crime of conspiracy or other crimes have been committed." Now that EPI had been added to the list of suspected quiz frauds, the legal machinery was set in motion to determine the final truth—whether the nation's television viewers had been victims of a deliberately perpetrated fraud. The casual network and sponsor investigations, so easily ended with producer assurances, were finished. The formal legal process had taken over.[38]

NOTES

1. *New York Times,* July 14, 1959, p. 1.

2. U.S., Congress, House, Committee on Interstate and Foreign Commerce, *Investigation of Television Quiz Shows,* before a subcommittee of the Committee on Interstate and Foreign Commerce, House of Representatives, 86th Cong., 1st sess., 1959, Davis testimony, pp. 97, 99–102, 106, Enright testimony, pp. 249–250, Ervin testimony, pp. 184–189, Franklin testimony, pp. 134–137, 140 (hereinafter cited as *Investigation*); *New York Times,* August 30, 1958, p. 17; *Investigation,* Stempel testimony, pp. 47, 52, 56.

3. "Out of the Booth," *Newsweek,* August 25, 1958, p. 58; Charles Van Doren, " 'Junk Wins TV Quiz Shows,' " *Life,* September 23, 1957, pp. 137–138, 140, 145–146, 148; *Investigation,* Van Doren testimony, pp. 627, 634.

4. "Fallen but Queenly," *Newsweek,* July 21, 1958, p. 52; "Lady with the Answers," *Time,* May 12, 1958, p. 70; "Lady with the Answers," *Newsweek,* June 9, 1958, p. 78; *New York Times,* July 8, 1958, p. 55; "A Prize Pupil of Higher Earning," *Life,* June 2, 1958, pp. 86–88; Loudon Wainwright, "The Trouble with Being Elfrida," *Life,* June 23, 1958, pp. 71–74.

5. *Investigation,* Jackson testimony, pp. 646–649, 654–656, 658–660; *Wall Street Journal,* December 4, 1973, pp. 1 and 16.

6. *Investigation,* Abrams testimony, pp. 981, 986–987, 992, Bernstein statement, p. 923, Carlin testimony, p. 798, Cohn testimony, pp. 678–683, 688, Charles Revson testimony, pp. 879–880, sworn statement of Wilton J. Springer as part of Charles P. Howze, Jr., testimony, pp. 677–678.

7. *New York Times,* December 1, 1957, sec. 2, part 1, p. 13, April 2, 1958, p. 63, April 6, 1958, sec. 2, p. 13; "The Parlor Pinkertons," *Time,* August 11, 1958, p. 36; "The Splurge—$250,000 for Winners," *Newsweek,* September 8, 1958, p. 86; "The TV Quiz—How Far?" *Newsweek,* May 5, 1958, pp. 107–108.

8. "The Giveaways," *Time,* July 7, 1958, pp. 66–67; Wasserman quoted in "The Parlor Pinkertons," p. 36; "The TV Quiz—How Far?" pp. 107–108.

9. *Investigation,* sworn statement of Edward Jurist as part of Howze testimony, p. 380; "The People Getters," *Time,* August 25, 1958, p. 65.

10. *New York Times,* February 9, 1958, sec. 6, pp. 16, 67; John Lardner, "Life Around the Booths," *New Yorker,* November 30, 1957, p. 1470.

11. *New York Times,* August 18, 1958, p. 39, August 24, 1958, sec. 2, p. 13; *Investigation,* transcribed kinescope of *Dotto* for May 20, 1958, as

part of Hilgemeier testimony, pp. 290–292, Huschle testimony, p. 265.

12. *Investigation,* Sy Fischer testimony, pp. 344, 352, 361, 368, Jurist testimony, pp. 315–318, 321.

13. Ibid., Jurist statement, pp. 380–381, Jurist testimony, pp. 318–319; "The People Getters," p. 65.

14. *Investigation,* Lieber testimony, pp. 347–348.

15. Ibid., Hillman testimony, pp. 278–280, 283, Jurist testimony, pp. 315–316, 321.

16. Ibid., Huschle testimony, pp. 264, 267, letter of Howard Monderer to Mary Jane Morris, April 13, 1959, as part of Doerfer testimony, p. 480, Pinkham testimony, p. 385.

17. Ibid., Jurist testimony, p. 333.

18. Ibid., Hilgemeier testimony, including his sworn affidavit, July 25, 1958, pp. 285–289; "TV Quiz Business Is Itself Quizzed About Fix Charges," *Life,* September 15, 1958, pp. 22–23.

19. *Investigation,* Hilgemeier testimony and affidavit, pp. 287–288, 297–298, Jurist testimony, p. 323.

20. Ibid., Hilgemeier testimony and affidavit, pp. 287–288, 298, Jurist testimony, p. 322.

21. Ibid., Doerfer testimony, p. 464, Fischer testimony, p. 358, Hilgemeier testimony and affidavit, pp. 298–301, Jurist testimony, pp. 322–323.

22. Ibid., Fisher testimony, pp. 433–434, 443–444, Jurist statement, p. 382, Pinkham testimony, pp. 385–387, 390, Stanton testimony, including a CBS Office Communication from Fisher, August 11, 1958, pp. 1099, 1116–1118.

23. Ibid., Doerfer testimony, pp. 464–465, CBS Office Communication of Fisher, August 11, 1958, August 14, 1958, as part of Stanton testimony, pp. 1117–1119, Hilgemeier testimony, p. 299.

24. *New York Times,* August 18, 1958, p. 39, August 24, 1958, sec. 2, p. 13; *Investigation,* Carlin testimony, pp. 799–800, Doerfer testimony, including a letter from Richard A. Forsling to Mary Jane Morris, August 18, 1958, pp. 466–467, Forsling letter also in the Fisher testimony, p. 437, minutes of Fisher and Walter Reynolds for the *Dotto* meeting at Colgate-Palmolive, August 15, 1958, as part of Stanton testimony, pp. 1120–1122; "The Law & the Limelight," *Time,* September 1, 1958, p. 39.

25. *New York Times,* August 18, 1958, p. 39, August 24, 1958, sec. 2, p. 13, August 26, 1958, p. 59, August 27, 1958, p. 59.

26. Ibid., August 29, 1958, p. 25.

27. Ibid.; Investigation, Davis testimony, pp. 102–103, Enright testimony, p. 252, Ervin testimony, p. 188, Franklin testimony, pp. 135, 140; *New York Times,* August 30, 1958, p. 17; *Variety,* September 3, 1958, p. 38.

28. *New York Times,* August 29, 1958, p. 25; *Investigation,* Davis testimony, p. 103, Ervin testimony, p. 188.

29. *New York Life,* August 28, 1958, p. 29, August 29, 1958, p. 25, September 5, 1958, p. 51; Herbert Brean, " 'Controls' and 'Plotting' Help in Showmanship," *Life,* September 15, 1958, p. 24; *New York Times,* August 12, 1958, p. 1; *Investigation,* Ervin testimony, pp. 188–189; "New York Steam Roller," *Newsweek,* September 8, 1958, pp. 26–28; *New York Times,* August 27, 1958, p. 20, September 1, 1958, p. 15; "Quiz Shows Face a Question," *Business Week,* September 6, 1958, p. 42.

30. *Investigation,* Davis testimony, pp. 104–105, Franklin testimony, pp. 138–139; *New York Times,* September 1, 1958, p. 15, August 30, 1958, p. 17.

31. *New York Times,* September 2, 1958, p. 27, September 3, 1958, p. 67, August 30, 1958, p. 17.

32. "Meeting of Minds," *Time,* September 15, 1958, pp. 47–48. *Time's* account of the taped conversation was more thorough than the trade journals *Variety* and *Broadcasting,* but it was still incomplete. The ellipses within the conversations were deletions made by *Time.* I made the deletions indicated by asterisks. The bracketed explanations were also made by *Time* and had the effect of deleting additional parts of the tape recording. I have rephrased these explanatory notes.

33. *New York Times,* September 4, 1958, p. 55; *Investigation,* Barry statement in Ervin testimony, p. 191; "Quiz Scandal (Contd.)," *Time,* September 8, 1958, p. 43; "TV Quiz Business Is Itself Quizzed," pp. 22–23.

34. *New York Times,* September 9, 1958, p. 70, September 7, 1958, p. 86, September 6, 1953, p. 35.

35. *Investigation,* Abrams testimony, p. 993; *New York Times,* June 3, 1958, p. 63; *Investigation,* Carlin testimony, p. 798.

36. *Investigation,* p. 991; Charles Revson testimony, p. 901; Meyer Weinberg, *TV in America* (New York: Ballantine Books, 1962), p.500.

37. *New York Times,* September 11, 1958, p. 67; *Investigation,* Carlin testimony pp. 799–800, Fisher testimony, pp. 434–435; "If You Ask Questions . . .," *Newsweek,* September 15, 1958; p. 62; *New York Times,* September 13, 1958, p. 13; *Investigation,* Charles Revson testimony, pp. 880–881.

38. *New York Times,* August 4, 1958, p. 55, September 13, 1958, p. 13.

5 | "ARE WE A NATION OF LIARS AND CHEATS?" — *Christian Century*[1]

The announcement of the grand jury empanelment caused more frantic activity at the offices of Barry and Enright. Art Franklin did not follow the advice of his lawyer to commit perjury himself, but he did tell former contestants to lie before the grand jury. For a while Franklin avoided the subpoena, but eventually he did testify truthfully. The producers of *Twenty-one* tried to determine what most of the former contestants would say in testimony. They did not, for the most part, engage in threats or pressure to encourage lies, but they wanted to evaluate the effect of the truthful testimonies as opposed to the perjured ones. What is especially significant about this entire episode is that the persons who produced *Twenty-one* and other quizzes did not have to encourage mass perjury. Most of the contestants did not tell the truth on their own. Why they did may never be known. Still the pressure from Enright and Freedman may have prompted some frightened ex-contestants into continuing their personal quiz-show cover-ups. Albert Freedman was particularly worried about what the parade of former contestants might tell the assistant district attorney, Joseph Stone, since he had done most of the coaching of contestants on *Twenty-one*. Freedman told a large number of his former recipients of aid that he was going to deny everything before the grand jury "to take the terror away" from their own appearances. To a nervous Van Doren, who had already publicly denied culpability, he assured, "They can break my legs." The producer's promise must have helped assure the young instructor. Van Doren appeared before Joseph Stone and the grand jury on October 10 and denied ever receiving any aid on *Twenty-one*. Freedman later explained his behavior:

> In my panic and not knowing very much of the ground rules of a grand jury—it was a brand new experience for me. We are not hardened criminals. We are in show business. And the only thing I knew about a grand jury is that it would make a good format for a dramatic show.... I was then producing *Twenty-one*. I had several concerns. I had the concern that the show should not go off the air. I had the concern for the contestants, who I felt, if their identities were revealed, would destroy these people. I felt that the jobs of many of my friends working for the organization would be in jeopardy.
>
> Consequently, when I went before the grand jury, my testimony was foolishly done to safeguard all these three.[2]

The foreman of the twenty-three-member grand jury was economist and historian Louis Hacker. He was also the former dean of the school of general studies at Columbia University, the institution that dominated both the right and the wrong sides of the quiz-show scandal. The grand jury began its lengthy task of investigation on September 18, 1958, with Eddie Hilgemeier as its first witness. Two days prior, in his first major address since assuming the network presidency, Louis Cowan had told the Pittsburgh Advertising Club that any quiz show found to have had prearranged contestants should be promptly taken off the air, even if no specific law had been violated. It was a strongly needed speech from the man most inadvertently responsible for the profusion of big-money quizzes, and it helped launch a vigorous network investigation.[3]

After one week the grand jury had found James Snodgrass, who had been hoping that he would not be called to testify. He certainly was not going to testify voluntarily, as several ex-contestants had already done. After the Stempel story became public and *Twenty-one* came under suspicion, Freedman had lunch with Snodgrass to discern his plans. He tried to convince the young artist that if he were called to talk with the district attorney and not the grand jury, he should lie since there would be no required legal oath. Snodgrass replied that he was not going to tell anyone about his quiz stint, but if subpoenaed he would have to tell the truth. Freedman resigned himself to this.

After Snodgrass testified before the grand jury, his ingenious evidential procedure of three times mailing registered letters containing the questions and answers to himself prior to his appearances was soon public knowledge, although for a while Snodgrass refused to identify Freedman as his supplier of information for the quiz. This was, perhaps, the best proof that *Twenty-one* had been a fraudulent program. The Snodgrass letter (see appendix 3) gave greater credence to Stempel's tale and finally caused NBC to investigate more fully into the schemes of their recently acquired property, Barry and Enright.[4]

The Snodgrass testimony changed the mind of NBC about *Twenty-one*. Tom Ervin then knew that Dan Enright had lied to him. The network tried to start an extensive investigation, including the interrogation of Snodgrass and other former contestants, but it was requested not to do so by the district attorney's office. NBC did manage, however, to circulate nine affidavits to the men of Barry and Enright, including Freedman and the lesser staff, denying the fix charges, which all of them dutifully signed. Within a week after the Snodgrass evidence, NBC took over production of the above-the-line elements of the Barry and Enright quizzes it owned: *Twenty-one, Tic Tac Dough, Dough Re Mi*, and the recently created, highly successful, and totally legitimate *Concentration*. Jack Barry remained as moderator for *Twenty-one*, but Bill Wendell took over his duties for *Tic Tac Dough*. The production staff for the daytime programs were to report directly to NBC's Roger Gimbel, not Enright or associates, while the prime-time staff owed their new allegiance, ironically, to Joe Cates, the original producer of *The $64,000 Question*, now with NBC.[5]

Publicly Enright said he had asked the network to take over so his organization might "devote more time to disproving the unfounded charges against the integrity of our programs." The Barry and Enright denials were less loud and frequent than they had been when their only accuser was Herb Stempel. Clearly the demise of *Twenty-one* was in sight. At the request of Joseph Stone, the grand jury was extended to at least February 1959, to continue investigating quiz shows. On October 16, 1958,

Twenty-one was replaced by *Concentration*. Pharmaceuticals, Incorporated, trying to mask its ill-deserved notoriety in connection with the program, said that ratings had caused the change. It was true that the quiz had fallen to a Trendex rating of only 10.3, but the sponsor declined to speculate publicly why people were no longer watching *Twenty-one*.[6]

Finally *The $64,000 Question* was cancelled on November 4, still untainted by the scandals at the time. Its ratings had sunk to an all-time low. After giving away $2,106,000 in prize money and twenty-nine Cadillacs in the three years, five months, and one week since its debut, *The $64,000 Question* departed from sight. The big-money television quiz-show phenomenon had ended under shadow of scandal and declining audiences. Forty-four quiz and game shows had come and gone since *The $64,000 Question* first caught the public fascination, and the combined network prime time allotted to quizzes was down to six half-hour time slots.[7]

Within a week after *The $64,000 Question* was dropped, the grand jury gave the now-burgeoning quiz-show scandal its biggest shock of the year: Albert Freedman was indicted on two counts of perjury, both for previously denying to the grand jury that he had given out answers. There was little legal doubt in the public eye that *Twenty-one* had been a fraudulent program. The maximum penalty for each count of perjury was five years' imprisonment and $5,000 fine. Freedman pleaded not guilty and was freed on $1,500 bail. NBC immediately publicized that Freedman was no longer a producer with the network, since NBC had taken over all Barry and Enright programs after the James Snodgrass story had broken.[8]

After the Freedman indictment, the quiz-show grand jury conducted its investigation relatively quietly. In January 1959, Dan Enright, Jack Barry, and Robert Noah, *Twenty-one*'s co-creator and one of the associate producers, were called as cooperative witnesses before the grand jury, but on the advice of their lawyer, Jacob Rosenblum, they declined to sign the waivers of immunity from prosecution. The grand jury excused them, and the three never testified. Joseph Stone conducted the grand jury quietly with very few news leaks as 1959 wore on.

The press was strangely quiet in its reaction during the first year of the scandal. Editorializing was scant compared to the amount that followed the congressional hearings in the fall of 1959. The paucity of press comment is baffling. Perhaps it was because a sufficient number of notable quiz champions were denying publicly that they had ever received any aid after many of them had told the same lie to the grand jury. Ted Nadler, however, could truthfully say, "They never told me a damn thing." Charles Van Doren was an established regular on *Today* with a daily five-minute slot during which he would often read and explain poetry or offer some other intellectual tidbit. His word that he was unaided on *Twenty-one* appeared beyond reproach to most people. In spring 1959 he finally received his Ph.D. and in July was made an assistant professor at Columbia. Van Doren liked his television role and rationalized what he had done as good for the educational life of the nation in the long run.[9]

There was some talk of scandal in the nine months or so after the last of the big-money quizzes left television, but it was only slight. *Time* called *quiz* "television's own four-letter word," and the *Reporter* chided, "The $64,000 question on television now is whether the quiz shows are real contests or an intellectual grunt-and-groan equivalent of wrestling." The *New Republic* also noted that the state of affairs was "quite a comedown from the claims which were made for the quizzes a year ago—that they had made the world safe for erudition." Both of the latter journals hoped the scandal would drive all quiz and game nonsense from the air. Thus they saw potential good coming from the crises. Jack Gould provided the most perceptive and witty analysis: "The only flaw with *The $64,000 Question* was that it was too good," meaning that the subsequent imitations tried to maintain the high excitement that the Cowan show produced, which was impossible as the glut of spinoffs flooded the networks. It was possible to duplicate the success of *The $64,000 Question*, according to some producers, only through a highly controlled program. Gould did not think the quiz revelations would drive the format from the air as others hoped:

The durability of gimmicks and the ups and downs of public preference favor the continuance of the quiz. . . . The harried quiz producer always can take solace in the fact that the television medium operates in a uniquely protective barrel: no one yet has seen the bottom.

Possibly the lack of comment on the quiz scandal during the first half of 1959 can be attributed to the deferred expectation on the part of the press that the secret work of the grand jury would be made public when the proceedings ended, and with more information available, more comment would naturally follow. Certainly it was the intent of assistant district attorney Stone that the grand jury's findings would eventually be made public. Key congressional members also believed that would happen. None of the parties concerned were prepared for the stunning legal roadblock placed upon the path to the truth. [10]

In June 1959 the grand jury was finishing its investigation; it had sat for fifty-nine sessions over nine months, and had heard over two hundred witnesses. It wrote its report under the able direction of its foreman, Louis Hacker. The grand jury had sat 150 hours, and Stone and Hogan were as proud of its thoroughness as Hacker was. Freedman's indictment was the only one to come out of the investigation. Technically another grand jury indicted the producer from the evidence of the original grand jury. Frank Hogan certainly had suspicions that many other witnesses had lied. The district attorney's office, though, could find no specific violation of the laws beyond perjury in spite of the fact that the grand jury had uncovered widespread rigging of quiz programs. Legally there was no fraud; most statutory frauds require a victim, someone who was injured, usually financially, and the lawyers could find no one who fit. It might be argued that the viewing public had been the victim of the frauds, but in the days before class action suits, such an indictment was never considered. Also there seemed to be no monetary loss involved. Nonetheless, reasoned Hacker, the public should be informed as to what had happened, and he and the jury prepared a twelve-thousand-page report (or presentment). Presentments have a long tradition in American legal history; they usually concern public officials and call attention to illegal activity but do not carry the onus of a legal indictment. The findings of the grand jury were given to Judge Mitchell D. Schweitzer in a presentment with the expectation that he would accept the report and then hold hearings on motions to expunge parts of it. To everyone's surprise, however, on June 10, the day he discharged the grand jury, Schweitzer took the presentment and declared it "expungable prima facie," meaning that the entire finding was sealed from public access. In reaching his decision Judge Schweitzer drew from the opinion of Federal Judge Edward Weinfield, whom he quoted:

A presentment is a foul blow. It wins the importance of a judicial document, yet it lacks its principal attributes — the right to answer and appeal. It accuses, but furnishes no forum for a denial. No one knows upon what evidence the findings are based.

An indictment may be challenged — even defeated. The presentment is immune. It is like the hit-and-run motorist. Before application can be made to suppress it, it is the subject of public gossip. The damage is done. The injury it may unjustly inflict may never be healed.[11]

Despite Schweitzer's judicial logic, his impoundment of the presentment was virtually without precedent. Every one of the 497 grand jury presentments in New York since 1869 had been made public, including the fifteen which had been prepared under Frank Hogan's district attorney's office since 1942. Hacker was furious:

We do not wish so much time and effort to be lost. There may be questions of law that are moot in this controversy. But what is not moot is that there has been moral wrongdoing. . . . If a $10 bribe to a building inspector is proper material for a presentment, then I am sure that bribes of many thousand of dollars to contestants were also proper material. . . .

Stone and Hogan were equally bothered by Schweitzer's decision. From the beginning of the grand jury, Hogan had told the jurors that they would be able to offer a presentment. Schweitzer delayed his final decision on the presentment to allow all interested legal parties to file briefs to attempt to prove why he should make the report public. A couple of months before the judge discharged the grand jury, attorney J. Norman Lewis, representing *The $64,000 Question* and *The $64,000 Chal-*

lenge, filed a brief with Schweitzer challenging the release of the anticipated presentment because it might name innocent contestants only marginally involved in the deceptive quiz practices. Hacker and the grand jury foresaw the possible damage that such a presentment might cause and had taken careful measures to avoid harming innocent reputations: they included not one specific reference to people's names, particular quiz shows, or even networks. It was a report that described in detail only the methods of quiz fixings and controls. J. Norman Lewis had no way of knowing that the presentment he challenged would be devoid of specificity, but Judge Schweitzer was won over, in large part, by Lewis's arguments, as well as by the fact that the presentment did not concern questionable behavior by public officials. With the common judicial procedure of allowing friends of the court (amicus curiae) to file arguments to try to change his mind, Schweitzer gave slight hope to those who believed the whole truth of the quiz show scandal should be made known. Originally the judge gave only until June 26 for the briefs to be filed, but the final date had to be moved back many times—there were more amicus curiae briefs than Schweitzer anticipated—and the legal battle dragged on throughout the entire summer of 1959.[12]

Joseph Stone was determined to have the presentment released. In the district attorney's brief, much of which was confined by the secrecy of what had happened with the grand jury and therefore not made public, Hogan concluded:

> It is hardly disputable that millions of viewers would feel shamefully cheated by a hoax which stole many hours of their time. Nor could the justice of their position and the basic immorality involved be sloughed off by protestations that the only deprivation was that of the viewing public's leisure "time," and that in any event, the public received "entertainment" even though its character was misrepresented.
>
> The very essence of the quiz program's appeal lies in its implied representation of honesty. Were it generally understood that these programs do not present honest tests of the contestants' knowledge and intellectual skills, they would be utterly ineffectual in acquiring the public's "time."

The thrust of Hogan's argument was the public's right to know to what extent it had been duped and cheated by the conniving quiz producers. In the immediate weeks following Schweitzer's initial decision to close the presentment, significant support came to the side of the district attorney in an effort to release the document. The Grand Jury Association of New York filed a brief against the impoundment, as did the Citizens Union. NBC denied the rumors that it was behind the suppression of the material and declared that it favored the release. But Judge Schweitzer was not without support. Briefs filed against the public release included those from the Association of Lawyers of the Criminal Courts of Manhattan and the Kings County (Brooklyn) Criminal Courts Bar Association. As the judge mulled over the legal arguments on his desk that summer, District Attorney Hogan guessed, correctly, that the only method by which his and the grand jury's investigative efforts could be made known to the public was through a congressional hearing.[13]

On July 30 Arkansas Congressman Oren Harris, chairman of the House of Representatives Committee on Interstate and Foreign Commerce, whose subcommittee had jurisdiction over the communications industry, and Senator Warren Magnuson, chairman of the Senate committee of the same name and function, announced that they planned to investigate the activities of the quiz shows under question. Both senior Democrats had deferred any hearings because they had assumed the grand jury's findings would be made public. Harris knew it was essential that his committee have some of the researched evidence of the grand jury to avoid a long and duplicative investigation on its part. He therefore requested the minutes of the grand jury as a guide for the congressional investigation. He promised Schweitzer that he would keep the minutes secret and use them to "screen out those who were relatively innocent." The district attorney's office thought there was "ample legal precedent" for release of the minutes to Congress, but Schweitzer worried about possible leaks and whether the secrecy of the grand jury might be violated. He finally decided that the request need not be tied in with his decision on the presentment and approved the release of the minutes to Harris within a week after the request. Senator Magnuson's committee decided against a joint committee investigation and left the matter to the House of Representatives, although it also received the minutes. Judge Schweitzer also ordered that all exhibits from the grand jury be turned over to Oren Harris's Special Subcommittee on Legislative Oversight, which would handle the probe of fraudulent quiz programs.[14]

The minutes transcription was begun August 4, and with the belief that the task would take from six to eight weeks, the hearings were scheduled to begin October 6. Louis Hacker continued to urge the release of the presentment, saying it would be a "terrible waste" for the subcommittee to sift through all the minutes of the grand jury proceedings; he also feared the congressional hearings might turn into a "circus" as had so many others during the previous decade. Schweitzer, however, was not about to be pushed into a hasty decision on the presentment and did not turn it over to the subcommittee.[15]

House resolution 56 was passed by the first session of the Eighty-Sixth Congress in early 1959 and authorized the House Commerce Committee or its subcommittees to investigate and study matters within its jurisdiction. These items included "advertising, fair competition, and labeling," the important operations and implementations of the Federal Communications Act of 1934 charged with ensuring that broadcast stations serve "public interest, convenience, and necessity," and the Federal Trade Commission Act articles charged with preventing "unfair methods of competition in commerce, and unfair or deceptive acts or practices in commerce." Both acts were broad enough to include a wide variety of interpretations as to whether the quiz-show producers had indeed done anything illegal. The rules of procedure for the subcommittee, adopted in May, included provisions that the hearings would be open to the public unless an executive session was requested by a witness and approved by the subcommittee. Robert W. Lishman, the chief counsel for the special subcommittee, said, however, that if any witness gave testimony that contradicted his or her grand jury testimony, then that part of the minutes could be made public as part of a prosecution of the witness. The subcommittee did not want to use its power to subpoena and called for voluntary witnesses. In addition to Chairman Harris, the other subcommittee members were Democrats Peter Mack, Jr., of Illinois, Walter Rogers of Texas, John J. Flynt, Jr., from Georgia, and John E. Moss of California and Republicans John B. Bennett of Michigan, William Springer of Illinois, Steven B. Derounian of New York, and Samuel Devine of Ohio. Counsel Lishman was assisted by principal attorney Beverly Coleman and four other lawyers. Also ably assisting Lishman was special consultant Richard N. Goodwin, a young lawyer soon to join the political bandwagon of the rising young senator from Massachusetts, John F. Kennedy.[16]

The Special Subcommittee on Legislative Oversight convened its hearings on the quiz shows on October 6, 1959. Chairman Harris opened the proceedings:

> We do not feel that the quiz programs under consideration are "mere entertainment" in the same sense that a movie or other dramatic production is entertainment. Everyone knows that dramatic productions are carefully rehearsed. The same can be said of professional wrestling matches which are required by law in some jurisdictions to be designated "exhibitions" and not as "contests" or "matches." ... The subcommittee is interested solely in whether commercial deceit has been practiced on a national scale by means of deliberate and willful holding out to the public as honest contests, performances which were rigged in advance.

Herb Stempel led off the hearings in open session with no lawyer and related the entire tale of his life with *Twenty-one* and Dan Enright complete with several showings of kinescopes of his key matches with Charles Van Doren. Goodwin declared that Stempel was the most important source of information for the investigation of rigged quiz shows. From the outset of the hearings, it was apparent that the central figure in the process would be the young assistant professor from Columbia. At the start of the congressional inquiry, Van Doren's repeated denials of involvement in any chicanery were still the public record. Van Doren proved to be the most elusive witness for Oren Harris and his subcommittee.[17]

The second star of the first day's hearings was James Snodgrass, who provided proof that Albert Freedman had given him questions and answers prior to his appearances on *Twenty-one* by means of the letters he had written. Snodgrass even opened one of his letters (that of May 17, 1957) for the first time in front of the subcommittee. His testimony was followed by a kinescope of the following show, which demonstrated Snodgrass's deliberate intent not to follow the instructions of Freedman and correctly answer the Emily Dickinson question (see appendixes 1 and 3).[18]

The hearings were divided into two parts; the first ran from October 6 to 10, 1959, and also October 12, and the second group commenced November 2 and ran through November 6. The October group of sessions focused on the Barry and Enright productions of *Twenty-one* and *Tic Tac Dough* and Marjeff's *Dotto*. The second day of the hearings lasted until past midnight, as the subcommittee heard from the many associates of Barry and Enright, including Alfred Davis, the advertising agent Edward Kletter, and Art Franklin, all leading up to the executive session testimonies of Albert Freedman and Dan Enright. Franklin was an unusual witness. He first seemed to characterize the network response to the initial hint of scandal as that of sleepwalking, yet he seemed to contradict himself by saying that NBC was "terrified" at the possible truthfulness in Herbert Stempel's story.[19]

Freedman's testimony set the stage for the appearance of Charles Van Doren. The producer declined to say whether he had coached the most famous contestant until Van Doren himself had a chance to testify. The subcommittee agreed, in part, with Freedman but had a difficult time in bringing the young instructor to the witness chair. In addition, the inimitable Drew Pearson floodlit the stage and greatly heightened the public interest; sources had told him that Freedman said he had coached Van Doren, and the *New York Mirror* emblazoned the former quiz idol on its tabloid front page with the allegation that he was merely acting out a rehearsed performance on *Twenty-one*. On the evening the hearings began, NBC ordered Van Doren to send a telegram to the subcommittee demanding to clear the cloud of suspicion surrounding one of the network's stars of the *Today* show. It told Van Doren that his contract with them would be suspended if he did not try to testify. Van Doren, who had not yet told the truth even to his lawyer, Carl J.

Rubino, wanted very much to retain his job with NBC, so on October 7 he sent off a message to the subcommittee:

Respectfully request you read following statement into the record of the proceedings before your committee, quote: "Mr. Van Doren has made himself available to members of the committee staff. He has advised them that at no time was he supplied any questions or answers with respect to his appearances on "Twenty-One." He was never assisted in any form and he has no knowledge of any assistance having been given to any other contestant. He further stated that he voluntarily appeared before the New York County grand jury and told that body under oath that he never received any assistance in any form from any person at any time. Mr. Van Doren has advised that he is available to this committee's staff." Unquote.

(Signed) Charles Van Doren[20]

Having met NBC's demand to testify, Charles Van Doren began to have pangs of conscience. The following day he told his lawyer the truth and asked to be temporarily released from his classroom and television duties. Then, for a week, Van Doren disappeared. He and his wife went driving through the New England hills, while a frantic Oren Harris tried to find him. No one knew where he had gone. The *Washington Daily News* headlined, "Where's Charlie?" and a befuddled congressional subcommittee had to adjourn its first group sessions and reluctantly use its power of subpoena to retrieve the absent Van Doren.[21]

Finally, on October 13, Van Doren returned and was startled to learn that he was subpoenaed to appear the next day. He lied to the press that day, saying he had no idea the subcommittee was interested in hearing his testimony, but it was to be his final day of publicly denying his involvement. Two days later Van Doren told the truth to his parents and to both Frank Hogan and Joseph Stone. He was then scheduled to be the first witness when the hearings reconvened in early November. As the time approached, Van Doren's appearances at the district attorney's office led to increased press speculation that his testimony might reverse all the months of denial.

On November 2, 1959, the quiz-show scandal reached its apex as the personal symbol of the quizzes made one of the decade's more memorable confessions. A huge throng gathered to hear his testimony. He began:

> I would give almost anything I have to reverse the course of my life in the last three years. I cannot take back one word or action; the past does not change for anyone. But at least I can learn from the past.
> I have learned a lot in those three years, especially in the last three weeks. I've learned a lot about life. I've learned a lot about myself, and about good and evil. They are not always what they appear to be. I was involved, deeply involved, in a deception. The fact that I, too, was very much deceived cannot keep me from being the principal victim of that deception, because I was its principal symbol. . . .
> I have a long way to go. I have deceived my friends, and I had millions of them.[22]

Van Doren outlined the course of his fraudulent run on *Twenty-one*, and the emotion of the young professor impressed the majority of the subcommittee. After the testimony was over, Chairman Oren Harris complimented Van Doren for coming forward to tell the truth, which initiated a string of similar compliments from most of the other men sitting across the witness table from the former quiz hero. Chief counselor Robert Lishman offered, "I would like to join with the chairman in commending you for the soul-searching fortitude that is displayed in your statement." Congressman Rogers said, "I have listened to many witnesses in both civil and criminal matters, but your statement is the most soul-searching confession I think I have heard in a long time. . . . I think the American people are against corruption but they are for forgiveness when a man comes in and tells the truth." Van Doren's testimony was all the more remarkable because of the outpouring of sympathy it produced from the subcommittee. The congressmen took turns praising the confession of the former idol and expressed hope that Columbia University and NBC wold not take the harsh action of dismissing him. Only Congressman Steven Derounian of New York remained unimpressed: "I don't think an adult of your intelligence ought to be commended for telling the truth." Still, the overall subcommittee response was one of open sympathy. Chairman Harris ended Van Doren's appearance by thanking him:

Mr. Van Doren, you have given a very dramatic, but in my humble judgment a very pathetic, presentation here today.... I think it was a great writer, you may remember, that said one time, "there is so much good in the worst of us and so much bad in the best of us, that it behooves any of us to talk about the rest of us."...
I think I could end this session with you by saying what your attorney did say to you the other day; that is, "God bless you." The subcommittee thanks you for your appearance here.[23]

After Van Doren's public confession the rest of the hearings were anticlimatic, though Mert Koplin went on the stand and admitted for the first time that *The $64,000 Question* was less than honest. The hearings lasted until November 6 as the second half, following Van Doren's testimony, focused on the fraudulent EPI quiz shows. The Reverend Charles Jackson, Jr., and Arthur Cohn, Jr., came forward to describe their experiences on *The $64,000 Challenge*. Shirley Bernstein could not appear in person but sent a statement confirming her role as contestant coach. The hearings ended with the testimonies of Robert E. Kintner, president of NBC, and Dr. Frank Stanton, president of CBS. Both said that the networks had been uninvolved until after the Hilgemeier story broke. Stanton seemed somewhat willing to accept the responsibility of monitoring for possible fraud on the airwaves more than Kintner and therefore received more praise from the subcommittee.[24]

The Harris hearings managed to unearth further fraudulence in quiz shows previously unknown to the public record. Robert Kintner announced that NBC had discovered a kickback on the quiz *Treasure Hunt*, which had occurred in spring 1959. Bernard Martin and Artie Roberts, the warm-up men for *Treasure Hunt*, had persuaded a potential contestant that they be given several thousand dollars in return for placing him on the show. Since no *Treasure Hunt* staff or personnel had testified before the grand jury, this was a new development for Frank Hogan and his prosecuting staff. Thomas Fisher, vice-president and general attorney for the CBS television network, revealed the pre-show humming that had gone on with *Name That Tune*. Fisher and CBS decided to let the quiz remain on the air, but each week before the show began, it was announced:

This is a game that everybody can play. We play tunes drawn from the types of music the contestants are most familiar with. Some of the tunes have previously been identified for us by our contestants. But you don't have to be an expert to win. All our tunes are songs you've heard and sung all your life.

It was reasoned that this disclaimer would allow the viewing public to decide for itself if it wanted to continue watching. Fisher also announced that CBS had discovered that *For Love or Money* was rigged. This quiz, which had been on the air from June 1958 to January 1959 featured three contestants who chose the value of their questions by what was called a "dancing decimal machine," which shifted the decimal point in a four-digit number in rapid sequence until one of the contestants stopped it with an electronic buzzer. The CBS investigators (positions created after the Hilgemeier and Stempel stories became known) discovered that the decimal machine had been electronically rigged to allow the decimal point never to rest at the far right of the four-digit number, thereby preventing a question from achieving a value of $1,000 or more. This was quiz-show fraud done for purely budgetary reasons.[25]

From a legal standpoint, two witnesses in the hearings deserve notice. On the last two days of the first half of the investigation, the congressional subcommittee heard from Earl W. Kintner, chairman of the Federal Trade Commission, and John C. Doerfer, chairman of the Federal Communications Commission. Doerfer was probably the most besieged witness of the hearings, criticized for his opinion that the FCC could do little about the quizzes jurisdictionally. Doerfer had written to District Attorney Stone earlier in the year saying the Federal Communications Act of 1934, as amended, was indefinite with regard to fixed programs, and he maintained the same position at the hearings. Doerfer said before the subcommittee about the quizzes:

It is a kind of deceit which the most important element is missing, and that is an extraction of a consideration from somebody who is harmed. You get down to the question as a homeowner, who didn't pay his way into the show or didn't buy the book or something like that, it just has not been that legal consideration.

Doerfer cited the 1953 Supreme Court decision that overruled the FCC when it tried to ban radio giveaway programs from air because the agency at that time maintained they were lotteries. The Supreme Court stated in *FCC v. ABC et al.* (1953):

> The Commission contends . . . that these programs "are nothing but age-old lotteries in a slightly new form." The new form results from the fact that the schemes here are illicit appendages to legitimate advertising. . . . The radio giveaway looks to . . . material benefit to station and advertisers from an increased radio audience to be expended in advertising. . . . Something more is required than just a benefit to the promoter. The participation of the home audience by merely listening to a broadcast does not constitute the necessary consideration.

The last sentence of the decision was crucial to Doerfer's intriguing query as to who had been harmed by the quiz shows. The subcommittee, however, was unimpressed, particularly the peppery Congressman Rogers, who attacked Doerfer as a defender of the status quo in big broadcasting. Rogers showed the following law to Doerfer:

TITLE 18, UNITED STATES CODE—CRIME AND CRIMINAL PROCEDURE

Sec. 1343. Fraud by wire, radio, or television.

Whoever, having devised or intending to devise any scheme or artifice to defraud, or for obtaining money or property by means of false or fraudulent pretenses, representations, or promises, transmits or causes to be transmitted by means of wire, radio, or television communication in interstate or foreign commerce, any writings, signs, signals, pictures, or sounds for the purpose of executing such scheme or artifice, shall be fined not more than $1,000 or imprisoned not more than 5 years, or both. Added July 16, 1952, c. 879, section 18(a), 66 Stat. 722, amended July 11, 1956, c. 561, 70 Stat. 523.

But Doerfer still held that fraud probably was not committed in the quiz-show scandal because there was no victim. He cited the fact that the FCC had no power to license networks, and, even if it did, most quiz shows were independent productions devoid of network control. Doerfer also raised the issue of censorship. Section 326 of the Federal Communications Act is the statutory ban on the FCC to censor radio and television programming, and Doerfer feared that the legislation to regulate programming in the electronic media might violate section 326. The FCC chairman declared: "When you consider legislation, you have to look at this almost as though you are going to try to impose censorship on newspapers and magazines."[26]

By contrast the appearance of the Federal Trade Commission chairman, Earl W. Kintner, was received with warmth bordering on praise by the majority of the subcommittee. Clearly the focus of the FTC was on deceptive advertising, and the commercials of the fixed quiz shows were not in question. Kintner had indicated to Chairman Harris before the hearings: " 'deceptive entertainment' constitutes simply the surrounding circumstances during which the nondeceptive advertisements were made.... The FTC Act (15USCA ss. 41-51) does not purport to establish a decalogue of good business manners or morals."[27] Like Doerfer, Kintner was a strong advocate of business self-regulation, and as did the FCC chairman, he made a good case in explaining the nagging ineffectiveness of government by independent regulatory agency, that peculiar American legislative response to technologies and techniques beyond the scope and expertise of lawmakers. The FTC division on television and radio, said Kintner, had only two attorneys, two monitors, and two clerks to confront a billion-dollar industry. The staffing for the FCC was even more pathetic. Six people had to investigate and decide on forty-four hundred broadcast renewals in 1958. The FCC received an average of over 120 complaints per week, and its monitoring staff was woefully small. Of the 590 television stations in the country, spot checks were run only on 100 of them. Both agency chairmen implied that Congress had to share some of the blame for creating independent regulatory agencies that could not adequately regulate through the meager funding it gave them.[28]

Even the enactment of the Wheeler-Lee Act of 1938, said Kintner, which amended the FTC act by adding "unfair or deceptive acts or practices" to the realm of regulation of the FTC, did not allow the commission any control over the airwaves beyond commercial advertising. Despite the comparatively friendly reception made by the subcommittee to the FTC chairman, Congressman Rogers could not resist gibing: "You seem to be living on tradition rather than responsibility."[29]

The congressional hearings on the quiz-show scandals produced a massive public reaction. Most of the focus for comment centered on the climax of the hearings, Charles Van Doren's testimony. For Van Doren, the initial reaction to the scandals produced not only public scorn and sympathy but permanent results. The day following his appearance, the trustees of Columbia University voted to accept his offer of resignation. (In a scandal fraught with irony, one of the voting trustees of Columbia was district attorney Frank Hogan; another was the chairman of the board of CBS, William Paley, but he did not attend the vote on Van Doren.) On the day after Columbia's action, NBC dismissed him. There was a student effort at Columbia to have him reinstated. Two students collected 650 signatures on a petition advocating Van Doren's retention as a teacher, and a rally that attracted about 500 students was held one evening on the Columbia quad. But student support for the former quiz idol was frequently interrupted by booing and shouts against Van Doren. One student, leaning out from a dormitory window, ended whatever effectiveness the rally had generated by shouting: "Charlie's going to be in the quad tomorrow to give out the answers to the Comparative Lit exam!" Within a few days, Columbia President Grayson Kirk responded to the student petition by refusing to overturn the trustees' decision. Charles Van Doren, though, was not without a job. He took a position as a columnist for a new magazine, *Leisure*. Appropriately his byline was entitled, "The Intellect at Leisure." Van Doren also received an offer from Stockton Junior College in California to be an instructor in English. The cruelest form of humor came a couple of weeks later when he was elected constable in the town of Hallock, Minnesota, by a write-in campaign.[30]

Swirling about the events that had befallen Van Doren was a flurry of opinions, both serious and otherwise, that analyzed the meaning of his notoriety. From Van Doren came this reflective view a few weeks after his congressional testimony:

I've been acting a part, a role, not just the last few years—I've been acting a role for 10 or 15 years, maybe all my life. It's a role of thinking that I've done far more than I've done, accomplished more than I've accomplished, produced more than I've produced. It has, in a way, something to do with my family, I suppose. I don't mean just my father, there are other people in my family. But I've been running.[31]

The *Reporter* called Charles Van Doren "hapless," *Life* magazine, the national Catholic weekly *America*, and respected television columnist of the *New York Herald-Tribune*, John Crosby, all saw a parallel between Van Doren and the baseball player "Shoeless" Joe Jackson, who took part in fixing the 1919 World Series. The foreign press also commented on the Van Doren testimony. *Izvestia* said his fraudulent participation on *Twenty-one* was "one of those many swindles which still exist and one of the few disclosed in America." The French newspaper *France-Soir* compared his testimony with the "Checkers" speech of Vice-President Nixon and drew this generalization: "In America, more than anywhere, contrition is a form of redemption. A sinner who confesses is a sinner pardoned."[32]

One of the more emotional reactions to Van Doren's confession came from his former supervisor at NBC, Dave Garroway. On the *Today* program two days after the former quiz hero shattered his public image, Garroway broke down in tears in the middle of his telecast and had to leave the show, saying he was "heartsick" at what had happened to his former co-worker.[33]

Much of the reaction regarding Van Doren did not focus on him as much as the subcommittee's treatment of him. Most press and public reaction expressed dissatisfaction with the inferential pardon granted to Van Doren by most of the congressmen. Columnist Arthur Krock voiced "widespread disgust" with the subcommittee's response, and the *Nation* called the congressmen's reaction sententious. The most interesting discussion of what might be called the "pro-Van Doren" or "forgiving" response came in a *New York Times* article, "Reaction to the Van Doren Reaction," by the distinguished political scientist and historian Hans J. Morgenthau. The author said the quiz-show scandal, with Van Doren at the epicenter, was not comparable to the earlier Boss Tweed, Teapot Dome, and

Samuel Insull scandals, which were merely pecuniary scandals in the familiar realms of politics and business; the Van Doren case was much more profound for the nation.

It arose in a sphere whose ultimate value is neither power nor wealth but truth. The professor is a man who has devoted his life to "profess," and what he is pledged to profess is the truth as he sees it. Mendacity in a professor is a moral fault which denies the very core of the professor's calling. A mendacious professor is not like a politician who subordinates the public good to private gain, nor like a business man who cheats. Rather, he is like the physician who, pledged to heal, maims and kills.[34]

Morganthau was particularly upset by the reaction of most of the subcommittee opposite Van Doren and appalled by the fact that 650 Columbia students petitioned to retain him after he had admitted his fraud. "The scholar's special commitment to the truth" and the violation of that commitment by Van Doren were the focuses of Morgenthau's outrage. He called the students' action "moral illiteracy." As for the future, Morganthau said that American society

cannot condemn him [Van Doren] without condemning itself. . . . Instead, it tends to absolve him by confusing the virtues of compassion and charity for the actor with the vice of condoning the act. Yet, by refusing to condemn Van Doren, it cannot but condemn itself. For it convicts itself of a moral obtuseness which signifies the beginning of the end of civilized society.[35]

Most of the published reaction to the quiz-show scandals did not focus upon the trial of Charles Van Doren so much as use the young college professor as a starting point from which to comment about the ethics and morals of television, specifically, and, ultimately, American society in general. Morgenthau dwelled on Van Doren, but he exemplified serious discussion as to the meaning of the quiz-show scandals.

Church officials were among the first to state that the quiz revelations tended to lower the national morale. Letters and editorial cartoons decrying the scandals proliferated. Norman Cousins, editor of the *Saturday Review*, used them to denounce television: "Fraud in TV is not represented *primarily* by a likable young college professor who accepted the shabby standards of television producers." The real fraud, he said, was its profuse utilization of crime and violence in the bulk of the medium's programming. The *Saturday Review's* tirade against television was only one of scores of similar attacks against the medium. The *Reporter* offered a more perceptive comment on the ills of television:

> The history of television is the history of a responsibility that never came to rest. The law appeared to distribute it in unequal measure between the FCC and the station owners. But neither has proved capable of dealing with the unforeseen economic pressures generated by the industry's dizzying growth. . . . The fact is that the tussle between the network and the sponsor (together with his ad agency) for the final say-so on programming has for years been a standard feature of the industry's family life. The one commands the dollars, the other the time on the air, and the balance of power has oscillated between them roughly according to the laws of supply and demand. [36]

Life was curious that the people responsible appeared to escape any legal punishment, saying, "A noncriminal fraud is still a fraud," and said of the state of television, "It seems to bring out the cupidity and silliness of human nature on both sides of the screen."

As television was attacked, two major television personalities, Jack Paar and Dave Garroway, suggested that newspapers and magazines had overblown the quiz-show scandals in an effort to cripple a competing advertising medium. There was little defense voiced for the current condition of the new electronic medium. *American Mercury* said the television industry "burned American morality almost to the ground," and *Business Week* entitled its editorial on the scandal, "TV Quiz: What Does E-t-h-i-c-s Spell?" [37]

The bulk of public reaction to the quiz-show scandals did not single out the institution of television for attack nor solely criticize Charles Van Doren and the lesser hoaxers. In the spirit of Hans Morgenthau's article, the most common focus for comment used the rigged quizzes as a springboard from which to launch into a larger discussion of the national morality. A good example was the article in the *New York Times* by philosopher

Charles Frankel, "Is It Just TV—or Most of Us?" Of the fallen quiz-show idols he said, "The events that have led to such tragedy for them reflect attitudes that are widespread. Indeed, they were cued by practices that have become normal in American society." Frankel posed the interesting notion: "In happier days it was said that quiz shows demonstrated that intellect was useful in playing games and winning money and that they therefore advanced the cause of learning and education. What is disturbing about such arguments is not that they are false, but that they are very probably true." Frankel also cited three features in American society that fostered the scandals: the emphasis upon success; the "domination of the market place and the ubiquity of the salesman's ethic," which transforms the standard for success into that which can attract the greatest numbers or dollars; and a vaguely defined feature, which he referred to as a lack of American institutions that "embody public purposes and that exist to protect and advance them."[38]

The *New Yorker* was not so appalled by the moral implications of the scandal as intrigued by its extent and impact upon the national psyche:

The mysterious and awful thing about the television quiz scandals is not that the jaded souls who ran the show were hoaxers but that dozens, and perhaps hundreds, of contestants, almost all of whom must have applied in the simplicity of good faith, were successfully enrolled in the hoax. Now, as we remember the flavor and ethos of that innocent era, we realize that the contestants, aside from their freakish passion for Hittite history or skeet-shooting statistics, were meant to be us—you and me and the bright boy next door. This was America answering. This was the mental wealth behind the faces you saw in a walk around the block. The appeal of the programs, with the rising challenge of Soviet brain power as a backdrop, was ultimately patriotic; the contestants were selected to be a cross-section of our nation just as deliberately as the G.I.s in a war movie are. There we bravely sat in our living rooms, sweating it out with this or that Shakespeare-reading poultry farmer or chemistry-minded chorus girl, and there they were on the other side of the blurred little screen, patting (not wiping) their brows with handkerchiefs, biting their tongues as instructed, stammering out rehearsed answers, gasping with relief at the expected cry of congratulation. And we sat there, a nation of suckers, for years. It's marvelous how long it went on, considering the number of normal

Americans who had to be corrupted to keep the cameras whirring, in all this multitude, not one snag, not one audible bleat, not one righteous refusal that made the news. The lid didn't blow off until, years after a winner, disgruntled because he had not won more, was moved to confess and purge his guilt.

We are fascinated by the unimaginably tactful and delicate process whereby the housewife next door was transfigured into a paid cheat.[39]

Not all discussions of morality were as perceptive as that of the *New Yorker*, but they were interesting nonetheless. In a bitter editorial for the *Saturday Review*, poet John Ciardi remarked:

Let Ike and the Congress turn their attention to what has gone flabby in the American mind, a flabbiness to which Ike's prose and the shenanigans of a Public Relations Congress have contributed as much as any sideshow in the land. Certainly a nation more dedicated to its best principles and less complacent about itself—a nation, let us say, with its mind tuned to Jefferson and Lincoln rather than to gobbledygook and the hard-sell—would have found no need to make so much of the incident.... What I want to say is: Bah! You asked for it. This is your life. The price is right enough. You've got no secrets. People are ... well, never mind. But tell me, boys and girls and Federal gentlemen, has anyone had time to think of Mr. Khrushchev lately?[40]

The New York State education commissioner, Dr. James E. Allen, Jr., said the quiz-show scandal actually carried some good because it forced the nation to reexamine its moral values. Unlike Ciardi, Allen berated those who treated the scandals as not worthy of attention as "more scandalous" than the hoaxers themselves. *New York Times* journalist James Reston saw a connection between the fixed programs and the crippling steel strike the country was experiencing:

There is an overwhelming feeling here that somehow we have lost our way. Nobody seems to know just how or why, but everybody feels that something's wrong.

It is not only the TV quiz scandal but the steel strike that has given the impression of haphazard greed, and a system debased and out of balance.[41]

If the rigged quizzes were enough to worry one of the more

distinguished reporters in the land, then it was inevitable that the state of television in 1959 should provoke comment from the nation's highest officeholder, President Eisenhower. The occasion was the November 4 presidential news conference. A number of reporters, including Reston, asked the president whether he thought the quiz scandal held any wider implications for the country. Eisenhower compared his attitude with the "Say it ain't so, Joe" feeling about the fixed 1919 World Series and stated, "I think I share the American general reaction of almost bewilderment that people could conspire to confuse and deceive the American people." In response to a question from ABC newsman Edward P. Morgan, President Eisenhower offered: "Selfishness and greed are occasionally, at least—get the ascendancy over those things that we like to think of as the ennobling virtues of man, his capacity for self-sacrifice, his readiness to help others, and so I would say this: the kind of things that you talk about do remind us that man is made up of two kinds of qualities." Whether the president clarified the national feeling over the scandal is, of course, debatable, but he did maintain firmly that there was no national indifference to questions of morality as exemplified by the Van Doren story.[42]

Among the public reaction to the frauds, there was a curious collection of defenders of the state of television. In what could be labeled a counteroffensive to the critics of the medium, the indicted producer of *Twenty-one*, Albert Freedman, issued a lengthy defense of his former show. He maintained that no one was hurt financially by the fixed quizzes, including the public who paid no admission to watch television. In a strange form of logic, Freedman said, "Our only error was that we were too successful. The stakes were too high and the quiz winners fused themselves into the home life and the hopes and aspirations of the viewers." He called the outcry about ethics inapplicable because quiz shows fell into the special category of entertainment and concluded: "It is about time the television industry stopped apologizing for its existence and begin to fight back. It should insist that sponsored programs be recognized and judged as entertainment and entertainment only."[43]

To counter the criticism of American television, the Westinghouse Broadcasting Company, one of the largest nonnetwork

broadcast groups, which owned eleven television stations, re-
produced an article from *Television* magazine in a two-page advertisement in the *New York Times*. The article, by Victor
Ratner, entitled "The Freedom of Taste," answered critics of the
televised medium by arguing cultural relativism. It proclaimed
that good and bad taste were relative and that "serious programming" was highly favored by television compared to the
small intellectual minority of the audience served by such fare.
Its basic thrust was that most complaints against television are
elitist, as it used the following analogy:

Thus, what seems to the groaning intellectual to be a swift lowering
of our cultural standards, through mass media, may be only the slow-
ing up of a train, as it takes on many millions of new passengers—who
ultimately will be carried to those higher plateaus of culture where only
a small fraction of the human race found itself in the good old days.

A word of caution: It would be a mistake to ask the train to speed too
fast while taking on its new passengers. Those getting on would only
be left behind.[44]

A more specific defense of television was made in another
full-page *Times* advertisement. NBC president Robert Kintner
and chairman of the board Robert Sarnoff published "A Statement on Television," which denied that the quiz scandals indicated an irresponsible industry or any representation of national character. The most colorful counter to the low image of
television was this justification by an unidentified *Dotto*
spokesman: "Look, this may be a quiz business to the house-
wives of America, but to us, it's the entertainment business.
There's no reason for the public to know what happens behind
the scenes. If you buy a $5.80 seat to a play, why should that
entitle you to go backstage?"[45]

Possibly the best indicators of public reaction to events in
modern America are public opinion polls. The quiz-shows
scandals were the subject of such survey research. CBS hired
George Gallup and his polling firm to determine how widespread was the public's familiarity with the scandal. Since the
poll was taken at the height of interest, understandably knowledge and recognition of the rigged quizzes topped all other
events, including the Salk vaccine for polio, the Sherman

Adams affair, and the Quemoy and Matsu crisis off Nationalist China. Pollsters Sindlinger and Company conducted one of the most interesting polls on the fixed quizzes. Like Gallup, Sindlinger did not conduct polls concerning television on a regular basis. For this survey Sindlinger used a sample of 2,289 households and projected the findings into the tens of millions to represent the entire United States adult population. What was uncommon about the poll was not the projection but the fact that it was transposed literally. The question asked by the Sindlinger poll, during the congressional investigation by Oren Harris and his subcommittee, was: "What is your opinion of the current quiz show investigation?" The results showed that 46,170,000 (42.8 percent) favored the investigation; 32,962,000 (30.6 percent) did not; 18,790,000 (17.4 percent) had no opinion; and 9,985,000 (9.2) percent gave evasive or qualified answers. The question itself was worded such that the poll may have been requested by some broadcasting people, but there is no evidence to indicate this. The relatively high percentage not favoring the congressional probe may be explained two ways. Possibly the respondents in that category included a great number of postwar Americans weary and disdainful of the publicity-laden, fact finding legislative processs of the congressional investigation. A more alarming theory to many commentators, however, was that the nearly one-third response not favoring the investigation indicated that they thought the rigging of quiz shows not worthy of the time necessary to find the truth of the matter. To Sindlinger's second question, "Even though contestants on quiz shows are helped, have you found the quiz programs educational and entertainment enough to want to see them on TV again?" 39.9 percent said yes, an answer that may be interpreted as an even sadder commentary on the national ethic.[46]

Elmo Roper's poll on the quiz scandal revealed more optimistic findings: "These disclosures show just how bad television is": 4 percent; "These practices are very wrong and should be stopped immediately, but you can't condemn all of television because of them": 65 percent; "No one can really be in favor of this kind of thing, but there's nothing very wrong about it either": 7 percent; "What happened is a normal part of show business and is perfectly all right": 7 percent.

A much less significant poll was the daily question of the *New York Daily News's* inquiring photographer, Jimmy Jernail. He asked scores of people on the streets of New York City: "Would you have any qualms about appearing on a TV quiz show if it were rigged and you knew you would win a large sum of money?" To the surprise of everyone except the cynics, four out of every six respondents said that they would appear on a fraudulent quiz show.[47]

The abrogation of morality in the quizzes was not told solely in terms of survey research. The Reverend Stanley Skeens, who won $48,000 on *The $64,000 Question* and *The $64,000 Challenge* with the category of the Bible, said: "Personally, I believe all the fuss being raised in the TV quiz investigation is by a lot of soreheads." Added Myrtle Power, an early winner on *The $64,000 Question:* "If somebody had been giving out the answers, I wouldn't have stopped at $32,000. . . . I'd have gone all the way." It was public opinion samples like these that helped give basis to the many attacks on American values in the fall and winter of 1959.[48]

The reaction to the quiz frauds went beyond moral indignation, statements deriding television, and discussion of the national ethic. Included in much of the commentary was a variety of proposals for the correction of the ills of television. Many of the reforms contained harsh criticism of the FCC. The *New Republic* called the agency the "weakest sister" of all regulatory bodies and dubbed the commissioners the "Seven Dwarfs," who "parcel it [the airwaves] out free to money-grubbers—just as we gave away our rivers, lakes, and forests, 100 years ago." The journal proposed a more strictly run government system of broadcasting, similar to the BBC, or, perhaps a system of pay television. John Doerfer and the FCC were rarely left unscathed by most of the press. Said the *Reporter:* "Not until the bubble burst did it occur to anyone that there was a significant connection between public morals and public entertainment. . . . The FCC, which has long regarded its function as helping the networks make money, remained supremely indifferent."[49] "Where, may we ask, was the FCC?" asked *Consumer Reports* and maintained that the agency had full right and power to correct the aired deceptions. Lawyer and journalist Anthony Lewis of the *New York Times* identified the problem as an FCC that had earlier missed its opportunity for reform. In 1957 the dean of the University of Cincinnati Law School, Roscoe Barrow, headed a study (which came to bear his name) to improve the FCC. The Barrow report was, in fact, initiated by the FCC, but the agency chose to ignore all its proposed reforms. Among the major items the report recommended were direct FCC regulations of the networks and a ban on "option time," whereby a network forces a station owner into block purchasing (for example, a station must purchase an entire evening's programs in order to get the one show it might truly want). It also criticized the FCC practice of casually renewing station licenses without holding public hearings.[50]

Many other proposals that came forth did not directly attack the FCC as much as suggest new structural reforms for the communications industry. Ex-United States Senator William Benton proposed a permanent presidential commission, separate from the FCC, to report on the progress, or lack of it, of radio and television's obligation to serve the public interest. The idea of a "commissioner of television" or "TV czar" with broad powers over the medium received a great amount of support from various quarters. Charles Revson favored one, as did Senator Jacob Javits. One of the most intriguing ideas came from Philip Cortney, president of the cosmetic firm of Coty, Incorporated, and a major competitor of Revlon; he proposed that sponsors of fraudulent quiz shows should donate their profits to charity (none of them ever did). Of all the suggestions that surfaced, the one that received the greatest amount of discussion was that of journalist and philosopher Walter Lippmann. He called for an American counterpart to the British Broadcasting System, a government-owned network with a board composed of public-minded persons who would choose what went on the airwaves. Lippmann reasoned:

There is something radically wrong with the fundamental national policy under which TV operates. . . . We should not shrink from the idea that such a network [his plan for a BBC-like network] would have to be subsidized and endowed. . . . Why should it not be subsidized and endowed as are the universities and public schools and the exploration of space and modern medical research, and indeed the churches—and so many other institutions which are essential to a good society, yet cannot be operated for profit?

Lippmann's plan flirted with such a fundamental change in the relationship between government and the communications industry that it frightened industry representatives into considering less drastic reforms that might not have been seriously discussed otherwise. Lippmann probably failed to consider the deep commitment of the lawmakers themselves to the status quo in communications as well as the power of the broadcasting lobby. At the time of the television quiz-show scandals, eleven United States senators and twenty-two congressmen either owned outright or had very large investments in television stations, including Senate Commerce Committee Chairman Warren Magnuson, who was a large shareholder in the Seattle radio and television station KIRO.[51] With the flurry of television reforms being brought forth and debated in 1959, it remained for Gilbert Seldes to put the rhetoric into perspective. More than a critic of television, Seldes has been one of the most serious analysts of what has come to be called "the public arts" (film, radio, and television). Calling himself "the only man who has no instant and comprehensive plan for regulating, reforming, rehabilitating, or destroying the broadcast industry," Seldes labeled most plans ridiculous and criticized those who were "looking upward for Power." Seldes, nearly alone, questioned the reforms as generally seeking someone at some level who would dictate the content of television rather than keep the current system, even with its imperfections. Only the much-maligned FCC chairman, John Doerfer, talked about "freedom" in regard to the extensive reaction to the quiz scandal and posed the very real issue of possible censorship as part of the proposed efforts to clean up the abuses. To Seldes the question was whether Americans wanted to preserve the freest communications system in the world, with all its programmatic defects and economic injustice, or risk a hasty imposition of censorship in an effort to prevent a repetition of fraudulent quiz shows. Much of Seldes's wise caution was borne out during the months following the Harris subcommittee hearings, but to say that the quiz scandal did nothing to affect the state of television would be incorrect.[52]

One immediate result of this scandal was that many quiz programs, legitimate and tainted, were banished from the air. CBS, under Dr. Frank Stanton's edict, was more active than the other networks in sweeping away the genre that had caused all the embarrassment. Stanton, more than any other network executive, believed that the networks had not monitored the independently packaged quizzes as closely as they should have. He was the most vocal proponent of industry self-regulation: "Television must . . . not throw up its hands in despair and pass the problem over to a committee of laymen." CBS quickly canceled *Name That Tune*, even though the network had inserted the announcement that the contestants had been "prepared" for the quiz by listening to melodies. It also canceled *Top Dollar* and *The Big Payoff*, ironically replaced by *The Millionaire*. NBC also eliminated some of its quizzes but did not adopt Stanton's blanket approach that all big-money quiz programs should be taken off the air. It countered Stanton by asking, "Can honesty be equated with the size of a prize?" Obviously, though, NBC had to get rid of the Enright production of *Tic Tac Dough*, replaced by *Truth or Consequences*, but retained most of its quiz and game shows and emphasized to the public that it was increasing its security measures and monitoring efforts for its money shows. Both NBC and CBS instituted departments of "fair practices." Stanton appointed Joseph H. Ream, former executive vice-president and general attorney for the network, to be vice-president in charge of the Department of Television Program Practices, and NBC hired former ABC vice-president Ernest Lee Jahncke, Jr., to serve as director of the Department of Standards and Practices. Jahncke thought of his job as that of a censor and promptly proceeded to delete what he thought was an off-color joke from Jack Paar's *Tonight* show, causing Paar to walk off the show and temporarily retire from show business.[53]

The results generated by the television industry in response to the scandal involved more than merely canceling quiz shows. CBS in particular attempted to institutionalize honesty. It banned canned laughter and applause from all programming unless announced. Musical and variety programs featuring entertainers who mouthed songs to previously recorded performances required a new CBS tab, "Certain portions of this program were pre-recorded." All CBS employees were questioned about income other than salary earned from broadcasting or paid airtime appearances. The network also banned the company identification on merchandise given away, an adjustment that affected only one afternoon game show. NBC would not ban the names of prize donors but did eliminate the prize rebate on its game shows whereby the producer would receive cash to use the merchandise as a gift on the show, a technique also referred to as "plugola." None of these reforms, though, became a permanent part of the television landscape.[54]

CBS's purification attempt approached extreme measures. The fine news-interview program *The U.N. in Action* was required to announce that the interviews presented were not spontaneous; the interviewees had been briefed by reporter Larry LeSueur on the areas of discussion beforehand. A serious rupture occurred when CBS attacked *Person to Person*. This interview program, hosted by Edward R. Murrow, went into the homes of its subjects and contained obvious elements of prearrangement between Murrow and the subject as to what would be discussed. Stanton was bothered that the appearance of spontaneity was not borne out by the facts of the show because a camera obviously could not enter the home of the weekly subject unannounced. He called *Person to Person* "rehearsed," and within two weeks after the first segment of the congressional hearings, to the fury of producers Jesse Zousmer and John Aaron, CBS cancelled the program, equating *Person to Person* with the fraudulence of the quizzes. Murrow, vacationing in England, made a swift response:

Dr. Stanton has finally revealed his ignorance both of news and requirements of TV production.... He suggests that *Person to Person*, a program with which I was associated for six years, was not what it purported to be. Surely Stanton must know that cameras, lights, and microphones do not just wander around a home.... The alternative to a degree of rehearsal would be chaos. I am sorry Dr. Stanton feels that I have participated in perpetuating a fraud upon the public. My conscience is clear. His seems to be bothering him.

Stanton was stunned by Murrow's reaction. He and the chairman of the board of CBS, William Paley, sent their general counsel over to London to obtain, according to Fred Friendly, "some kind of face-saving apology from Murrow or his resignation." Edward R. Murrow neither resigned nor apologized, but his split with Frank Stanton was never healed, and the bitterness between the two men increased in the next year until Murrow finally left the network he helped create.[55]

Another victim of Stanton and CBS's newly found righteousness was Louis Cowan, the man whose work had initiated the quiz show. Unfortunately for Cowan, during the Harris special subcommittee investigation of the quizzes, he was hospitalized with phlebitis in his left leg and could not appear to testify as president of the CBS Television Network. His absence at the hearings seemed too convenient to some critics and cast suspicion over his role in the fraudulent quiz shows, although Merton Koplin's testimony cleared him of any knowledge of the method of Entertainment Productions' operation of his $64,000 quizzes after he went to CBS. To the careful observer, there was no question that Cowan was blameless, and few network presidents of CBS had been more committed to the News Division than Louis Cowan, once he had joined forces with Murrow and Friendly.

In June 1959, according to Stanton, Cowan told his superior that he would be leaving the network in about a year. In the months after the hearings, Stanton hastened the departure of his network president. Cowan explained his uneasy position in his resignation statement to Stanton:

> During recent weeks you have expressed, both publicly and privately, your complete confidence in me and in the fact that I had nothing to do with the rigging of quiz shows. Nevertheless, in spite of my record and your confidence in my integrity, you have suggested repeatedly, directly and indirectly, that I should resign. Newspaper stories have referred regularly to my impending resignation.
>
> And during these past two weeks you have asked me not to communicate with anyone at the office. I find myself completely at a loss to understand your actions.
>
> I have asked you explicitly whether the real reason you did not want me as president of CBS television network is that, at this particular

moment, you do not want a man who has had an association with quiz shows, even though his association was completely honest and honorable. But you have told me emphatically that this is not the reason for your desiring my resignation.

You have insisted that any public statement place primary responsibility for my resignation upon my health. I have insisted on greater accuracy; my health is now excellent. In consequence, we have been unable to write a joint statement.

Stanton returned this response:

It is true that I have urged you to give up your post as president of the CBS television network. The reasons for this feeling, I have tried, in our private conversations, to make clear to you.

In the first place, we must have strong and decisive leadership and a man with outstanding administrative skills as the chief operating executive of the CBS television network—particularly in these times. Your talents and proven abilities are many indeed, but as you yourself have said many times, administration is not your forte. . . .

I told you that your lengthy absence in a fast moving situation had led me to the conclusion that it would be most upsettting to the organization to have you return and then leave again within six months.

To Stanton, the fact that the creator of *The $64,000 Question* was also president of the television network branch at a time of the medium's harshest criticism was detrimental to the image of CBS and the industry itself, despite the fact that Louis Cowan was innocent of any wrongdoing.[56]

In spite of Stanton's ill-conceived treatment of Louis Cowan and Edward R. Murrow, his response to the shame of the quizzes far outshone any other industry spokesman. Unlike his counterpart at NBC, Robert Kintner, he offered no law or commission-like review as a possible solution; he stated simply that the networks had failed in their duty. Stanton received more praise for his testimony before the Harris subcommittee and subsequent speeches than anyone else in television. Even Fred Friendly, who could hardly be called an admirer of Dr. Stanton, said: "Most of the spokesmen for the other networks were dazed, frightened, inarticulate towers of jello whose public statements only seemed to compound the faults that the quiz scandals had brought to light. In his austere, brutally frank willingness to assume responsibility rather than seek a scapegoat, Stanton may have saved the industry."[57]

To Oren Harris and the men who sat across from Charles Van Doren at his confession, industry self-regulation was not enough, and a legislative response was forthcoming. In the months following the hearings, the special subcommittee prepared a report on legislative means to establish greater control over the technically noncriminal practices of Dan Enright and his industry compatriots. Prior to that, however, the executive branch joined to present a united front against fraudulent quizzes. President Eisenhower, at his October 22 news conference, directed Attorney General William Rogers to investigate the scandal and prepare a report by January 1, 1960. The Rogers report preceded the interim report of the Harris subcommittee by a couple of months, but both contained essentially the same recommendations.

The Rogers report maintained that the FCC had the authority "to take appropriate measures" to guarantee that quiz shows are honest contests. Even though such measures were already available, the report also recommended additional legislation. More surprising, the attorney general made the bold suggestion that networks should be licensed by the FCC. The interim report, which soon followed, recommended the addition of criminal penalties for programmatic deception on television and a short-term suspension of stations proven guilty of broadcasting such deceit; it justified its stance by calling "it . . . contrary to the public interest for a radio or television station to be used for broadcasting any programs which . . . deceive viewers or listeners." The report also recommended licensing networks directly, but it recognized the fact that the networks were most vulnerable through the legally limited number of profitable affiliates owned outright.[58]

In the midst of the slow legislative process, John Doerfer's career as chairman of the FCC ended. Early in January, days after the release of the Rogers report, he vacationed aboard a yacht for about a week. The yacht was owned by his friend, George B. Storer, who owned several radio and television stations. This indiscretion was the final outrage to Doerfer's critics. Pressure quickly mounted that he resign to help regenerate the image of the FCC. He denied he had violated any regulations, but the appearance of television's chief regulator as a guest of a station owner led to his downfall. On March 10 he resigned as chairman, and Frederick W. Ford, another commissioner, was appointed to succeed him. The press presumed that he, along with Robert Lee and Robert Bartley, two other commissioners, who publicly dissented from Doerfer's contention that the agency had no authority to do anything about the prearranged quiz contests, would favor a more active regulatory commission.[59]

The course toward a law to make illegal a television practice, which to most observers was unlikely ever to occur again, moved inexorably forward. In late March 1960 Oren Harris introduced two bills onto the floor of the House of Representatives, one to license the networks directly and the other to make broadcasting fraudulent quiz shows a crime. The legislative course of action following the disclosure of the fixes seemed absurd to more than one observer. Anthony Lewis said, "This horse is so dead that this seems . . . like demanding a law against the hoop skirt monopoly"; Charles Van Doren compared the bill to "using a pile-driver to kill a mouse"; and the New Republic used a similar analogy for the legislation: "Killing flies with a sledge."[60]

Nonetheless the proposed amendments to the Communications Act pressed on. By late June Congressman John Bennett's provision to license the networks failed to pass on the House floor 149-35, while Oren Harris, responding to Doerfer's January cruise, succeeded in passing an amendment to prohibit honoraria and gifts to the FCC members. The House weakened another part of the initial amendments, which provided a $10,000 fine and a ten-day license suspension for stations guilty of violating FCC regulations, by putting the burden of proof upon the regulatory agency. The majority of congressmen seemed to think the restrictions too harsh and specified that such sanctions be made only if the violation was the result of "negligent or intentional" actions.

By the time the bill got to the U.S. Senate, it was weakened further by the Commerce Subcommittee on Communications chairman, John Pastore (Democrat-Rhode Island), who struck out the suspension provision and left only the fine. Senator William Proxmire (Democrat-Wisconsin) tried to restore the penalty, which might have put stations off the air briefly, but he was thwarted by Pastore. The senator from Rhode Island reasoned that the television-viewing audience would be penalized more than the stations by any suspensions. The new FCC chairman, Frederick Ford, favored the House version, but his opinion could not sway the Senate. Therefore the bill that President Eisenhower signed into law on September 13, 1960, was a fairly mild reformation of the broadcast industry. It allowed the FCC to require license renewals of less than the legally required three years if the agency believes such action would be in the public interest, prohibited gifts to FCC members, and declared illegal any contest or game with intent to deceive the audience. The flurry of proposals for substantive television reform that followed in the wake of Van Doren's congressional confession had faded into a rather innocuous piece of legislation.[61]

At the same time as the bill to outlaw rigged quizzes was proceeding toward law, Oren Harris's subcommittee was investigating other areas of deceit and public fraud. As a direct result of the quiz-show scandals and investigation, the "payola" crisis struck the American psyche, and a new scandal soon followed. Although the investigation of widespread payoffs to radio disc jockeys by record companies to promote their recordings on the air was a dramatic story, the Harris subcommittee also launched another important investigation as a result of the quiz investigation. The FTC fell under congressional scrutiny nearly equal to that endured by the FCC as months of hearings and discussion about deceptive advertising competed for the space with the "payola" scandal and the waning comment about the fraudulent quiz shows.[62]

More important was the response of the advertising industry to the quiz-show scandals regarding the relationship between television sponsorship and television programming. The response was slow in coming, but after the dialogue among advertisers began, there was a massive internal debate. Rarely had the advertising industry gone through a period of greater self-examination. Carl Spielvogel, the *New York Times* reporter assigned to the advertising industry, labeled advertisers basically quiet and fearful in the first few weeks after the nation learned of the machinations of Martin Revson and his associates. Frederick Gamble, president of the American Association of Advertising Agencies, which contained over 75 percent of all agencies, was one of the first in the industry to suggest that advertisers should discuss "morality in advertising." Soon thereafter one of the top advertising men in the country, Fairfax M. Cone, chairman of the board of Foote, Cone, and Belding, suggested that advertisers and their agencies divorce themselves from television programming. This concept was the "magazine-ad" approach, which was discussed within the advertising firms for months. Unlike virtually all other kinds of media used by advertisers, television was the only one in which sponsors frequently attempted to determine content.

Days after the Cone statement, Donald Frost, chairman of the Association of National Advertisers, called many sponsors together for a closed meeting to discuss responsibility in television programming. The meeting turned into a bitter fourteen-hour debate when several sponsors suggested that advertisers should have no control over the content of the shows they sponsor. The dictates of Revlon upon *The $64,000 Question* and *The $64,000 Challenge* may have been the extremes of sponsor influence, but meddling was an all-too-frequent event to television producers and network officials. As an example, Chevrolet once deleted the dialogue "fording a stream" from a program it sponsored because of the reference to a competitor.

In the late 1950s, it could be argued, the television networks were little more than conveyances for advertisers. When the magazine-ad concept was broached as possibly applicable to television, CBS quickly endorsed the idea. The more timid advertisers welcomed the shifting of responsibility to the networks, presumably more knowledgeable about broadcasting anyway. The image of advertising had fallen almost as far as that of television following the quiz revelations, and the industry forcefully sought to improve its relationship to the medium. Another change that was also becoming popular was to consider a new way to charge sponsors for airtime. At the convention of the Association of National Advertisers in late 1959,

Rodney Erickson, a vice-president of Warner Brothers, suggested that the networks should charge varying rates for
advertisers depending on the size of the audience reached; this
method would ensure the advertisers that they were paying
more proportionately for what they were getting and dilute the
temptation to interfere with the programming to increase the
ratings. CBS was already proceeding with the varying-rate system for the news show CBS Reports, and the practice gradually
expanded in the following years.

As a result of the furor created by the quiz-show scandals, the
advertising industry helped change the inner structure of the
television industry substantially. It was a gradual process not
really solidified until the early 1960s, but what it eventually
meant was that sponsorship (strong identification between advertiser and program) came to an end. The strong sponsor gave
way and the networks increased their power enormously, especially as the lessons of Twenty-one and Dotto marked the rapid
decline in independently produced packages being aired on
networks. The varying-rate schedule was also gradually instituted, which increased the impact of the ratings incalculably.
Nevertheless, as the sponsor system changed, another arose:
"overcommercialization. When the advertiser was sponsor it
behooved him to be sensitive to the frequency and length of his
program interruptions. As a buyer of minute packages which
disperse his message over an assortment of programs on various nights of the week, he is unburdened of that aesthetic de-
cency as well as other responsibilities."[63] Perhaps the greatest
irony of all is that while the advertiser and the network have
wrought a significant change in the way television is run, the
change in the content of television has been almost impercepti-
ble.

Even though the fraudulence on the rigged quiz shows was
found to be noncriminal and therefore unpunishable, the scandal did lead to the prosecution of some of the people involved,
all of them contestants (except for Albert Freedman). Shortly
after the Van Doren testimony and soon after district attorney
Frank Hogan announced that he estimated that only about 50 of
the 150 witnesses who appeared before the grand jury em-
paneled late in 1958 had told the truth, about 30 former witnes-

ses called Hogan and said that they wanted to change their testimony. The legal process of prosecution for former contestants who had perjured themselves was slower than the legislative method that outlawed deceptive programming. It was not until July 1960 that a new grand jury was formed to reinvestigate the ex-contestants. Again the prosecution was headed by Joseph Stone. The first indictments handed down were to Artie Roberts and Bernard Martin, who had bribed contestants on *Treasure Hunt*. No former contestants from the EPI quizzes, *The $64,000 Question, The $64,000 Challenge,* or *The Big Surprise,* were indicted because the prosecutors reasoned that there was no collusion on those shows: the contestants were unaware that their pregame interview would manifest itself as part of the questions they received until they were inside the isolation booth. All the other prosecutions were against former contestants of either *Twenty-one, Tic Tac Dough,* or *Hi-Lo,* creations of Dan Enright. Enright himself had never testified before the grand jury earlier and therefore was unindictable for perjury the second time around.[64]

On October 7, 1960, eighteen people were indicted for second-degree perjury, and in the days following, they made their pleas at the district attorney's office. The ex-contestants included Van Doren, Vivienne Nearing, Elfrida Von Nardroff, and Hank Bloomgarden (the opponent of James Snodgrass), all of them big winners on *Twenty-one*. Lesser-known indicted winners from that quiz were Morton Harelik, Paul Bain, Richard Klein, and Ruth Miller. From *Tic Tac Dough* came Henrietta Dudley, Tim Horan, Joseph Rosner, Patricia Sullivan, Dr. Mike Truppin, Patricia Nance, Ruth Klein, Terry Curtis, Neil Wolf, and Richard Klein, who had also appeared on *Twenty-one*. The biggest winner of *Tic Tac Dough,* Army Captain Michael O'Rourke, was not indicted, but he was forced to resign his commission. Terry Curtis, who had also appeared on the same quiz, was one of the biggest winners on *Hi-Lo*. Some of those indicted had won relatively small amounts of money for their connivances. Rosner won only $1,600 on *Tic Tac Dough,* and Richard Klein has received only a $1,000 check for his efforts on *Twenty-one*.

The trials and hearings for the defendants did not start until

May 1961 when Vivienne Nearing pleaded guilty and received a suspended sentence from Judge William Ringel. Henrietta Dudley and Roberts and Martin soon followed with the same pleas and received the same suspended sentences. Nearing, in the following year, was suspended from the practice of law for six months. By the end of 1961, four others had offered up guilty pleas and received similar treatment, including Dr. Truppin, a professor who was also publicly reprimanded and censured by the New York State Board of Regents. In late January 1962, Charles Van Doren, Elfrida Von Nardroff, Hank Bloomgarden, and the remaining twelve ex-contestants received the same punishment meted out to the participants in a now nearly forgotten scandal. Van Doren had pleaded not guilty in his initial arraignment, but the treatment of those defendants who preceded him probably convinced him and his lawyer to change the plea. With the end of the final suspended sentence given to Ruth Klein the legal resolution of the quiz show scandal had ended. All of those prosecuted were convicted not for collusion in a televised fraud but for lying to a grand jury. Albert Freedman was the only television executive who received an indictment.[65]

NOTES

1. "Are We a Nation of Liars and Cheats?" *Christian Century*, November 18, 1959, p. 1334.

2. "A Big Quiz for Quizzes," *Life*, October 19, 1959, p. 52; U.S. Congress, House, Committee on Interstate and Foreign Commerce, Investigation of Television Quiz Shows, before subcommittee of the Committee on Interstate and Foreign Commerce, House of Representatives, 86th Cong., 1st sess., 1959, Franklin testimony, p. 139, Freedman testimony, pp. 223–226, Jackman testimony, pp. 132–133 (hereafter cited as *Investigation*); *New York Times*, October 11, 1959, p. 5, November 6, 1959, p. 1; *Investigation*, Doren testimony, pp. 627–628.

3. September 17, 1958, p. 75, September 18, 1958, p. 63, September 19, 1958, p. 55, June 11, 1959, p. 19.

4. "Quiz Scandal (Contd.)," *Times*, October 6, 1958, p. 50; *New York Times*, September 27, 1958, p. 42; *Investigation*, Snodgrass testimony, pp. 63, 75, 86–87; "Telling Tales on '21,' " *Newsweek*, October 6, 1958, p. 52.

5. *Investigation*, Ervin testimony, pp. 190–192, 199; *New York Times*, October 4, 1958, p. 43.

6. *New York Times*, October 17, 1958, p. 58, October 4, 1958, p. 43.

7. Ibid., November 5, 1958, p. 71; "Come and Gone," *Newsweek*, October 27, 1958, p. 88; "Quiz Man in a Jam," *Newsweek*, November 17, 1958, p. 63; "Squeeze on the Quiz," *Newsweek*, October 27, 1958, p. 88.

8. *New York Times*, November 8, 1958, pp. 1, 43; "Quiz Man in a Jam," p. 63.

9. Herbert Brean, " 'Controls' and 'Plotting' Help in Showmanship," *Life*, September 15, 1958, p. 25; *New York Times*, January 21, 1959, p. 63; *Investigation*, Van Doren testimony, p. 627; Meyer Weinberg, *TV in America* (New York: Ballantine Books, 1962), p. 10.

10. "Basketball Scholarship," *Time*, April 6, 1959, p. 45; *New York Times*, September 28, 1958, sec. 6, pp. 12, 64–65; Henry Popkin, "The Trouble with the Quiz Shows," *New Republic*, October 13, 1958, pp. 22–23; "A Ray of Hope," *Reporter*, September 18, 1958, p. 2.

11. *New York Times*, June 11, 1959, p. 19, June 12, 1959, pp. 1, 55; "A Tawdry Hoax," *Newsweek*, June 22, 1959, p. 46.

12. *New York Times*, June 12, 1959, pp. 1, 55, July 14, 1959, pp. 1, 59, June 24, 1959, p. 64, June 11, 1959, p. 19, August 4, 1959, p. 55; "Tawdry Hoax," p. 46.

13. *New York Times*, July 14, 1959, pp. 1, 59, June 19, 1959, p. 51, June 24, 1959, p. 64, July 11, 1959, p. 29, July 18, 1959, p. 35, July 23, 1959, p. 53, June 11, 1959, p. 19; "Tawdry Hoax," p. 46.

14. *New York Times*, August 6, 1959, p. 29, July 31, 1959, pp. 1, 43, August 1, 1959, pp. 1, 37, August 14, 1959, p. 6, August 4, 1959, p. 55, August 5, 1959, pp. 1, 55.

15. Ibid., August 7, 1959, p. 46, August 5, 1959, pp. 1, 55, September 5, 1959, p. 17.

16. Ibid., August 6, 1959, p. 29; *Congressional Index, 1959–1960* (New York: Commerce Clearing House, 1960), I: 2008, 2022, 2027, 2046, 2054, 2064, 2069; *Investigation of Television Quiz Shows*, pp. 1–3, 7.

17. *New York Times*, October 7, 1959, pp. 1, 47; Richard N. Goodwin, *Life*, November 16, 1959, p. 30; Harris statement in *Investigation*, p. 9.

18. *New York Times*, October 7, 1959, pp. 1, 47; U.S. Congress, House, Committee on Interstate and Foreign Commerce, Interim Report, *Investigation of Regulatory Commissions and Agencies*, H. Rept. 1258, 86th Cong., 2d sess., February 9, 1960, pp. 8–9 (hereafter cited as *Interim Report*).

19. *Investigation*, Franklin testimony, pp. 136–137.

20. Ibid., Freedman testimony, p. 461, telegram as exhibit in part of

Harris statements, p. 619; *New York Mirror*, October 12, 1959, pp. 1, 2; *Investigation*, Van Doren testimony, pp. 628, 629.

21. "Big Quiz for Quizzes," p. 51; *Investigation*, Van Doren testimony, p. 629.

22. *New York Times*, October 24, 1959, p. 1; *Investigation*, Van Doren testimony, pp. 624, 629.

23. *New York Times*, November 3, 1959, pp. 1, 20; statements of Oren Harris, Walter Rogers, and Robert Lishman within *Investigation*, Van Doren testimony, pp. 624–646.

24. *Investigation*, Bernstein statement, pp. 922–926, Cohn testimony, pp. 678–692, Jackson testimony, pp. 646–676, Robert Kintner testimony, pp. 1025–1085, Koplin testimony, pp. 742–788, Stanton testimony, pp. 1087–1128.

25. "Big Quiz for Quizzes," p. 52; *Investigation*, Fisher testimony, pp. 433, 435, 438–440; *New York Times*, July 9, 1960, p. 1; *Investigation*, Kintner testimony, pp. 1045, 1066.

26. *Investigation*, Doerfer testimony, including the legal citations and exhibits and a letter from Doerfer to Joseph Stone, February 18, 1959, pp. 478, 486–487, 507–508, 510–511, 513, 515, 517, 526, 531.

27. Ibid., letter of Earl Kintner to Oren Harris, September 3, 1959, as part of Kintner testimony, p. 47.

28. Ibid., Doerfer testimony, p. 536, Kintner testimony, pp. 553, 555; "Two-Fisted Crackdown," *Newsweek*, May 30, 1960, p. 108.

29. *Investigation*, Kintner testimony, including Rogers's remark, pp. 551, 568.

30. *New York Times*, November 6, 1959, p. 17, November 7, 1959, p. 13; "Out of the Backwash of the TV Scandals...," *Newsweek*, November 16, 1959, p. 66; *New York Times*, November 4, 1959, p. 29, October 15, 1959, p. 1, November 3, 1959, pp. 1, 24.

31. "Van Doren on Van Doren," *Newsweek*, November 9, 1959, pp. 69–70.

32. "The Blame For TV Fixes," *Life*, October 26, 1959, p. 38; "Quizlings," *Reporter*, October 29, 1959, p. 2; "Quiz Quiz: Critics-Across-the-Sea," *Newsweek*, November 1, 1959, p. 67; "Say It Ain't So, Charles," *America*, October 24, 1959, p. 98.

33. *New York Times*, November 5, 1959, p. 30.

34. Ibid., p. 34, November 22, 1959, sec. 6, p. 11; "The Uses of Scandal," *Nation*, November 14, 1959, p. 341.

35. *New York Times*, November 22, 1959, sec. 6, pp. 11, 106.

36. Ibid., October 12, 1959, pp. 1, 39; Norman Cousins, "The Real Fraud," *Saturday Review*, November 21, 1959, p. 27; Robert Horton, "The Economic Squeeze On Mass TV," *Reporter*, April 28, 1960, pp. 19–20.

37. "Blame for TV Fixes," p. 38; Frank Bain, "Who's to Blame for TV's Deadly Sins," *American Mercury* (November 1950): 59; "A Question of Freedom," *Time*, December 7, 1959, pp. 47–48; "TV Quiz: What Does E-t-h-i-c-s Spell?" *Business Week*, November 14, 1959, p. 184.

38. "Is It Just TV—or Most of Us?" *New York Times*, November 15, 1959, sec. 6, pp. 15, 105.

39. John Updike, *Assorted Prose* (New York: Alfred A Knopf, Inc., 1965), pp. 86–87. Reprinted with the permission of Alfred A. Knopf, Inc.

40. John Ciardi, "Exit a Symbol," *Saturday Review*, November 21, 1959, pp. 27–28, 59.

41. James E. Allen, Jr., "The TV 'Fixes' and Teacher Responsibility," *School and Society*, April 23, 1960, p. 202; *New York Times*, November 24, 1959, p. 30.

42. *New York Times*, November 5, 1959, p. 16.

43. Ibid., November 9, 1959, p. 27.

44. Victor Ratner, "The Freedom of Taste," reprinted from *Television* magazine for the *New York Times*, December 28, 1959, pp. 14–15.

45. "Scandal of the Quizzes," *Time*, September 1, 1959, p. 38; *New York Times*, November 29, 1959, sec. 2, p. 12.

46. *New York Times*, December 4, 1959, p. 22; part of Sindlinger data exhibited in *Investigation*, Robert Kintner testimony, pp. 1083–1084; "Out of the Backwash," p. 66.

47. "Out of Backwash," p. 66; Elmo Roper, "Rigged Quizzes: The Public's View," *Saturday Review*, February 13, 1960, p. 36.

48. "Out of the Backwash," pp. 66–67.

49. *New Republic*, November 9, 1959, p. 7, October 19, 1959, p. 2; "Quizlings," p. 2.

50. *New York Times*, November 8, 1959, sec. 4, p. 1, November 9, 1959, p. 27; "Where, May We Ask, Was the FCC?" *Consumer Reports* (January 1960): 9–11.

51. *New York Times*, November 11, 1959, p. 34; John Fischer, "New Hope for Television?" *Harper's* (January 1960): 12; Fred W. Friendly, *Due to Circumstances Beyond Our Control* (New York: Vintage Books, 1967), p. 116; *New York Times*, November 9, 1959, p. 27; Lipmann article originally appeared in the *Christian Science Monitor*, reprinted in "Prostitute of Merchandising," *Time*, November 9, 1959, p. 58; *Investigation*, Charles Revson testimony, p. 880; *New York Times*, October 28, 1959, p. 75.

52. *New York Times*, December 31, 1959, p. 37; Gilbert Seldes, "No Broom at the Top," *Saturday Review*, December 19, 1959, p. 23.

53. *New York Times*, October 19, 1959, p. 58, November 20, 1959, p.

62; "After Appomattox," *Time*, February 22, 1960, p. 74; *New York Times*, November 26, 1959, p. 50, December 27, 1959, sec. 2, p. 13, October 17, 1959, pp. 1, 26; "Purity Kick," *Time*, November 2, 1959, p. 43; *New York Times*, October 18, 1959, pp. 1, 45.

54. *New York Times*, December 15, 1959, p. 70, October 20, 1959, p. 1, December 3, 1959, p. 75, December 5, 1959, p. 47.

55. Ibid., October 27, 1959, p. 74; Friendly, *Due to Circumstances*, pp. 108–110, 124–125; *New York Times*, October 20, 1959, p. 1, October 23, 1959, p. 1, October 25, 1959, p. 1.

56. *New York Times*, December 9, 1959, pp. 1, 53, December 13, 1959, sec. 2, p. 21; Friendly, *Due to Circumstances*, pp. 93, 112–112; *Investigation*, Koplin testimony, pp. 743, 748–749, Stanton testimony, pp. 1088 and 1099.

57. Friendly, *Due to Circumstances*, p. 102; *New York Times*, November 8, 1959, sec. 4, p. 7, November 27, 1959, p. 28; "Stanton in the Augean Stables," *Nation*, November 7, 1959, pp. 322–323; "TV Blows a Fuse," *Fortune* (December 1959): 96, 98; "TV Quiz: What Does E-t-h-i-c-s Spell?" p. 184.

58. *New York Times*, January 1, 1960, pp. 1, 10, 12, Feburary 7, 1960, pp. 1, 62; *Congressional Quarterly Almanac* (Washington: Congressional Quarterly, 1960), 16: 357, 359–360; *New York Times*, October 23, 1959, p. 1; Interim Report, pp. 38–40, 64, 87, 90. (The last three pages are cited from the Rogers Report, which is appendix E in the Interim Report); *U.S. News and World Report*, January 11, 1960, p. 61.

59. *Congressional Quarterly*, p. 358; "TV 'Policeman'—Who Would Be It?" *Newsweek*, November 9, 1959, p. 71; "Two-Fisted Crackdown," p. 108.

60. *New York Times*, November 8, 1959, sec. 4, p. 7, February 25, 1960, p. 59, March 24, 1960, p. 27; Frank B. Pierson, "Killing Flies with a Sledge," *New Republic*, November 23, 1959, p. 20.

61. *New York Times*, September 14, 1960, p. 88; *Congressional Quarterly*, pp. 356, 358–361; *New York Times*, June 1, 1960, pp. 1, 64, June 29, 1960, p. 1, August 11, 1960, p. 53; U.S. Congress, House, *Communications Act Amendments, 1960*, 86th Cong., 2d sess., June 13, 1960, pp. 1–8.

62. *New York Times*, November 2, 1959, pp. 1, 61, November 8, 1959, p. 1; "Drive on Cheats," *Time*, January 4, 1960, p. 66; *New York Times*, November 11, 1959, p. 1.

63. "Admen Face the TV Issue," *Business Week*, November 21, 1959, pp. 115–117; Les Brown, *Television: The Business Behind the Box* (New York: Harcourt Brace Jovanovich, 1971), pp. 64–65; *New York Times*, November 18, 1959, pp. 1, 83, November 19, 1959, p. 79, October 20,

1959, p. 63, November 8, 1959, sec. 3, p. 12, November 10, 1959, pp. 1, 42, November 18, 1959, p. 67.

64. *New York Times*, November 7, 1959, p. 1, July 6, 1960, pp. 1, 27, July 9, 1960, pp. 1, 41, March 24, 1960, p. 35.

65. Ibid., January 18, 1962, pp. 1, 16, October 19, 1960, p. 91, October 21, 1960, p. 67, October 22, 1960, p. 41, October 25, 1960, p. 71, October 28, 1960, p. 7, June 6, 1961, p. 74, June 16, 1961, p. 43, November 28, 1961, p. 39, December 16, 1961, p. 23, December 20, 1961, p. 67, January 23, 1962, p. 40, June 30, 1962, p. 47, October 27, 1962, p. 14; "Out of the Backwash," p. 66; *New York Times*, October 8, 1960, p. 1, October 18, 1960, pp. 1, 78, December 2, 1960, p. 59, April 1 1961, p. 41, May 9, 1961, p. 41, January 11, 1962, p. 35.

CONCLUSION

Why did the fixed quizzes occur? Much of the reasoning must be economic. Meyer Weinberg emphasizes this cause. He showed that Geritol's annual sales jumped from $10,482,000 in 1956 (before *Twenty-one* began) to $13,975,000 in 1957 and $12,379,000 in 1958, when the show was on the air. They fell to $10,600,000 when it was cancelled. Geritol sales, then were approximately 25 percent higher while *Twenty-one* was being aired. Geritol did not interfere with the quiz's workings, nor was *Twenty-one* a huge success in the ratings. For Revlon and *The $64,000 Question*, the figures are even more impressive. Before 1955, when the first big-money quiz was aired, Revlon's annual average net profit (1950–54) was $1,200,000. From 1955 to 1958 it rose to $7,680,000 and averaged $11,078,996 in the years 1959 and 1960. Money, according to Weinberg, was the prime motivating factor for producers to arrange the outcome of quizzes they hoped would increase the ratings and, in turn, the sponsor's profits and interest in remaining with the show. Revlon demonstrated a strong relationship between television ratings and sales, but this correlation did not exist for many other shows.

There is more to the meaning of the quiz frauds than saying that they demonstrate the avarice of American corporations linked with advertising agencies and the television industry. There is more significance to the scandals than proving a theory of materialistic determinism even though greed, arguably, may have been the most prevalent human behavioral trait displayed throughout this entire tale.

From the viewpoint of the contestants, the monetary lure was reason enough for many to deceive, but other factors also figured in their participation. From the novels of Horatio Alger to Frank Norris to Sinclair Lewis, the American success ethic usually has been demonstrated materialistically, and to those who wanted success enough, the quiz show provided an instantaneous demonstration of American savvy translated into dollars. To be successful meant to be rich, and the quizzes offered this to many; the means of attainment on the shows were immaterial. However, some contestants were lured into the deception by altruism and fame. Here the instrument of television offered unique opportunities. No other communications medium can produce facial familiarity more than television. No larger audience can be reached for a contestant desirous of promoting his charity or organization than that afforded by television. The newest electronic medium had opened the door into millions of homes, and uninvited guests "were admitted into every household through the small electronic screen." Mixed in with all the other motives of contestants was the willing and eager belief that somehow it was all part of entertainment, a kind of showmanship that everyone practiced and that therefore softened somewhat the wrongness of the act. Herbert Stempel thought that the deceptions were a normal part of quiz shows; so did Charles Van Doren and many others. The real blame for the manifestations of that conviction, however, belonged not to the contestants but to people like Albert Freedman and the other quiz executives who deliberately lied to the on-screen participants in their hoaxes.[1]

The big-money quiz shows are a fascinating part of recent Americana. They drew upon every institution and tradition for improving the appeal of the show. The military was used with the appearances of Richard McCutchen, always resplendent in his Marine Corps uniform. Gino Prato and Teddy Nadler fortified the belief of success in America for immigrants and the children of immigrants. Herbert Stempel was the ex-GI working his way through college. Baseball was a popular category as shown by Myrtle Power and others. Religion was exploited often, but never more crassly than with Catherine Kreitzer who "graduated" from her quiz winnings to do Bible readings on America's longest-running television replacement for vaudeville, Ed Sullivan's *Toast of the Town*. Every corny homily an emcee could use was designed to place the quiz show into the mainstream of American life. At the same time the originality of each show was promoted. The facet of American life most exploited by the designers and producers of the quiz shows was education. *The $64,000 Question* and *Twenty-one* were purported to be educationally sound and beneficial by a variety of people. The successful quizmaster was held up as a model for schoolchildren, particularly one as charming as Charles Van Doren. Hundreds of teachers were heartened by the programs' pithy remarks on the value of studying. Van Doren was touted as the scholar as hero, which for most educators in the 1950s was a new and exciting climate of opinion, a remarkable state of affairs, especially since the likable teacher's on-screen 'heroics' occurred nearly a year prior to the Soviet Union's launch of the world's first satellite, an event that almost overnight profoundly affected how most Americans regarded the teaching profession. In a large measure, perhaps, the image of Van Doren helped prepare that transition of American opinion.

The big-money quiz was the most outrageously new use of television and, at the same time, was disguised as an American staple of both entertainment and education, something akin to a spelling bee on a grandiose scale. The most important elements in the quizzes, though, were not their exploitation of contestants and institutions but the materialistic tenets they presented. Apart from the fraudulence, probably nothing else of the quiz shows has been emphasized in this work as much as their pecuniary nature. Success as measured by money has been one of our strongest social gospels, and rarely was this more entertainingly and quantitatively demonstrated than by contestants who successfully answered questions for money. The shows were both damned and praised for their materialistic appeal. One critic would condemn a quiz for its cultivation and display of greed; another could argue that the quizzes merely duplicated what was already present in society: a competitive acquisition of dollars. In particular, the dual isolation booth quiz shows such as *Twenty-one* and *The $64,000 Challenge* could be portrayed as a lively representation of the businessman's credo: knowing more than your competitor means more dollars for you. The rags-to-riches overnight American success story had found one of its oddest and yet most popular outlets in *The $64,000 Question* and its imitations.

One pattern the quiz-show scandals demonstrated was similar to what happened to radio during the 1920s. Technology was moving so rapidly during the 1950s and so drastically altering the leisure-time uses of Americans that it far outstripped the abilities of government and industry to anticipate and handle such a situation. The scandals were a non-criminal fraud without victims in the context of a new electronic medium. The response of Congress to the jamming and questionable radio programming of the 1920s was to create the Federal Communications Commission. The response of Congress to the television scandals was an almost needless little piece of legislation. The congressional response to the scandals in 1960, in addition to making such deceptions illegal and providing more funds and personnel to a woefully understaffed FCC, point to another meaning the quiz scandals hold, one that has a common line throughout U.S. business history. Given the spectre of new government interference or even regulation, both the television industry and the concomitant advertising industry moved relatively quickly toward an apparatus of self-policing their domains. This has been a frequent response from any business or industry caught in the throes of scandal or abusive conduct. It is disheartening to realize that the fair-practices departments established by the networks as a result of the quiz scandals have turned their energies elsewhere, evolving into offices of censorship that render recent motion pictures incomprehensible on television and snip at bits of creativity in television programming judged unfit for the nation's airwaves.

One would have imagined that the television industry, having survived its worst scandal, would never again permit high-stakes quizzes on television, but the big-money quiz shows reemerged to become a continuous and ongoing phenomenon. In the summer of 1963, slightly more than three years after the last big-money quiz left the air and approximately one and a half years after Charles Van Doren received his suspended sentence, ABC announced the return of the big-money quiz in the form of *100 Grand*. This program was developed by producer Robert Stivers, an inventive man new to television, whose greatest claim to fame had been the development of the cardboard container for orange juice. Even though ABC purchased the idea, the network had a difficult time locating a sponsor, but it finally pursuaded El Producto Cigars and Alberto-Culver Products that the big-money quiz could make a popular comeback. The quiz was due to enter the fall lineup of new shows and pitted two contestants against each other (in twin "bubbles" rather than isolation booths). One contestant was an "expert" designated by any local chamber of commerce, who received a nominal $500 per appearance. The chamber of commerce selected by the program, however, received $10,000. Opposing the "expert" was an "amateur" selected by the show who could achieve a potential $100,000 in winnings. Each contestant prepared questions to ask the opponent. The security surrounding 100 Grand was extremely tight. Contestants were sequestered in hotel rooms to prepare their questions and not released until just prior to airtime. One of the early "experts," Professor Peter Paul Fuchs of Louisiana State University at New Orleans, was ordered to travel to New York under an assumed name. The questions were verified intensely, and the rulebook for 100 Grand numbered 199 pages. Unfortunately for the quiz, what occurred on screen was not nearly as interesting as the off-screen security precautions. The show went on the air on September 15, 1963, with an inordinate amount of time in the first half of the show taken up with an explanation of how 100 Grand could not contain the deceptions of the earlier big-money quizzes. In spite of all the ballyhoo and precaution accompanying 100 Grand (or perhaps because of it), the show was one of the biggest ratings flops of the season; it was canceled after only three weeks.[2]

Even more surprising was the appearance in 1976 of a quiz show derived directly from The $64,000 Question. In spring of 1975, Viacom Enterprises, which had purchased the rights to The $64,000 Question, sold the idea of a remake of the famous quiz to scores of CBS-affiliated stations to fill their 7:30 P.M. time slots, which the FCC had recently ruled in its prime-time access decision that network programming previously filling that time period must be dropped so that local stations might meet the needs of their communities more adequately, as well as increase their profits from advertising. In the rush to fill the extra half-hour of prime time given to them, many local stations opted for prepackaged syndicated programming rather than develop their individual local shows. Viacom's remake was a syndicated program that filled the void for many stations. There was some talk of using the original name, but the quiz was dubbed *The $128,000 Question* when it aired in the fall of 1976. Little else was changed on the show. Many of the same categories, including the Bible, remained as did the ever-present isolation booth. Viacom sought the same type of contestant who drew the adulation and interest back in 1955, or as Viacom's president, Henry Gillespie, said, "We will be searching for the ideal contestant who I like to think of as the blue-collar guy with the white-collar mind." The flourishing of syndicated shows for the 7:30 P.M. time slot also heralded the return of *Treasure Hunt* to the air along with *The $100,000 Name That Tune*. Despite the scandals and the fleeting nature of television programming, it appears that the big-money quiz show has achieved a certain degree of permanence on television, albeit in syndication. In an effort to recapture the past, Viacom even hired Steve Carlin and Mert Koplin to produce *The $128,000 Question*.[3]

Perhaps the most significant thing that can be said about one of the most noted nonpolitical scandals was how little change occurred as a result. In the words of Jack Gould:

The scandal caused no lasting loss in income audience size, or general acceptability of the medium.... In many ways the peril of TV is greater since the scandal. An industry that so simply survived a storm of such huge proportions is going to be less inclined than ever to see merit in proposed changes. The status quo has been undeniably hardened.

The problem of television entertainment remains precisely what it was before the contestants showed up: how to make a practical case for higher standards in programming when the public will look at whatever it receives free of charge rather than turn off a set. To the solution of that dilemma of the video age the quiz scandal and its aftermath appear to have contributed nothing.

If the status quo of big broadcasting was indeed strengthened after the quiz frauds, was it partially the result of the moral apathy of the later years of the Eisenhower presidency as historian Eric F. Goldman alluded in *The Crucial Decade—and After?* Goldman connected the Van Doren confession with similar events occurring at approximately the same time: the Sherman Adams scandal, a widely publicized letter from John Steinbeck to Adlai Stevenson attacking the "cynical immorality" of the nation, and a University of Pennsylvania study, which reported that nearly 40 percent of all college students had cheated on examinations. As fascinating as Goldman's speculations are, they are selective examples of what is probably the most difficult topic in history to discuss—national character—and must be treated with cautious judgment. Nonetheless some generalizations should be attempted.[4]

The public apathy in the wake of the quiz scandals demonstrated a startling degree of national cynicism. Most social commentators were more alarmed by this feeling than by the actual riggings. In the absence of any large outcry to reform television, the American public settled back to watch another full decade of mediocre programming. This is not to say, however, that just because television remained largely unchanged, the public indifference to the scandals carried over into other realms. Certainly political attitudes changed. If the years 1958 through 1960 displayed a national listlessness toward moral and ethical concerns, in contrast, the New Frontier years immediately following appear even more buoyant than they might have been in actuality. In a relative sense then, the quiz-show scandals, the Sherman Adams scandal, and the U-2 incident, as foci of deceit and unethical behavior during those years, assisted the image of the administration of President Kennedy as a time of change in attitude for Americans—from apathy to social consciousness, from political boredom to political concern. Highly defined lines of national character separating presidential administrations are arguable divisions at the very least, and such is the case here; 1960 was one of the most popular years for President Eisenhower as evidenced by his triumphant worldwide tour. That year also marked the beginning of extensive white participation in the civil-rights movement, more noticeably in the black-inspired freedom rides and sit-ins in the

South. This was a demonstration of social consciousness that was missing five years earlier at the birth of the modern U.S. civil-rights movement, the Montgomery bus boycott led by the Reverend Martin Luther King, Jr.

It would be more accurate to say that the quiz-show scandals represent the nadir of a brief cycle in recent history during which the American people and their concerns regarding the unethical behavior of their leaders, whether business, political, or media, were largely undemonstrative. The public silence and apathy indicated not only a degree of condolence with the crimes but a stronger feeling of helplessness in resolving such television distortion. It especially aggrieved one's sense of justice to witness the fact that every person legally punished for the frauds was a contestant, not someone who worked for the fixed programs. The image of the system protecting the powerful while prosecuting the weak was reinforced by the several perjury convictions of contestants.

The quiz riggings add to the accumulated fact that hoaxes, frauds, and deceit have been present throughout American history. The 1920s, in particular, exhibited similar materialism and similar chicanery. The big-money television quizzes and their disgraceful end were but small indicators in our recent electronic past in which an infant (or adolescent) medium, television, reflected a laxity in ethics common to all ages. The nation's greatest philosopher, William James, wrote in 1912:

But will vice never cease. Every level of culture breeds its own peculiar brand of it as surely as one soil breeds sugar-cane, and another soil breeds cranberries. If we were asked that disagreeable question, "What are the bosom-vices of the level of culture which our land and day have reached?" we should be forced, I think, to give the still more disagreeable answer that they are swindling and adroitness and cant, and sympathy with cant—national faults of that extraordinary idealization of "success" in the mere outward sense of "getting there," and getting there on as big a scale as we can, which characterizes our present generation.[5]

NOTES

1. Brown, p. 61; Kletter testimony, p. 167; Weinberg, pp. 25-26, and 46-47.

2. "Out of Isolation," *Newsweek*, August 5, 1963, p. 67; Chris Wel-

PN 1992.8 Q 545

Quiz Shows

les, "No Rig, No Fix and No Quiz," *Life*, October 18, 1963, pp. 133, 135.

3. *New York Times*, March 14, 1975, p. 70, April 8, 1975, p. 75.

4. Goldman, pp. 314-327; *New York Times*, October 23, 1960, sec. 2, p. 13.

5. William James, *Memories and Studies* (New York: Longmans, Green and Co., 1912), p. 351.

Appendix 1

TRANSCRIBED KINESCOPE OF TWENTY-ONE, MAY 20, 1957

BARRY. Good evening. I'm Jack Barry. To date, Hank Bloomgarden has won over $50,000. Because of a series of ties he must play the next game at $3,000 a point, which means that in just a few brief minutes he could increase his money winnings to over $100,000 or, he could lose all of his winnings. To learn the outcome, let's meet our first two players as Geritol, the high potency tonic that helps you feel stronger fast, presents "Twenty-One."

ANNOUNCER. Back for the fourth week—Mr. James Snodgrass. And returning with $52,000, Mr. Hank Bloomgarden.

BARRY. Gentlemen, welcome back to "Twenty-One." This is getting to be like old home week—your familiar faces here on the television screen standing beside me each week. Have you been getting lots of advice during this past week, Hank?

BLOOMGARDEN. Oh, I certainly have, Jack. Not only from family and friends, but from hundreds of people all over the country who have taken the trouble to write me and I certainly appreciate their interest. I certainly appreciate their advice, too. But you know, it's a peculiar thing, this is just an individual game, and I guess I have to make up my own mind as to what to do, notwithstanding all of this wonderful and thoughtful advice that I've gotten.

BARRY. I'm sure people in writing telling you how you should play the game are doing it really with your best interest, but as you say, you have to play it the way you see fit.

BLOOMGARDEN. Right.

BARRY. How about you, did you get any advice, Jim?

SNODGRASS. Well, yes, I have been getting lots of advice but I'm afraid it's—it's just adding up to confusion with me.

BARRY. Well—let's hope that confusion will not overrule the wonderful thinking you have been doing so far.

Gentlemen, you are as familiar as anybody with what has happened here. You tied a number of times. We're going to play at $3,000 a point, which means that $63,000 in overall is at stake. Hank you could either be wiped out completely or you could end up with over $100,000. Jim, you could wind up with $63,000 or anywhere in between that. Hank, you know in the excitement of the game last week, I got kind of carried away myself and mentioned a number of times to you how much you could lose. I didn't mean it to in any way un-nerve you, and I'll try very hard not to do that again tonight.

And now, if you fellows are ready to play, suppose you take your places in studios, put on your earphones and the best of luck to both of you.

Neither player inside can hear anything until I turn their studios on, they cannot see anybody in the studio audience, nor can they hear the studio applause. I'm going to turn both studios on right now. Can you hear me, Jim?

SNODGRASS. Fine, thank you, Jack.

BARRY. How about you, Hank?

BLOOMGARDEN. Very well, thank you.

BARRY. All right, fellows, the most monumental game in the history of our program is about to take place. I think you deserve a few seconds to relax in there and get ready for the big—the giant game about to come—so, take it easy if you will. And we'll get on with the game in just a moment, but first I wonder, if we could turn the cameras around, would we see something like this?

[Commercial Break at this time.]

Now, on with the game. Hank, remember, $3,000 a point, your $52,000 is at stake and I'll get back to you in a moment.

All right, Jim, it's unnecessary to point out the rules of the game, you've played it enough, you have to try to get to 21 as fast as you can. The first category is American—American literature. You grade yourself—how many points do you want from 1 to 11?

SNODGRASS. I'll take 11, please.

BARRY. That would be our most difficult question on American literature, 11 points.

I will read you lines from four of America's greatest poets—in each—in each case tell us the name of the poet—first, "I hear American singing—the very carols I hear"; second, "The fog comes on little cat feet"; Third, "Hope is the thing with feathers that perches in the soul"; fourth, "I shot an arrow into the air—it fell to earth. I know not where." What I want is the names of the poets. Shall I take them one at a time?

SNODGRASS. Ah, yes, please.

BARRY. All right, for 11 points. First, "I hear American singing—the very carols I hear."

SNODGRASS. Ah, that is—Walt Whitman.

BARRY. That is right. Second, "The fog comes on little cat feet."

SNODGRASS. That is ah—the poem—"The Fog" or "Fog" by Carl Sandburg.

BARRY. That's right. Three, "Hope is the thing with feathers, that perches in the soul."

SNODGRASS. "Hope is the thing with feathers—that perches in the soul." That is—ah—actually one of my favorite poets—Emily Dickinson.

BARRY. You're right. Fourth and finally, which would give you a full 11 points—and have you off to a flying start, "I shot an arrow in the air—it fell to earth, I know not where."

SNODGRASS. Henry Wadsworth Longfellow.

BARRY. You're right. For a full 11 points. All right, Jim, you couldn't get off to a better start and I'll get back to you in just a moment.

Hank Bloomgarden, here we go—for $3,000 a point. The category, American literature. How many points do you want from 1 to 11?

BLOOMGARDEN. Ten.

BARRY. Ten points—one of our more difficult questions. Tell us the name and author of the books in which the following are major characters. First, Victor Joppolo, J-o-p-p-o-l-o, whose attempts to rebuild a war-torn town are brought to an abrupt end by order of a superior; second, Dick Diver, writer and psychologist, whose marriage to a patient was followed by the dissipation of his genius and the ruin of his promising career; third, when a school building collapsed and killed several children as he had predicted, Willie Stark was catapulted into a powerful political career which ended with his murder; I want the name and author of the books in which the following are major characters. Shall we take it one at a time?

BLOOMGARDEN. Please.

BARRY. Victor Joppolo, whose attempts to rebuild a war-torn town are brought to an abrupt end by order of a superior.

BLOOMGARDEN. Victor Joppolo appeared in John Hersey's book "A Bell for Adano."

BARRY. Correct. Dick Diver, writer and psychologist, whose marriage to a patient was followed by dissipation of his genius and the ruin of his promising career.

BLOOMGARDEN. Dick Diver—that was in "Tender is the Night" by F. Scott Fitzgerald.

BARRY. Also correct. Finally, for 10 points, when a school building collapsed and killed several children as he had predicted, Willie Stark was catapulted into a powerful political career which ended with his murder. For 10 points.

BLOOMGARDEN. Willie Stark—that was in "All The King's Men."

BARRY. Right.

BLOOMGARDEN. "All The King's Men" was written by—Robert Penn Warren.

BARRY. You're right—and you've got ten points. I'll get back to you in just a moment, Hank.

Jim Snodgrass, you have 11 points—the category—Armed Forces. Armed Forces. How many points do you want?

SNODGRASS. I have 11?

BARRY. Yes.

SNODGRASS. I'll take 10 please—get to 21 if I can.

BARRY. You're going to take 10 points, which would give you 21 if answered correctly. Because you are trying for 21, you may have some extra time if you need it. If you do answer correctly, please remember that Hank's—Hank Bloomgarden still has one more turn to go—so hold on, even if you get 21. Here it is—for 10 points. Give me the present locations of the training academies of—first, the U.S. Army; second, the U.S. Navy; third, the U.S. Merchant Marine; fourth, the U.S. Air Force; and fifth, the U.S. Coast Guard. Want some time to think this over?

SNODGRASS. Ah, yes—please.

BARRY. All right—I'll tell you when your time is up.

SNODGRASS. All right. Thank you.

BARRY. Your time is up, Jim—let me repeat the question. This is an important moment for you, ten points would give you 21. I want the locations —the present locations of the training academies of the U.S. Army, U.S. Navy, U.S. Merchant Marine, U.S. Air Force, and U.S. Coast Guard.

SNODGRASS. All right—uh—let me see if I can get the Army, Navy and ah—Coast Guard first.

BARRY. All right—how about the U.S. Army?

SNODGRASS. That is—ah—the U.S. Military Academy at West Point, New York.

BARRY. Correct. You asked next for the U.S. Navy?

SNODGRASS. Yes sir. Ah, that is—the U.S. Naval Academy at Annapolis, Maryland.

BARRY. That is correct. Did you ask now for the—

SNODGRASS. Coast Guard, please.

BARRY. Coast Guard. All right. Let's skip down to the Coast Guard.

SNODGRASS. That —ah—the Coast Guard is in—ah—New London, Conn.

BARRY. Correct. You have three of them. You need two more for 21 points. U.S. Merchant Marine.

SNODGRASS. Let's see—it used to be at Sheepshead Bay—it's ah—Kings Point on Long Island, here in New York.

BARRY. Correct. Finally, if you can give me the location of the Air Force, you will have 21 points.

SNODGRASS. Um—this is where the word "present" comes in—

BARRY. Yes.

SNODGRASS. Ah—let's see, they're building the new Air Force Academy at Colorado Spring in—ah—Colorado. That's not done yet. I think—ah—wait—yes, yes—at the Lowery Air Force Base in Denver, Colorado.

BARRY. That is right, and you've scored 21 points. Jim Snodgrass, you've done it again—you've got 21 points—you still have to wait to see what Hank Bloomgarden does—I'm gonna give you some—I'm gonna let you listen, but please do not divulge your score or speak in any way.

Hank, you have 10 points—the category is Armed Forces. Armed Forces. How many points do you want, from 1 to 11?

BLOOMGARDEN. Eleven, please.

BARRY. You're going all the way for 21? I can tell you now that your opponent has already scored 21 points. It means once again and I'm not gonna point this out, that everything is at stake—if you answer correctly we'll have another tie and we'll have to play again at $3,500 a point. If you miss, of course, you'll be wiped out. Here is your question—because you're trying for 21, I'll give you some extra time to think it over. The highest rank currently held in the U.S. Army is General of the Army. The highest rank in the Navy is Fleet Admiral. There are at present three Generals of the Army and two Fleet Admirals on active duty. Name these five men. Understand the question all right? Want some extra time to think it over?

BLOOMGARDEN. Please.

BARRY. I'll tell you when your time is up.

BLOOMGARDEN. Could you, could you run through that again, please—the question?

BARRY. Yes. I think the only important part you have to know is the actual last part. There are at present three Generals of the Army and two Fleet Admirals on active duty. Name these five men. Want to think it over?

BLOOMGARDEN. Please.

BARRY. All right—I'll tell you when your time is up.

Your time is up, Hank. For 11 points which would give you 21—and another tie, or, if you miss you will be wiped out—the question again. The highest rank currently held in the U.S. Army is General of the

Army. The highest rank in the Navy is Fleet Admiral. There are at present three Generals of the Army and two Fleet Admirals on active duty. Name these five men.

BLOOMGARDEN. Well, the Army. President Eisenhower was a General of the Army, but he had to resign from the Army when he assumed the Presidency, so that let's him out. General George Marshall is one.

BARRY. That's right.

BLOOMGARDEN. General Douglas MacArthur is another.

BARRY. You've got two.

BLOOMGARDEN. Oh—Omar Bradley. Omar Bradley.

BARRY. That is right. You've got three of the generals—now, two fleet admirals—if you answer this successfully you will have 21 points.

BLOOMGARDEN. Nimitz is one.

BARRY. That is correct. One more will give us another tie.

BLOOMGARDEN. Leahy, Leahy.

BARRY. That's right—and you scored 21 points.

Gentlemen, I don't have to tell you both what's happened—there's the 21 up and both of you've done it again—21 points, and I'm sorry, we're gonna have to put you through some more of what is ob—ob— obviously torture for both of you in there. We'll have to play another game, this time at $3,500 a point. I'm not even gonna stop to figure out how much it could be—it probably is o—over $70,000 will be involved. Will both of you relax for a moment or so? If you can, and we'll get back to you in just a moment.

We'll—uh—we'll get on with the next game in just a moment but first there is a word about another one of our fine products.

[Commercial]

BARRY. I'd say that was pretty good advice, wouldn't you? Incidentally, all questions used on "Twenty-One" have been authenticated for accuracy and order of difficulty by the editorial board of the Encyclopedia Britannica.

I want to turn both these studios on right now. Hank , the boys in the control room—the producers have asked me to ask both of you if you both feel at this tremendous amount—I want to point out that in the next game $73,500 will be at stake. As far as I know, that is the greatest amount of money ever at stake in any quiz program on television anywhere in the world. Do you feel you can continue on with this, Hank? All right—tonight—but you look a little bit shaken—you're all right—Jim are you OK?

SNODGRASS. Yes, I'm fine.

BARRY. Both of you ready to go on?

SNODGRASS. Yes.

BARRY. All right boys, it's up to you. Here we go—it's set for $3,500 a point—I'll get back to you in a moment, Hank.

OK, Jim—the category—Queens—Queens. How many points do you want, from one to eleven?

SNODGRASS. I'll take ten, please.

BARRY. Ten points. One of the more difficult questions, again. This Queen of Hungary and her husband Francis the First had many children, one of whom became a famous queen of France. Tell us first the name of this Queen of Hungary, second the name of her daughter who became Queen of France, and third the name and number of the King of France who married her daughter. Let's take the first one—the name of the Queen of Hungary.

SNODGRASS. I think her name was Maria Theresa.

BARRY. That's right. Second, the name of her daughter who became Queen of France.

SNODGRASS. The ah—name of the daughter that became Queen of France was—ah—Marie Antoinette.

BARRY. That is correct. Finally, the name and number of the King of France who married her daughter.

SNODGRASS. Well, let's see—that was Louis—the—the—I was going to the last of the Louis—uh—Louis the Sixteenth.

BARRY. That is correct—you've scored ten points. I—ah—I have a feeling the audience is more stunned than you are in there, Jim. That was the end of the question and he scored his ten points. We'll get back to you in just a moment.

Hank Bloomgarden, at $3,500 a point, the category is Queens—how many points do you want, from one to eleven?

BLOOMGARDEN. I'll take 10 on that.

BARRY. For ten points. This Queen of Hungary and her husband Francis the First had many children, one of whom became a famous Queen of France. Tell us first the name of this Queen of Hungary, second the name of her daughter who became Queen of France, and third the name and number of the King of France who married her daughter. First, the name of the Queen of Hungary.

BLOOMGARDEN. The name of the Queen of Hungary—was—Maria Theresa.

BARRY. Correct. Second, the name of her daughter who became Queen of France.

BLOOMGARDEN. That was Marie Antoinette.

BARRY. That is correct. Third, the name and number of the King of France who married her daughter, for a full ten points.

BLOOMGARDEN. Oh, it was Louis—which one—Louis the Sixteenth.

BARRY. Correct. You've got ten points. I'll get back to you in just a moment.

Jim, you have ten points—the category is Biology—Biology. How many points do you want, from one to eleven?

SNODGRASS. I'll try for 11.

BARRY. You'll try for 11.

SNODGRASS. I'll try for 11.

BARRY. Which would give you 21 if answered correctly, but remember Hank still has a turn to go so—take it easy—if you answer correctly.

The bones in our backbones or vertebrae are arranged in five groups and named for their positions in the spinal column. Name these five groups. Understand it all right?

SNODGRASS. Aah—yes.

BARRY. Want some time to think it over?

SNODGRASS. Yes, please.

BARRY. I'll tell you when your time is up. Good luck, Jim.

SNODGRASS. Thank you.

BARRY. For 11 points which would give you 21, the bones in our backbone or vertebrae are arranged in five groups and named for their positions in the spinal column. For 11 points and 21, name these five groups.

SNODGRASS. Aah—I imagine the sacrum is part of it—

BARRY. I beg your pardon?

SNODGRASS. The sacram—or sacram. S-A-C-R-U-M.

BARRY. I'm sorry to have to call for a ruling on this, Jim—

SNODGRASS. Or sacroiliac, it may be also.

BARRY. I'll have to call for a ruling on that, too. One of the groups is called S-A-C-R-A-L—the producers say "no"—cannot accept. I'm sorry, Jim. Sacral is actually the name—

SNODGRASS. Sacral—

BARRY. And we'll have to get it precisely from both—I'm sorry you lose your 11 points—it puts you back down to zero—better luck on the next round.

SNODGRASS. Well, let's see what happens.

BARRY. All is not lost yet—Hank still has to answer.

Hank Bloomgarden, you have ten points. The category is Biology—how many points do you want, from one to eleven?

BLOOMGARDEN. Eleven.

BARRY. You're gonna try for 21.

BLOOMGARDEN. Right.

BARRY. Here is your question for 11 points—the bones in our backbone—

BLOOMGARDEN. Doesn't he have 21?

BARRY. I beg your pardon?

BLOOMGARDEN. Doesn't he have 21?

BARRY. As you know, if he had 21, I would have told you so, Hank.

BLOOMGARDEN. Oh.

BARRY. Here we go. The bones—we'll have to go along here—the bones in our backbone or vertebrae are arranged in five groups and named for their positions in the spinal column. Name these five groups. Want time to think it over?

BLOOMGARDEN. Please.

BARRY. I'll tell you when your time is up and good luck. For 11 points, which would give you 21, Hank, name the five groups in the spinal column.

BLOOMGARDEN. The lumbar—

BARRY. Lumbar is one.

BLOOMGARDEN. The sacral—

BARRY. Two.

BLOOMGARDEN. The—the thoracic—

BARRY. That is correct. You've got three of them. Two more to give you a victory.

BLOOMGARDEN. The cervical—

BARRY. Right. You need one more for 21 points.

BLOOMGARDEN. I'm not sure of the pronunciation of this—I'll spell it for you—you'd better pronounce it. Aah, c-o-c-c-y-x I think it's coccyx or coccyx—I'm not sure. c-o-c-c-y-x.

BARRY. I, I have no idea how to pronounce it, but you're right—you have 21 points.

Congratulations, Hank—Ladies and gentlemen, would you all hold your applause, please—one moment—Jim, I think you've heard what happened. Our time is running out—you've just won another victory—you've won by a score of 21 points—at $3,500 a point—you've won $73,500—added to your previous $52,500, your winnings—$126,000. Congratulations, Hank Bloomgarden.

What do you—what do you say after that? I believe that that's the greatest amount of money ever won in one fell swoop on television—congratulations—Jim, how do I thank you—the magnificent showing—we were playing for $3,500 a point. I know you're going to have an art exhibit down at the Village at the end of the month and this $3,500 that you're gonna get as a consolation will go toward making your career as an artist even a more secure one. Congratulations—a tremendous hand for Jim Snodgrass.

Congratulations! Congratulations again! Whoo—we'll be back in 30 seconds to continue, but right now here's my friend Bob Sheppard who seems to have his eye on the calendar—Bob—

[Commercial.]

BARRY. I said that right, didn't I—$126,000—that's the amount. We won't be on next week—Producer's Showcase is going to have the Festival of Magic with Ernie Kovacs as the host and with a whole bunch of wonderful magicians—but I think it'll be very worthwhile if you're back with us in two weeks to see what Hank Bloomgarden does with $126,000. I don't know about you, but we had a wonderful time here. Good night. Thank you, everybody. Good night.

[Commercial.]

Source: Testimony of James Snodgrass, U.S., Congress, House Committee on Interstate and Foreign Commerce, *Investigation of Television Quiz Shows,* before a subcommittee of the Committee on Interstate and Foreign Commerce, House of Representatives, 86th Cong., 1st sess., 1959, pp. 78-84.

Appendix 2

TRANSCRIBED KINESCOPE OF DOTTO, MAY 20, 1958

RALPH PAUL. In just a few moments, the first phone call. Stand by. You may be phoned. You'll be asked if you can identify this face. If you can, you will win a fabulous prize. All you have to do is watch—watch these dots. "Dotto." "Dotto," the exciting new quiz game, brought to you by Colgate Dental Cream. Fight tooth decay with Colgate's while you stop bad breath all day. And here's your host for "Dotto," Jack Narz. [Fanfare].

NARZ. Hi, everybody. Thank you very much. Tonight, on behalf of Colgate, may I welcome all of you to "Dotto." New York is all aflutter this morning; we have two very famous people visiting us. President Eisenhower is here, and Van Cliburn, the young Texan pianist who scored such a big hit over in Moscow, is also in town and repeated his triumph last night here in New York. And with two famous people in town, we are going to have a big parade this afternoon, and it's gonna be one of those great-big ticker-tape parades, you know. He just can't seem to shake pianoplayers, this guy, does he! This is the show, you know, that used to be on every day, Monday through Friday, here on CBS. And what we do is, we have a series of dots back here which, when they are connected, form a picture, and those pictures turn into dollars for our studio contestants. Now, today we'll be making our first phone call to you at home to see if you can identify our home "Dotto" picture and maybe win the cavalcade of three fine cars. We will find out in just a few moments, but right now let's meet our first two guests. Ralph, please?

PAUL. Well, Jack, getting us off on a solid note—returning for the second day, Colgate Dental Cream welcomes back our new champion from New York, Miss Marie Winn, and her challenger from Mountain Park, Okla., Mrs. Yeffe Kimball. [Applause.]

NARZ. Now, first of all, let's talk to our new champ, who yesterday won $440. I guess that makes you feel pretty good, doesn't it, Marie!

WINN. Oh, I guess it does.

NARZ. Well, good enough. What are you going to do with all that loot? Spend it all in one place or are you going to keep it?

WINN. Well, I haven't decided, but—

NARZ. How did you spend your evening—tossing?

WINN. Oh, I really had a swell time, Jack. I spent some little time with Latin, then with symbolic logic, then with music—

NARZ. Marie, you know, I hate to say this, but I don't think we're gonna have any questions concerning those subjects on "Dotto" this morning. Maybe you were studying the wrong thing. We'll find out in a moment. Let's talk to your challenger now. Yeffe Kimball, from Mount Park, Okla.—

KIMBALL. Mountain Park.

NARZ. Mountain Park. I'm sorry; Mountain Park, Okla. You're part Osage Indian?

KIMBALL. Right.

NARZ. Uh, huh. And your husband is an atomic scientist. You are a specialist on Indian work. May I ask you, first of all, what the name Yeffe—and that's spelled Y-e-f-f-e—what does it mean?

KIMBALL. Wandering Star.

NARZ. Wandering star? You mean like Sonny Tufts, or somebody like that? No? [Laughter.] Do you understand Indian—the dress too, may I ask, is this authentic?

KIMBALL. Well, this is the Sisuki Indian dress that the Rio Grande Valley Indians copied from the Spaniards' shirts when they came out there in the early 16th century.

NARZ. Were these worn in those days?

KIMBALL. The men wore those shirts, and then the women copied them for themselves.

NARZ. Would you step out front here where we could get a shot of it and have everybody take a look at the dress. Isn't that beautiful? It's very colorful. Yeffe, real nice. [Applause.] How about Indian sign language? Do the Osage use sign language?

KIMBALL. The Indians all use sign language.

NARZ. Do you understand it? Can you use it?

KIMBALL. Yes. Let's say I had to ride a horse all the way here to get to this program—

NARZ. In New York City, boy, yeah. Yep—

KIMBALL. I would start out early in the morning and I would get on my horse and I would ride all day until sundown at night, then I would lie down and go to sleep, then I would get up on my horse and I would ride all night long and come back to sunrise and I would be here.

NARZ. And that would just about cover going across town here in New York. Believe me, that's about as fast as you can make it in a cab. Well, Yeffe and Marie, we'll start our first match in just a moment. Right now, a word to you folks. Do you know who was the first to put toothpaste in a tube? Colgate, that's right. And now, who was the first with an aerosol toothpaste? Colgate! Watch.

[Commercial break at this time.]

NARZ. And Yeffe and Marie, for each of you we have some Colgate Dental Cream with Gardol and Power-Packed Colgate. OK, all set now to go with our first match. Good luck, ladies, and would you take your positions back at the Dotto boards, please. And now let's reveal the Dotto pictures, today worth $1,000. Now as you know, you have identical pictures. However, you cannot see each other's. And remember the sooner you identify the picture the more money you'll make. We'll pay you $20 for each dot that remains unconnected. Yeffe, would you try your Dotto button, please? [Buzzer.] OK, and Marie? [Buzzer] OK, fine, they both work and we're ready to go. Yeffe our first category, documents of history. Now you have your choice of 5, 8, or 10 dots. Now think carefully because if you miss the questions the dots you ask for will be connected in your opponent's picture. Documents of history —

KIMBALL. Well, I'd better play it safe and take 5.

NARZ. Five. Was the great religious reformer who tacked his 95 theses to the church door Martin Luther or John Wesley?

KIMBALL. Martin Luther.

NARZ. That is right. Yes, ma'am, and here are your 5 connected dots, Yeffe. OK, 5 dots connected 45 unconnected. Your picture is worth $900, Yeffe. Marie, documents of history is our category. Five, eight or ten for you?

WINN. Well, you know I did take a history course. I think I'll try 10.

NARZ. Ten. Name the man who wrote the famous "Fourteen Points."

WINN. Woodrow Wilson.

NARZ. That is right, yes, ma'am, here are your 10 connected dots. All right, 10 dots are connected in your picture, 40 unconnected. It's worth $800. And all of our questions are verified by the editorial board of the Encyclopedia Americana. I see Yeffe squinting, working real hard over there. You recognize it yet? We'll go on with —

KIMBALL. Not yet.

NARZ. American short stories is our next category, Yeffe. American short stories — 5, 8 or 10?

KIMBALL. Well, I'll try 10.

NARZ. Ten. Here we go. Surgeon, soldier, sailor, spy, dreamed Thurber's great creation. Though Walter's life was mighty dry, he had imagination. Name that story.

KIMBALL. Will you repeat that, please?

NARZ. [Repeats] Can you name that story — [bell rings]. Oh, you

don't know? It's one of my favorites. "The Secret Life of Walter Mitty."
Yeffe, I'm sorry you didn't answer that question, and because you fell
through, the 10 dots you asked for will now be connected in Marie's
picture. Marie, 10 dots for you. [Music—dots being connected.] OK,
now you have 20 dots connected in your picture, Marie. You can go for
your first clue on this question. The category, American short stories.

WINN. I think maybe I know it.

NARZ. Well, you can do whatever you want to. You can press your
button for dotto, we'll give you a chance to make the identification, or
you can go one more question to go for the first clue, whatever you
want to do.

WINN. All right, I'll go for one more question. I'll take the five.

NARZ. OK, to give you the clue. All right. A horror story of greed and
hate as—Poe did spin it; a cellar of wine was the bait, the man was
walled within it. Was the story "The Cask of Amontillado" or "The
Telltale Heart?"

WINN. "The Cask of Amontillado."

NARZ. You are right. Here are your five connected dots. Here's your
clue. [Music—dots being connected.] All righty, there are 25 connected dots in your picture. $500 riding on your answer. Marie, you
understand that if you are mistaken you'll be eliminated from the
game? OK. All right, Yeffe will not be able to see your answer. Just step
right over and write it out, please. [Music.] You are absolutely right,
Marie. Now please stand by. Yeffe, she has identified her picture, and
oh boy, let's see how you do. Now. You have only five dots connected
in your picture. I know you have been squinting at it real hard. Let's
see if you can put those dots together and come up with the right
answer and tie up our game. Good luck, Yeffe. [Music.]

KIMBALL. Gee, I don't think I can, but I'll take a guess.

NARZ. All right, you're entitled to a guess.

KIMBALL. It looks like Winston Churchill.

NARZ. No, I'm sorry. That means that Marie Winn remains our dotto
champion. She correctly identified Barry Fitzgerald. [Applause.] Of
course the first clue was Abbey player—that arm chair would have
helped you a lot. Thanks so much, Yeffe for playing dotto for us. The
makers of Colgate have for you a check for $25, Yeffe. Thanks again.
Good luck. Marie you have won another $500, you now have a total of
$940. You are still our champion and in a very short time we'll have a
brand new challenger for you, so please stand by. And in just a moment we will connect 10 more dots to our home dotto picture and make
our first phone call. But right now, here's the story about the greatest
washday development of our time.

[Commercial.]

And now I recommend we all take a look at the home dotto picture as Mr. Ralph Paul connects 10 more dots.

PAUL. Thank you, Jack. That phone call in a moment, but first the 10 dots. Each day 10 dots are connected in our home dotto picture. Now the first person that we call at home who can identify this face will receive a fabulous prize. And now here are the 10 dots for today. [Music—dots being connected.]

NARZ. OK, there are the 10 dots for today. Now it's time for our first phone call, and Ralph, whose card was drawn today?

PAUL. Well, Jack, we received cards from all over these United States, and today our call goes all the way to New York, to Brooklyn—

NARZ. Yea-a-a, Brooklyn.

PAUL. Where "Dotto" is seen over WCBS-TV, and Jack, you'll be talking to Mrs. Georgia B. Phillips.

NARZ. Thank you very much Ralph. Hello there, Mrs. Phillips.

MRS. PHILLIPS. Hello, Mr. Narz.

NARZ. Can you hear me all right?

MRS. PHILLIPS. Yes, I can. I'm looking right at you.

NARZ. Well, good, and good luck to you, Mrs. Phillips. And in just a moment I'll be asking you the big question—asking you to identify this home dotto picture. And if you can, listen to what we will send you.

[Commercial break at this time.]

MRS. PHILLIPS. Ah, you know, I missed two of the clues.

NARZ. Yes, I do—but I'm not—I beg your pardon?

MRS. PHILLIPS. I missed two of the clues, and if you had called me last week I would have won that beautiful kitchen.

NARZ. Yeah, but this is this week, Mrs. Phillips, and there's another picture. Do you have any idea who it is?

MRS. PHILLIPS. I'm going to take the wildest stab in the world. I don't know. Was he a writer?

NARZ. I beg your pardon?

MRS. PHILLIPS. Was he a writer?

NARZ. I'm sorry, I can't answer that. I can't tell you anything.

MRS. PHILLIPS. Well, I'm gonna take a wild guess and say Shakespeare.

NARZ. Well, I'm gonna make a wild answer and say "No," Mrs. Phillips, it is not Shakespeare. Sorry. However, because your card was drawn, Mrs. Phillips, we're going to send along to you a full year's supply of all the Colgate products seen here on "Dotto." OK?

MRS. PHILLIPS. All right.

NARZ. Thanks very much for entering our contest. Bye, bye.

MRS. PHILLIPS. Call me again sometime.

NARZ. Well, let's hope so.

MRS. PHILLIPS. When I have the answer.

NARZ. OK, when you know the answer. All right, you let us know when you know the answer. OK, Mrs. Phillips, thank you and goodbye. Bye, bye.

Well, that means tomorrow we'll make another telephone call and later today another word clue to help you identify this picture. Now, Mrs. Phillips proved how important the clues are, so write 'em down, won't you? And if you'd like to enter the home dotto game, here's all you have to do.

[Promotional announcement followed by a commercial.]

NARZ. Thank you, Bess. Marie, ready to go onward and upward?

WINN. Sure thing, Jack.

NARZ. Let's try, shall we? Ralph, would you introduce our next player, please.

PAUL. Jack Narz, Florient Air Deodorant welcomes Mr. Michael Hayden of Old Greenwich, Conn.

NARZ. Hi, Mike [Applause.] Now let's see, Mike, we'll find out about you. You're a single fellow, huh?

MIKE. Yes, sir.

NARZ. Well, we'll find out in just a few minutes if you can make lots of money. You're a pilot by trade, is that true?

MIKE. Right—with Pan American.

NARZ. With Pan Am—where do you fly, between here and there?

MIKE. Well, we go as far as Teheran, the pilots in the Atlantic division. There's three divisions of Pan American.

NARZ. Well, let's see how you do on this division of CBS, which is studio 62 on 47th Street. May I present each of you with some Florient Air Deodorant, which comes in four fragrances, spice, mint, pine and floral. There you are—and good luck to you. And now would you step back, please, to the dotto boards and we'll get along.

And let's reveal the new dotto picture, worth $1,000. These are identical pictures, however you cannot see each other's. And Mike, the sooner you identify the picture the more money you will make. Want to try the dotto button there on the desk in front of you? [Buzzer.] OK, fine. Now the first category, songs about bands. Now you have a choice of a 5- or 8- or 10-dot question. If you fail to answer, the dots you ask for will be connected in your opponent's picture. Do you want to ask a question, Mike?

MIKE. Yeah, there's nothing up there yet.

NARZ. That's right. That's why we ask you the questions, and then if you answer the questions correctly then we'll put something up there. And Mike, our first category is songs about bands.

MIKE. I'll take 8 points.

NARZ. Eight. In this band song there's a flute player named Hennessey, and the music is something grand. Can you name that band?

MIKE. That's McNamara's band.

NARZ. That's right. Now we'll put something up there, eight connected dots. [Applause—music—dots being connected.] Mike, the picture is vorth $840. Marie, the category, "Songs about Bands."

WINN. Mike took eight, didn't he?

NARZ. He did.

WINN. Well, I'm gonna try 10.

NARZ. All rightee. According to this song, this is the bestest band what am, honey lamb. Name that band.

WINN. "Alexander's Ragtime Band."

NARZ. Sure it is. And here are 10 connected dots for you, Marie. OK, 10 dots connected in your picture, 40 unconnected it's worth $800. And Mike, our next category, "Russia, Now and Yesterday;" 5, 8 or 10?

MIKE. Ten points.

NARZ. Name the Russia cultist murdered in 1916, who was known as the Mad Monk.

MIKE. Rasputin.

NARZ. That's right. And here's 10 more dots for you. [Music—dots being connected.] I'm as confused as you are, believe me. OK, I think you have 18 dots connected, 32 unconnected. The picture is worth $640. Marie, Russia, now and yesterday.

[Buzzer, by Mike.]

NARZ. You think you know who it is, Mike?

MIKE. I'll give it a try.

NARZ. Well, I'll tell you what. We're gonna give you a good fair chance at it and also you, Marie. We're gonna give you another 60 seconds to study that picture and study it hard. I'm as confused as anybody here in the studio right now. In the meantime, we'll be back to get your answer in just a moment, Mike. Right now, I think it looks like my old Buddy, Ralph Paul, has a little something going for him over there on his "Dotto" board. It looks like maybe it's a kind of a problem. What's going on over there, Ralph?

[Commercial.]

NARZ. Ah, thank you, Sparkle. And boy, this is one time when both contestants really used that 60 seconds you gave them, Ralph. They've both been peering and squinting and taking all different views on this thing. OK, Mike, you have 32 unconnected dots in your picture and that means that $640 is riding on this answer. Now if you are mistaken we will have to eliminate you from the game. OK, Marie will not be able to see your answer if you will step right over there to the Dotto-graph and write it out, please. [Music.] And his is right. Yes, that's who it is. [Applause.] I'm as much in the dark as anybody—had to get this—wait a minute, I beg your pardon. Then what do we do now? We'll make a ruling about it? He's right actually in the identification. He didn't put all—he has a partial answer down—you'll make a ruling later? In the meantime we'll go over to Marie. All right, Marie, he has identified his picture. He's on the right track. He has made almost a complete identification. We'll have to make a ruling on his answer a little later. But in the meantime we're gonna give you an opportunity to stay in our game by coming up with your identification if you can. Now you have had 60 seconds to look at them. You want another 10 to study it?

WINN. Yes.

NARZ. All right. Good luck then, Marie.[Music.]

WINN. It looks to me by that thing down there, something like a duck. So is it Donald Duck? or little ducks?

NARZ. Well, I can accept one answer from you, Marie. Could you give me just one?

WINN. Donald Duck's little nephews?

NARZ. Well, you are right. Now that is right—it is Donald Duck's nephews. And I think we have—well I know we have a tie game now, so that solves our problem. Actually I think Mike chose the hard way to write his answer. If he had written Donald Duck's nephews we would have accepted that answer, but you wanted to give us the names. And I— believe it's Huey, Dewey, and Louie. Is that right, Louie's the third one? OK, but in the meantime I think he was right in identifying the nephews, and I know Marie was, so we have a tie game. We'll have them both back here tomorrow. OK, we'll play "Double Dotto" then. Thanks, Mike, thanks, Marie, we'll see you tomorrow. Tomorrow they'll be playing for $40 for each unconnected dot and the next picture you folks see will be worth $2,000. Right now we want you folks at home to see your word clue on the Home Dotto picture, so here it is, and write it down. [Music.] Friend of royalty. Get your cards in as soon as possible. Our address for the Home Dotto game, Dotto, Box 503, New York 46, N.Y. That's about it for today. Tomorrow we'll add 10 more dots in the Home Dotto picture and make another phone call. We'll see you then. Goodbye, everybody. See you tomorrow.

[Commercial.]

Source: Testimony of Edward Hilgemeier, Jr., U.S. Congress House Committee on Interstate and Foreign Commerce, *Investigation of Television Quiz Shows,* before a subcommittee of the Committee on Interstate and Foreign Commerce, House of Representatives, 86th Cong., 1st sess., 1959, pp. 290–296.

Appendix 3

SECOND AND THIRD LETTERS OF JAMES SNODGRASS PRIOR TO APPEARANCES ON TWENTY-ONE

May 11, 1959

To whom it may concern:

The following are some of the questions, specifically the one I will be asked for the television quiz show "Twenty-One" on the night of May 13 (Monday).

First category: "Movies"—I take 11 points. The question is worth 11 points.

In the story of "Snow White and the Seven Dwarfs," after she is banished from the palace of her stepmother, the Queen, Snow White goes to live in the forest with seven dwarfs. In the Walt Disney version, what were the names of the seven dwarfs?

(I shall answer in this sequence—Sleepy, Sneezy, Dopey, Happy (pause) the grouchy one, Grumpy (pause) Doc (pause) Bashful.

Second category: "England—I take 10 points.

What was the name of the ruling houses to which the following monarchs belonged—Richard II, Henry VII, Edward V, George VI?

(I shall answer something like this. Richard II was the last of the Plantagenets; Henry VII was a Tudor. I shall then ask to come back to Edward V. George the Sixth of course was the House of Windsor. Then I think about Edward V and mention that he was the kid murdered in the Tower of London by Richard III; he was not a Tudor, he was of the House of York.)

That ends the first game with a score of 21. Presumably Bloomgarden and I shall be tied.

First round game 2: "Presidents."

The first President of our country was a General as was President Eisenhower. Identify the following Presidents who also were generals. This man won fame by defeating the British at New Orleans during the War of 1812? (I answer correctly—Andrew Jackson.) This general led the American forces at the Battle of Thames in 1813? (I stress the fact that Thames is in Ontario, Canada, also during the War of 1812. William Henry Harrison.) This man enlisted in the army as a private, was appointed a brigadier general and fought with General Scott in capture of Mexico City—(According to the plan of the show I am to miss this question. I am to say "Ulysses S. Grant" which is wrong. The proper answer is "Franklin Pierce." This general defeated Santa Ana at the Battle of Buena Vista? (Zachary Taylor.)

Second round—"The Twenties" (I again try for 11 points since I am at zero.)

The following authors were awarded the Pulitzer prize in the twenties. Name the work for which they received this prize.

Stephen Vincent Benet ("John Brown's Body"), Edna Ferber (for her novel "So Big"), Edith Wharton (for "The Age of Innocence"), Thornton Wilder ("The Bridge of San Luis Rey").

(Signed) James Snodgrass

May 11, 1959

To Whom It May Concern:

The following are the questions for the first game on the television quiz program to take place at 9 o'clock Monday evening, May 20, 1957.

Round 1: Category "American Literature," 11 points:

Identify the major American poets who wrote the following lines of poetry: "I hear America singing . . . the varied carols" (Walt Whitman); "Fog comes in on little cat feet" (Carl Sandburg); "Hope is a thing with feathers, it whispers to the soul" (Emily Dickinson); "I shot an arrow in the air, where it fell I know not where" (Henry Wadsworth Longfellow).

Round 2: Category "The Armed Forces," 10 points:

Where are the present academies of the following branches of the United States Armed Forces: Army (U.S. Military Academy at West Point, N.Y.): Navy (U.S. Naval Academy at Annapolis, Md.): Coast Guard (The Coast Guard Academy is at New London, Conn.); Merchant Marine (King's Point, Long Island); Air Corps (While the Air Corps Academy is being constructed at Colorado Springs the present academy is in Denver, Colo.)

According to the plan I am to miss the first question, specifically the lines by Emily Dickinson. I've been told to answer Ralph Waldo Emerson. I have decided not to "take the fall" but to answer the question correctly.

James Snodgrass

Source: Testimony of James Snodgrass, U.S., Congress, House Committee on Interstate and Foreign Commerce, *Investigation of Television Quiz Shows,* before a subcommittee of the Committee on Interstate and Foreign Commerce, House of Representatives, 86th Cong., 1st sess., 1959, pp. 63, 75.

BIBLIOGRAPHY

PUBLIC DOCUMENTS

Congressional Index, 1959-1960. New York: Commerce Clearing House, 1960. Vol. 1.

Congressional Quarterly Almanac. 86th Cong., 2d sess. Washington: Congressional Quarterly, 1960.

U.S. Congress. House. Committee on Interstate and Foreign Commerce. *Communications Act Amendments, 1960.* H. Rept. 1800, to Accompany S. 1898, 86th Cong., 2d sess., 1960.

——. *Investigation of Regulatory Commissions and Agencies.* H. Rept. 1258, 86th Cong., 2d sess., 1960.

——. *Investigation of Television Quiz Shows.* Hearings before a subcommittee of the Committee on Interstate and Foreign Commerce, House of Representatives, 86th Cong., 1st sess., 1959.

NEWSPAPERS

Daily Worker, 1955
New York Herald Tribune, 1955.
New York Journal-American, 1955
New York Mirror, 1959
New York Times, 1955-1962, 1975.
New York World-Telegram and Sun, 1957.
Variety, 1955-1956, 1958.
Wall Street Journal, 1973.

BOOKS

Agnew, Clark, and O'Brien, Neil. *Television Advertising.* New York: McGraw-Hill Book Company, 1958.

Brooks, John. *The Great Leap.* New York: Harper and Row, 1968.

Brown, Les. *Television: The Business Behind the Box.* New York: Harcourt Brace Jovanovich, 1971.

Evans, Jacob. *Selling and Promoting Radio and Television*. New York: Printers' Ink Publishing Company, 1954.

Friendly, Fred W. *Due to Circumstances Beyond Our Control*. New York: Vintage Books, 1967.

Goldman, Eric F. *The Crucial Decade—and After: America, 1945-1960*. New York: Vintage Books, 1960

Hickok, Eliza Merrill. *Quiz Kids*. Boston: Houghton Mifflin, 1947.

Hofstadter, Richard. *Anti-Intellectualism in American Life*. New York: Vintage Books, 1962.

James, William. *Memories and Studies*. New York: Longmans, Green and Company, 1912.

Kando, Thomas M. *Leisure and Popular Culture in Transition*. St. Louis: C. V. Mosby Company, 1975.

Potter, David M. *People of Plenty*. Chicago: University of Chicago, Press, 1954.

Schlesinger, Arthur M., Jr. "Sources of the New Deal." In *Paths of American Thought*, edited by Arthur M. Schlesinger, Jr. and Morton White. Boston: Houghton Mifflin, 1963.

Weinberg, Meyer. *TV in America*. New York: Ballantine Books, 1962.

ARTICLES

Ace, Goodman. "The $64,000 Answer." *Saturday Review*, August 13, 1955, p. 23.

"Admen Face the TV Issue." *Business Week*, November 21, 1959, pp. 116-117

"After Appomattox." *Time*, February 22, 1960, p. 74.

"All Aboard for Rainbow Land!" *Christian Century*, September 14, 1955, pp. 1044-1045.

Allen, James E., Jr. "The TV 'Fixes' and Teacher Responsibility." *School and Society*, April 23, 1960, p. 202.

"The American Dream." *Commonweal*, February 22, 1957, pp. 523, 525.

"Another $64,000 Question." *Christian Century*, August 3, 1955. p. 885.

"Are TV Quiz Shows Fixed?" *Look*, August 20, 1957, pp. 45-47.

"Are We a Nation of Liars and Cheats?" *Christian Century*, November 18, 1959, p. 1334.

"The Artful Jockey." *Newsweek*, April 30, 1956, p. 78.

Bain, Frank. "Who's to Blame for TV's Deadly Sins?" *American Mercury* (November 1960): 59.

"Banker." *New Yorker*, September 24, 1955, pp. 35-36.

"Basketball Scholarship." *Time*, April 6, 1959, p. 45.

"Battle of the Bones." *Time*, June 3, 1957, p. 68.

Bernstein, Lester. "The Wizard of Quiz." *Time*, February 11, 1957, pp. 11, 44-46, 49-50.

Bester, Alfred. "Life Among the Giveaway Programs." *Holiday* (May 1957): 115-116, 174.

"The Big Money," *Time*, September 3, 1956, pp. 37-38.

"A Big Quiz for the Quizzes." *Life*, October 19, 1959, pp. 51-52.

"The Blame for TV Fixes." *Life*, October 26, 1959, p. 38.

Brean, Herbert. " 'Controls' and 'Plotting' Help in Showmanship." *Life*, September 15, 1958, p. 24.

Broadcasting, April 16, 1956, p. 19.

————. August 6, 1956, p. 14.

Brogen, Wendall. *New Republic*, August 8, 1955, p. 23.

"Challenger." *Time*, March 11, 1957, p. 51.

Ciardi, John. "Exit a Symbol." *Saturday Review*, November 21, 1959, pp. 27, 28, 59.

"Come and Gone." *Newsweek*, October 27, 1958, p. 88.

Cousins, Norman. "The Real Fraud." *Saturday Review*, November 21, 1959, p. 27.

Crosby, John. "It Was New and We Were Very Innocent." *TV Guide*, September 22-28, 1973, p. 7.

"Drive on Cheats." *Time*, January 4, 1950, p. 66.

"The Enormity of It." *Time*, September 19, 1955, p. 88.

"Fallen but Queenly." *Newsweek*, July 21, 1958, p. 52.

Fischer, John. "New Hope for Television." *Harper's* (January 1960): 12.

"Fort Knox or Bust." *Time*, August 22, 1955, p. 47.

"45-19-39," *Time*, September 10, 1956, pp. 95-96.

Frank, Stanley. "Television's Desperate Numbers Game." *Saturday Evening Post*, December 7, 1957, p. 150.

"Fun and Games." *Time*, January 21, 1957, p. 40.

Gehman, Richard. "How to Think Big." *Cosmopolitan* (December 1955): 77, 79, 80, 81.

————. "The Real Meaning of Intelligence." *Cosmopolitan* (September 1957): 28.

"Getting Rich on TV." *Newsweek*, March 25, 1957, pp. 63-65.

"The Giveaways." *Time*, July 7, 1958, pp. 66-67.

Goodwin, Richard N. *Life*, November 16, 1959, p. 30.

"High Court Takes Giveaway Issue." *Broadcasting*, October 19, 1953, p. 44.

Hiken, Nat. "The Big Money." *Time*, September 3, 1956, pp. 37, 38.

Hoffman, Betty. "Famous Overnight." *Ladies' Home Journal* (November 1957): 161, 163, 164, 190, 192, 193.

Horton, Robert. "The Economic Squeeze on Mass TV." *Reporter*, April 28, 1960, pp. 19-20.

"How They Got $74,000." *Newsweek*, July 23, 1956, p. 70.

"How to Get on a TV quiz show." *Changing Times* (June 1956): 46.

"Human Almanac." *Time*, March 18, 1957, pp. 63-64.

"If You Ask Questions..." *Newsweek*, September 15, 1958, p. 62.

"Knowing Your Wife." *Newsweek*, January 9, 1956, p. 63.

"Know-It-All." *Newsweek*, January 28, 1957, p. 60.

"Lady with the Answers." *Newsweek*, June 9, 1958, p. 78.

"Lady with the Answers." *Time*, May 12, 1958, p. 70.

Langman, Anne W. *Nation*, April 28, 1956, p. 370.

Lardner, John. "The Ear and the Overshoot." *New Yorker*, August 9, 1958, pp. 70-72.

———. "Life Around the Booths." *New Yorker*, November 30, 1957, pp. 147, 149-50

———. "The Summit of Culture." *Newsweek*, September 26, 1955, p. 72.

———. "Take It, Myrt, Take It." *Newsweek*, October 10, 1955, p. 104.

"The Law and the Limelight." *Time*, September 1, 1958, p. 39.

"The Little Boy Blew It." *Newsweek*, April 16, 1956, p. 77.

Mannes, Marya. "The Million Dollar Surprise." *Reporter*, December 1, 1955, pp. 38-40.

March, Hal. "Could You Answer the $64,000 Question?" *American Magazine* (December 1955): 81-82.

"Meeting of Minds." *Time*, September 15, 1958, p. 47-48.

"The Misuses of Money." *Life*, March 25, 1957, p. 42.

"Moderation." *Time*, July 25, 1955, p. 68.

New Republic. November 9, 1959, p. 7.

———. October 19, 1959, p. 2.

Newsweek, April 30, 1596, p. 78.

———. February 27, 1957, p. 65.

New Yorker. October 24, 1959, p. 33.

"New York Steam Roller." *Newsweek*, September 8, 1958, pp. 26-28.

"No Question That It Sells." *Broadcasting*, September 19, 1955, p. 46.

"Now the Sponsors Call the Tune." *Business Week*, April 19, 1958, pp. 53-56.

"$128 Bust." *Time*, October 1, 1956, p. 70.

"$100 a Week for 20 Years." *Time*, December 19, 1955, p. 46.

"On Getting Rich Quick." *Newsweek*, February 11, 1957, p. 74.

"Out of the Backwash of the TV Scandals..." *Newsweek*, November 16, 1959, p. 66-67.

"Out of the Booth." *Newsweek*, August 25, 1958, p. 58.

"Out of Isolation." *Newsweek*, August 5, 1963, p. 67.

"Papa Said Stop." *Newsweek*, August 22, 1955, p. 85.

"The Parlor Pinkertons." *Time*, August 11, 1958, p. 36.

"The People Getters." *Time*, August 25, 1958, p. 65.

"The Philippian Way." *Newsweek*, July 25, 1955, p. 59.

Pierson, Frank B. "Killing Flies with a Sledge." *New Republic*, November 23, 1959, p. 20.

"Poor Loser." *Newsweek*, April 23, 1956, p. 58.

Popkin, Henry. "The Trouble with the Quiz Shows." *New Republic*, October 13, 1958, pp. 22-23.

"Portrait of a Winner." *Newsweek*, April 15, 1957, p. 70.

"A Prize Pupil of Higher Earning." *Life*, June 2, 1958, pp. 86-88.

"A Prodigy Rings the Bell." *Life*, May 7, 1956, pp. 88, 90.

"Prostitute of Merchandising." *Time*, November 9, 1959, p. 58.

"Purity Kick." *Time*, November 2, 1959, p. 43.

"Question and Answer." *Newsweek*, July 23, 1956, p. 69.

"A Question of Freedom" *Time*, December 7, 1959, pp. 47-48.

"Quiz Crazy." *Time*, February 27, 1956, pp. 74-75.

"Quizlings." *Reporter*, October 29, 1959, p. 2.

"Quiz Man in a Jam." *Newsweek*, November 17, 1958, p. 63.

"Quiz Quiz: Critics-Across-the-Sea." *Newsweek*, November 16, 1959, p. 67.

"Quiz Scandal (Contd.)," *Time*, September 8, 1958, p. 43.

"Quiz Scandal (Contd.)," *Time*, October 6, 1958, p. 50.

"A Ray of Hope." *Reporter*, September 18, 1958, p. 2.

"A Rich Marine Eats His Words." *Life*, September 26, 1955, pp. 181-183.

"Say It Ain't So, Charles." *America*, October 24, 1959, p. 98.

"Scandal of the Quizzes." *Time*, September 1, 1958, p. 38.

Seldes, Gilbert. "No Broom at the Top." *Saturday Review*, December 19, 1959, p. 23.

Seligman, Daniel. "Revlon's Jackpot." *Fortune* (April 1956): pp. 236, 239, 240.

"Semper Chow." *Time*, September 26, 1955, pp. 17-18.

Sharnik, John. "Giveaways: Little Men, Big Money." *House and Garden* (November 1956): 45-47.

Shayon, Robert Lewis. "Come and Get a Million." *Saturday Review*, June 16, 1956, p. 34.

"The Tragedy of $64,000." *Saturday Review*, September 24, 1955, p. 26.

"64,000-Dollar Carpenter." *American Magazine* (July 1956): 43.

"The $64,000 Question." *Newsweek*, September 5, 1955, pp. 41-45.

"The $60 Million Question." *Time*, April 22, 1957, pp. 78, 80, 82.

"The Splurge—$250,000 for Winner." *Newsweek*, September 8, 1958, p. 86.

"Squeeze on the Quiz." *Newsweek*, October 27, 1958, p. 88.

"Stanton in the Augean Stables." *Nation*, November 7, 1959, pp. 322-323.

Stearn, Jess. "How to Win a Quiz Show." *American Mercury* (August 1957): 38.

"Stop Wherever You Are." *Fortune* (September 1955): 85.

"The Swedish Shark." *Newsweek*, February 25, 1957, p. 66.

"A Tawdry Hoax." *Newsweek*, June 22, 1959, p. 46.

"Tearjerker." *Time*, July 9, 1956, p. 40.

"Telling Tales on '21.' " *Newsweek*, October 6, 1958, p. 52.

"Think Hard." *Newsweek*, June 13, 1955, p. 102.

Time, April 30, 1956, p. 90.

———. April 22, 1957, p. 47.

"TV Blows a Fuse." *Fortune* (December 1959): 96, 98.

"TV 'Policeman'—Who Would Be It?" *Newsweek*, November 9, 1959, p. 71.

"TV Quiz Business Is Itself Quizzed About Fix Charges." *Life*, September 15, 1958, pp. 22-23.

"The TV Quiz—How Far?" *Newsweek*, May 5, 1958, pp. 107-108.

"TV Quiz: What Does E-t-h-i-c-s Spell?" *Business Week*, November 14, 1959, p. 184.

"TV's Figures Won't Quite Add." *Business Week*, September 29, 1956, p. 45.

"Two-Fisted Crackdown." *Newsweek*, May 30, 1960, p. 108.

"The Ultimate Responsibility." *Time*, November 16, 1959, pp. 78-79.

"The Uses of Scandal." *Nation*, November 14, 1959, p. 341.

U.S. News and World Report, January 11, 1960, p. 61.

Van Doren, Charles. "Junk Wins TV quiz shows." *Life*, September 23, 1957, pp. 137-138, 140, 145-146, 148.

"Van Doren on Van Doren." *Newsweek*, November 9, 1959, pp. 69-70.

Wainwright, Loudon. "The Trouble with Being Elfrida." *Life*, June 23, 1958, pp. 71-74.

Wakefield, Dan. "The Fabulous Sweat Box." *Nation*, March 30, 1957, pp. 269-271.

Weaver, William. "Letter from Rome." *Nation*, June 2, 1956, pp. 478-479.

Welles, Chris. "No Rig, No Fix, and No Quiz." *Life*, October 18, 1963, pp. 133, 135.

"When Winners Pay." *Newsweek*, April 1, 1957, p. 10.
"Where, May We Ask, Was the FCC!" *Consumer Reports* (January 1960): 9-11.
"Whither Charley?" *Time*, March 25, 1957, p. 50.
"Winner Take All." *Newsweek*, December 19, 1955, pp. 44-45.

INDEX

About the Author

Kent Anderson was awarded the Ph.D. in history by the University of Washington in 1975.